Durable Trades

Durable Trades

Family-Centered Economies
That Have Stood the Test of Time

by
RORY GROVES

Foreword by
ALLAN C. CARLSON

Front Porch Republic *Books*

To Ivar, Elsie, Harriet, Alden, and Elias, and my children's children.

Contents

PART III: DURABLE FOUNDATIONS

Foreword

FEW BOOKS ARE ACTUALLY groundbreaking in concept and execution. Fewer still—no more than a handful each year—accomplish this in more than one way. *Durable Trades: Family-Centered Economies That Have Stood the Test of Time*, by Rory Groves, is one of those very few.

There are recent volumes by the thousands that claim to be career guides. There are thousands more in the related realm of "how to choose a college." None of these, however, have asked the key questions found in *Durable Trades*: What jobs or trades have survived the tumultuous upheavals—what Joseph Schumpeter has called "the creative destruction"—of industrial capitalism over the course of 250 years? What means of earning a living actually reinforce, rather than undermine, family bonds and a vital home economy? In this careful and most readable book, Mr. Groves provides rich and compelling answers.

Where almost every other "career book" buys into the argument that workers will need to completely retrain every five to seven years just to keep a job, this author proves that there are many rich and rewarding forms of labor with astonishing records of durability. Where the prophets of Artificial Intelligence and robotics claim that these forms of smart automation will displace almost all current forms of human labor, Mr. Groves offers an alternate vision forward: there are human-scale tasks aplenty where the robots and super computers will find few opportunities . . . where they cannot compete.

On the superficial level, the author—himself a computer programmer—does make the outrageous claim: "Forget computer engineering . . . become a shepherd!" And yet, this book is full of mighty wisdom about the nature of human work and, indeed, about the nature of human beings. Above all, Mr. Groves recovers a profound truth: a job is not an end in itself; it is rather one means—and only one means—toward building a rich and satisfying life, toward human flourishing.

Mr. Groves is particularly adept at reconnecting work and homelife. The most fundamental change wrought by the industrial revolution was the manner in which it wrenched apart one's place of work from one's place of residence. Woman, man, and even child (in the early years) were pulled out of their artisan shops and off their farms into separate factories to serve the machines. In this volume, the author offers sound and practical ways to heal this breach . . . and the result is revolutionary (or perhaps counter-revolutionary) in its own right.

A second original aspect of *Durable Trades* comes from its opening discussion of the historical developments that led modern societies to the point of apparent human obsolescence. He draws on the insights of some well-known analysts—ranging from Joseph Tainter in *The Collapse of Complex Societies* to Rod Dreher in *The Benedict Option*—to clarify our current predicament. Along the way, though, he provides important insights of his own. As a sampling:

- "But material abundance, along with its sister decadence, is a lagging indicator. The institutions and social contracts that have supported our way of life for centuries—marriage, family, faith, community and morality—have been utterly decimated";

- "The biblical idea of work as worship had to be undone before people were ready to submit to the idea of leisure, comfort, and wealth as acceptable pursuits in and of themselves";

- "It was the collapse of cultural boundaries combined with the ascendancy of humanist thought about the nature of work that unleashed the amoral, and immoral, use of technology."

Most strikingly, Mr. Groves' historical discussion of job specialization in industrial society led to an astonishing realization . . . by me, at least. In 1800, the number of distinct "occupations" found in the new United States was 70; in the year 2000, 30,959. All of the increase came as human beings adjusted their labor to accommodate the new machines, to enable the mechanical devices to become ever better, to help them in a way to "evolve." In our time, however, all of those new jobs—all!—are the very ones threatened by the culminating triumph of the machines, in artificial intelligence and robotics. The human enablers, it seems, are becoming ever less important . . . and may soon not be needed at all.

All of which underscores this book's focus on durable trades. These are the forms of work that are truly human and so resistant, at least, to the victorious march of the machines. These are the ways in which the unsettling disruptions of the Industrial Revolution can be deflected or overcome and through which vital, function-rich home economies can be built again as the essential material foundation for strong and child-rich families.

Finally, and perhaps most importantly, *Durable Trades* is a powerful Christian meditation. Mr. Groves uses Scriptural passages throughout the volume to remind readers of the profound importance given to human labor by the Hebrew prophets, by Jesus of Nazareth, and by His apostles. In doing so, he contributes in an important way to the resanctification of work . . . an absolutely necessary task in the building again of a Christian culture.

Allan C. Carlson, Swallow Farm
Winnebago County, Illinois
March 22, 2019

Dr. Allan C. Carlson is the John A. Howard Distinguished Fellow for Family and Religious Studies at the International Organization for the Family and Editor of The Natural Family: An International Journal of Research and Policy. *Dr. Carlson is the author of 15 books including* The Natural Family Where It Belongs: New Agrarian Essays.

Author's Note

*Such is the destiny of all who forget God; so perishes
the hope of the godless. What they trust in is fragile; what they rely on is a spider's web.*

—JOB 8:13–14 (NIV)

AS THIS BOOK GOES to press, the world is in the throes of global pandemic. In January reports of an obscure virus emerged from Wuhan province, China, where 40 cases of the novel Coronavirus had been confirmed. Two months later there are 800,000 cases in 178 countries, with infections doubling every six days. The Centers for Disease Control has estimated a worst-case scenario of 1.7 million deaths in the U.S. Around the world, drastic measures are being taken: emergency declarations, border closures, quarantines. We now stand on the precipice of a severe economic recession, if not depression. After reaching an all-time record high in February, the U.S. stock market plummeted nearly 37 percent in a mere four weeks. The Federal Reserve has pledged $1.5 trillion to protect the banking system, and Congress has passed a $2 trillion stimulus bill to stave off recession. Global supply chains are strained to the breaking point as manufacturing facilities shut down due to lack of laborers. And consumers are encountering a phenomenon they have never seen before: empty shelves in every grocery store in America.

What is being heralded as *unprecedented* is, in fact, quite precedented. Global pandemics occur with frightening regularity. In the last four centuries, there have been three pandemics each century: two minor and one major. The last major pandemic was the Spanish Flu of 1918, which infected half the globe and claimed 50 million lives at a time when only 14 percent of the world's population lived in cities.

But what astounds most is not the seriousness of the illness, but the fragility of the infrastructure on which our society depends—a central theme of this book. The world's supply chain, finely tuned for maximum profitability and just-in-time delivery, cannot keep pace with demand. As store shelves empty and drug shortages begin, Americans are discovering just how many of their necessities are Made in China. They are beginning to question whether our reliance on long supply chains and distant manufacturing plants are in our national best interest. They are questioning whether efficiency and profitability are the only measures that matter.

While the primary research for this book was completed over a year ago, the key tenets are proving true today: resilient nations rely on resilient communities, which rely on resilient families. Historically it has been decentralized, interdependent families and communities working together that have best weathered the storms of adversity. It will be the same today. A durable future depends on resilient family economies, close-knit communities, and "a firm reliance on the protection of Divine Providence"—it always has.

March 31, 2020

Preface

IN HIS SEMINAL WORK, *The Course of Empire,* Thomas Cole traces the rise and fall of a fictitious empire through a series of five paintings. The series begins with the primitive *Savage State,* followed by the idyllic *Pastoral State,* leading up to the *Consummation of Empire,* in which the imperium reaches its apex of wealth and power, only to be followed by *Destruction* and finally *Desolation*, in which savagery reasserts its dominance. The fact that these paintings were created in the mid-nineteenth century, just as the Industrial Revolution was drawing to a close (with America's "consummation" soon to follow), causes me to wonder whether Cole was more a prophet than a painter.

We live in a paradoxical time. As Western nations revel in unprecedented wealth and power, we are increasingly preoccupied with collapse. We closely monitor every uptick and downtick in the stock market indices but ignore the health of social institutions that undergird our way of life. Corporately we have specialized in every field of knowledge. But individually we lack the basic understanding to feed, clothe, and shelter ourselves— knowledge that has been passed down through every generation except the last two or three. We are abundant with things but wracked with loneliness and starved for meaning.

Faced with this reality, I desired to build something that would survive and thrive in an uncertain future, something that would tap into the historical context of work, family, and faith that has been practiced for thousands of years—in other words, something that will last. And if I'm going to spend the next 20 years building a family-centered economy, I want it to be one that doesn't die with me—or with the next recession, invention, or global supply-chain disruption. So I began to research people, places, and professions that have endured upheaval in the past and continue to do so today. This work is the culmination of that effort. It presents professions that have proven to be the most durable throughout history, place, governments, economic cycles, invention, and collapse; it examines the historical record with an eye for modern challenges.

Simply put, the purpose of this research is to identify which family-centered vocations are still viable to those who want to build durable futures for their families. If "a good man leaves an inheritance to his children's children," then this effort is the beginning of that inheritance.

Rory Groves
December 20, 2019

Acknowledgements

THERE IS NO MORE foundational truth about family than what God spoke in the garden: "it is not good for man to be alone." My deepest appreciation goes to my wife Becca without whom nothing I do or achieve would be worthwhile. She makes possible a joy-filled, family-centered home by her tireless dedication to our children and their best interests. Her witness inspires me to walk into the calling God has for our family. We are truly one flesh, two halves of the same whole.

I also want to thank Allan Carlson whose writing on the natural family and where it belongs greatly impacted us and spawned many late-night conversations about the future direction of our family.

Thank you to Jason Peters and the Front Porch Republic team for believing in this project and investing so much time and effort to bring it to life. Thank you to Chris Wiley, Kevin Swanson, Mike Cheney, Israel Wayne, Paul Gautschi, Lois Johnson and others who have encouraged me along the way and helped to shape this work.

And to our friends, family, and readers of the Grovestead Newsletter. Thank you for sharing in all that we are loving and learning from our life in the country.

Introduction

Against Obsolescence

AFTER MOVING TO A hobby farm several years ago, I began researching alternatives to the career path I have been on most of my life. Our experiences here with farming, stewarding land, and raising animals (and children) have stirred a deep desire in me to spend more of my time building things that will last. As a computer scientist, I have seen my share of obsolescence. Nothing can be more temporary than what comes out of Silicon Valley. I vividly remember my first day as a self-employed computer consultant many years ago, bright-eyed and cheery, working for myself for the first time. My client had hired me to help with a custom software project and had given me a tour of the sprawling dot-com startup's headquarters with its few hundred employees. The supervisor showed off the free soda machines, communal working environments, and break rooms replete with ping pong tables and other games. I was told about a forthcoming jumbotron on which movies would be screened every Friday afternoon. The next day everyone was laid off. Including me. It was the beginning of the dot-com collapse.

That experience, so early in my career, was formative to me in understanding how disposable we all are in the modern economy. We live in a time when companies employ "planned obsolescence" to make sure things they produce wear out and need to be replaced, so we need to keep earning money to buy the replacements. Even things that do not wear out on their own become targets of obsolescence by their manufacturers, as was discovered with older-model iPhones: Apple was deliberately degrading performance in order to force customers into newer versions (or so the 32 class-action lawsuits in the U.S. claim).[1]

And, increasingly, people are becoming obsolete. It is said the average person will work seven careers in his lifetime, which means he switches

1. Tung, "iPhone throttling."

careers about every five to seven years. According to the Bureau of Labor Statistics, a worker will switch jobs within those professions every 2.5 years.[2] If it takes roughly five years working full-time to become an expert in a given skill, it is doubtful that all of these people are voluntarily choosing to abandon their professions at the peak of their ability. For many, if not most, this way of life is forced upon them. Indeed, a person in my field who does not continuously retrain will become obsolete in about three years.

We are told to be good consumers, which means using things up and throwing them away. We are told that this is the foundation on which our prosperous economy depends. But we're a long way off the normative flow of history, in which self-reliance was the rule and where handmade furniture and tools were passed down for generations because they were made to last for generations.

When things broke down, they were fixed. What couldn't be fixed was used elsewhere. Garbage trucks did not pick up 96-gallon bins every Tuesday and bring them to landfills, because nothing was thrown out. Neither were people disposable. A person's worth was not the net total of his paycheck. Children were viewed as gifts from God and the elderly revered as the well-spring of wisdom. Everyone from cradle to grave had value and purpose and was needed by the community if the community were to survive.

Careers didn't become obsolete every half-decade. They lasted for hundreds of years. There was no need for perpetual purchasing because people knew how to make virtually everything they needed, and make it well. "Up to 1840, boot and shoemaking was wholly a handicraft," noted historians at the U.S. Department of Labor in 1928. "Shoemaking could be performed adequately . . . by any frontier farmer in his colonial kitchen."[3]

In his book *The New Agrarian Mind*, Allan Carlson writes about pre-Industrial life in America: "Before 1840, homespun cloth, homemade clothes, hand-wrought furniture, domestically produced candles, and home educated children were the rule, in city and countryside."[4] Of these people Thomas Jefferson wrote in 1785: "They are the most vigorous, the most independent, the most virtuous, and they are tied to their country and wedded to its liberty and interests by the most lasting bands."[5]

In the course of researching this book, I have had difficulty finding comparative wage data and living standards for pre-Industrial professions. Farming, though idealized by Jefferson, is not even listed as an occupation

2. BLS, *National Longitudinal Surveys,* "Number of Jobs Held in a Lifetime."
3. BLS, *History of Wages,* 103.
4. Carlson, *The New Agrarian Mind,* 1.
5. Jefferson, letter to John Jay, August 23, 1785.

in *The Statistical Abstract of the United States* 1752–1885, despite the fact that the vast majority of people were farmers during that period. To the industrialists, money was the only measurement, and whatever could not be measured was not worth mentioning.

With the Industrial Revolution, *efficiency* became our highest virtue, and with it generational stability collapsed. The factory replaced the family as the primary means of sustenance. Opportunity for apprenticeship, relationship, and cross-generational continuity of values and culture disappeared.

Is all this simply romanticizing the past? Don't we live vastly wealthier lives today? I guess it depends on how you define wealth. In terms of material abundance, yes, we are vastly richer than our forebears. But it's hard to put a price on self-sufficiency. In terms of relationships to each other, to the land, and to God, our forebears were much richer than we. In *The Benedict Option*, Rod Dreher writes, "The long journey from a medieval world wracked with suffering but pregnant with meaning has delivered us to a place of once unimaginable comfort but emptied of significance and connection."[6] If quality of life consists merely of the abundance of possessions, if our value to society is based solely our productive capacity, if money, things, careers and people are perpetually becoming obsolete, what have we profited by gaining the whole world?

This book is an attempt to answer the question: is there another way? Is it possible to reclaim some of the lost practices of previous generations— and lost rewards of strong families and resilient communities? Is it possible to build something that will last, something that becomes an inheritance, even to our children's children?

In the pages that follow, I outline how our modern way of life is resting on fragile foundations and discuss a few of the many challenges that lie ahead (Part I). I also present a catalog of what I call Durable Trades: historical, family-centered professions that have survived some of the worst upheavals in history—and are still thriving today (Part II). To each trade listed I assign a score based on metrics such as historical stability, family-centeredness, and resistance to automation (the complete list of criteria can be found in the Appendix). Finally, I offer some reflections on this research and discuss how families can prepare for an uncertain future by examining the past (Part III).

I intend this work to be a starting point. Family-centered trades are not only the most durable throughout history; they are also the ideal context by which parents can pass their values, faith, and culture on to the next

---

6. Dreher, *The Benedict Option*, 46.

generation. My hope is that this book inspires readers in some way to begin building a lasting inheritance for their families.

PART I

Brittle Systems

Men always build their towers so high they fall down.
— FRANCIS SCHAEFFER

1

The Challenge Ahead

We all have grown up in complex societies, so we consider complexity to be normal, and we consider it to be the natural state of affairs. The problem with this view is that it's historically inaccurate. We are in fact an anomaly of history. We don't realize that low complexity is the normal state of affairs and the way we live today is very unusual.[1]

—JOSEPH TAINTER

RESEARCH INTO THE TOPIC of "durable trades" invariably leads to the causes of decline. After all, why bother investigating such a topic unless there is an underlying sense that the way we live today is not indefinitely sustainable? If such a project is worth undertaking, what assumptions are being made about the way things are?

Jobs in the building trades are projected to increase faster than jobs in every other sector in America over the next decade—faster even than health care and technology.[2] Over the same period, many white-collar jobs requiring 4-year college degrees will cease to exist. Why is this?

---

1. Tainter, "Will Our Society Survive Complexity?"
2. Manyika et al., "Jobs Lost, Jobs Gained."

To answer these questions, we must examine the more serious cracks in modernity's foundation so that we can understand the need for more durable alternatives for those living in the twenty-first century.

Complexity & Specialization

In his renowned work, *The Collapse of Complex Societies*, historian Joseph Tainter posited a new theory for the cause of decline and collapse in civilizations. Prior to his work, theories of societal collapse ranged from "such catastrophes as nuclear war, resource depletion, economic decline, ecological crises, or sociopolitical disintegration."[3] But Tainter's theory differed from other literature on the subject. Tainter asserted that societies collapse not because of external pressures forced upon them, but because of increasing levels of complexity from within:

> Human history as a whole has been characterized by a seemingly inexorable trend toward higher levels of complexity, specialization, and sociopolitical control, processing of greater quantities of energy and in formation, formation of ever larger settlements, and development of more complex and capable technologies.[4]

As societies face problems, they increase in complexity in order to solve them. Eventually, Tainter argues, the complexity overwhelms a society's ability to maintain it, and the result is a "rapid loss of complexity in a society," otherwise known as *collapse*.

To prove his point, Tainter documents the collapse of 18 civilizations through history, from the Old Egyptian Empire (2181 BC) to the Roman Empire (AD 476), to the Chacoan (AD 1300) and Mayan (AD 900) civilizations in North and South America, all of which were at their heights—some having lasted thousands of years—when collapse came suddenly.

One way to measure complexity in a society is to look at the stratification of professions—that is, job specialization. As societies increase in complexity, the labor force must continually re-orient itself to meet new demands and challenges, subdividing complex tasks into simpler ones. In America, as with the rest of the industrialized world, we have seen a logarithmic rise in the number of occupations over the last two centuries.

At the founding of our country, there were at most a few dozen distinct occupations. Within 100 years that number had risen to over 8,000. Today

3. Tainter, *The Collapse of Complex Societies*, 3.
4. Tainter, *The Collapse of Complex Societies*, 3.

there are over 30,000 occupations, with dozens of new specialties being invented daily.

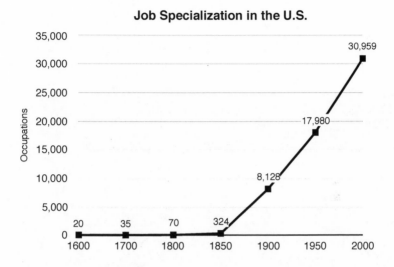

Job Specialization in the U.S.

Sources: Virginia Center for Digital History; Colonial Williamsburg; US Census 1850; US Census 1900; IPUMS USA; 1950 Census, Alphabetical Index of Occupations and Industries; Census 2000 Occupational Index; Data for 1800 is estimated.

To analyze the rapid increase in specialization and complexity, twentieth-century economists developed models to interpret the data. The Three-Sector Theory, developed by Allan Fisher, Colin Clark and Jean Fouraste, proposed organizing job specialties into three "megasectors" of economic activity: primary, secondary, and tertiary. Later a fourth sector was added, the quaternary.

"This categorization is seen as a continuum of distance from the natural environment," explains geographer Matt Rosenberg. "The continuum starts with primary economic activity, which concerns itself with the utilization of raw materials from the earth such as agriculture and mining. From there, the distance from the raw materials of the earth increases."[5]

Primary Sector activities include raw material extraction, namely, farming, mining, fishing, forestry, and hunting. The Secondary Sector produces finished goods from the activities of the Primary Sector. This includes manufacturing, processing, and construction. The Tertiary Sector is broadly known as the services industry. Activities in this sector involve selling goods

5. Rosenberg, "The 5 Sectors of the Economy," para. 1.

made by the Secondary Sector and providing services—transportation, banking, healthcare, and law—to people in all sectors. The more recently defined Quaternary Sector consists of intellectual activities known as the knowledge economy—scientific research, education, government, and information technology.

Clark codified this theory into a time-series chart to illustrate how civilizations progress from Primary Sector activities to Tertiary and Quaternary Sector activities as they mature and industrialize.

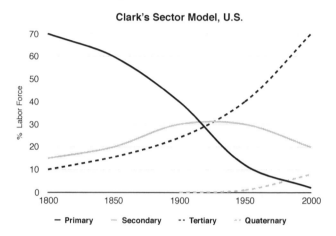

In pre-industrial America (prior to 1790), more than two-thirds of the population was directly involved in such primary activities as farming and forestry, with a small minority involved in manufacturing and even fewer in services. Today these allocations have reversed dramatically, with only a small minority involved in primary activities, while the vast majority are employed by the service (tertiary) and knowledge (quaternary) economies.

Keep in mind that the names given these various sectors are Primary, Secondary, Tertiary, and not First, Second, Third. While the expansion of subsequent sectors correlates to an increase in prosperity for the society being measured, these sectors still depend on precedent-sector activities. In other words, before scientists, computer programmers, and biotech engineers can be employed in a society, there must be robust construction, manufacturing and service sectors. And before there can be robust construction and manufacturing, there must be farming, forestry and mining. Even the theoretical astrophysicist has to eat.

Consider viewing these sectors as a pyramid. In simpler societies, the foundation consists of a broad base of Primary Sector activities: agriculture, mining, and forestry—and a broad base of laborers to work those professions. Upon this foundation rests manufacturing, processing, and construction activities. Towards the top of the pyramid we see the Tertiary (service) and Quaternary (knowledge) sectors.

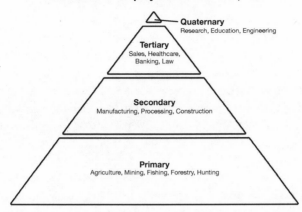

Distribution of Employment in the U.S., 1900

A society that is formed thus would be inherently stable and self-sufficient. External impacts such as supply-chain disruptions would have limited, if any, impact. With its broad foundation of primary activities, such a society maintains the essential knowledge to feed, clothe, and shelter itself without being overly dependent on secondary and tertiary activities. But imagine if the pyramid were inverted. What if the foundation is minuscule and has to support the weight of the entire rest of the economy? How stable would that society truly be?

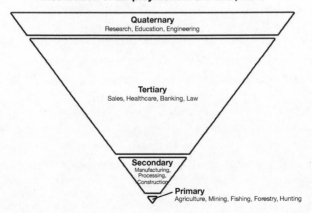

Distribution of Employment in the U.S., 2010

When illustrated in this way, such a society appears unstable and top-heavy. Yet this is how all modern, post-industrial societies are organized today. Within a relatively short timeframe, Western nations have come to rely on a minuscule proportion of their fellow citizens to supply the vast majority of their needs. Some nations are entirely dependent on others (i.e., imports) to provide for basic subsistence. In historical terms, we refer to those nations as subjugated.

Some may point to raw material imports and modern global trade, which offsets declines in domestic primary and secondary sector activities. Others may point to the fact that, despite declines in employment, America still manufactures as much as before. But over the long run of human history, this degree of specialization has never truly been tested. We are the "anomaly" that Tainter describes. Should there be any significant disruption to Primary or Secondary Sector activities, how stable would the more advanced sectors be?

It was not that long ago that every American citizen, regardless of occupation, possessed the skills to provide his or her own food, shelter, and clothing, should the need ever arise. Today, so far along the "continuum of distance from the natural environment," how many of the service and knowledge workers who drive our economy could do the same?

Slave to the Lender

Perhaps the most glaring crack in the foundation of our modern way of life is debt. At no time in history has the world's wealth been so vastly eclipsed by its debt. In truth it is difficult to distinguish how much of our prosperity and material abundance is the product of innovation and productivity, as is claimed, and how much is the result of profligate spending.

Total federal debt in America surpassed $23 trillion in 2019, not including state and municipal debt, which amounts to another $3 trillion.[6] The federal government currently spends over $5 trillion per year but only collects $3.4 trillion. Combined with state and local spending, total government debt is increasing by well over $1 trillion per year, and the *rate* of increase keeps increasing. To put this into perspective, as if perspective could be had with numbers so staggering, we are borrowing $2 million a minute.[7]

Americans pay $380 billion annually just to service the interest on this debt, and this at historically low interest rates. If rates were ever to return to the historical average of 5 percent, it would cost $1.2 trillion annually just to

---

6. Source: US Treasury, Congressional Budget Office, US Census, Federal Reserve, USDebtClock.org

7. Paul, *Proceedings and Debates of the 11th Congress*, 126.

pay the interest—one-quarter of the total U.S. budget and nearly twice the entire military defense budget.

Total unfunded liabilities, which are future benefits the government has promised to pay but does not actually have the income to support, are estimated to be north of $210 trillion.[8] That's a $342,000 liability for every man, woman, and child in this country. However, it will mostly fall to our children and their children to bear the consequences of these promises. If Solomon was correct that "a good man leaves an inheritance to his children's children,"[9] what do the wicked leave behind?

Thomas Jefferson, America's third president, strongly condemned debt-financed spending, writing in 1816 that "the principle of spending money to be paid by posterity, under the name of funding, is but swindling futurity on a large scale."[10] Unfortunately, few Presidents since Jefferson have held such strong misgivings about debt. Early on, from our nation's founding until the Civil War, the national debt doubled at the rate of once every 200 years.[11] But since abandoning the gold standard in 1971, the national debt has been doubling every eight years, with the exception of the Reagan presidency, during which the national debt tripled.

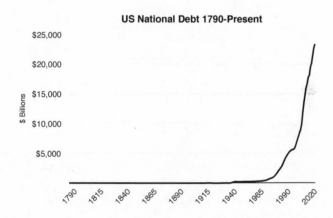

US National Debt 1790-Present

Source: US Dept. of Treasury

However, spiraling national debt is not a uniquely American phenomenon. While America is the world's largest economy, it is not alone in

8. Kotlikoff, "America's Hidden Credit Card Bill," para. 9.

9. Prov 13:22

10. Jefferson, letter to John Taylor, May 28, 1816.

11. Over the 71 period from 1790 to 1861 federal debt increased 27 percent: Bureau of the Fiscal Service, U.S. Department of the Treasury.

fueling its prosperity through borrowed money. Total combined sovereign
debt around the world is estimated to be $217 trillion—325 percent of world
GDP—and this does not include private debt: credit cards, mortgages, auto
loans and student loans, or commercial business debt.[12] Such a calculation
worldwide has yet to be made. But if other countries bear any resemblance to
America, where total household debt stands at $14 trillion, then the tally of
all worldwide debt and unfunded liabilities may require another comma.[13]

Top Debtor Nations (trillions)	
USA	$23.5
Japan	$11.4
China	$8.6
UK	$3.4
Italy	$2.9
France	$2.8
India	$2.5
Germany	$2.4
Brazil	$1.8
Canada	$1.7
Spain	$1.5

Source: USDebtClock.org (March 2020)

Don't be fooled by the monetary theorists: we are in the parabolic
blow-off stage of debt accumulation. Fifty years ago, when federal debt was
a "mere" $350 billion, no one could have imagined the staggering levels of
debt that we would find ourselves in today. Few would have predicted that
our debt-financed prosperity could go on this long.

Wisdom of the ages tell us that "the rich rule over the poor, and the
borrower is slave to the lender."[14] But the Gods of the Copybook Headings
are utterly out of touch with the Hopes that our World is built on. Like our
untested experiment in specialization, global debt will continue to accumulate until it can't—until, as Kipling warns, "we have plenty of money, but
nothing our money can buy."[15]

12. Rabouin, "Total global debt tops 325 pct of GDP."

13. Federal Reserve Bank of New York, "Household Debt Tops $14 Trillion."

14. Prov 22:7

15. Kipling, "The Gods of the Copybook Headings," line 27.

The Ghost of Money

In 1913 a pound of butter cost 37 cents, a two-piece men's suit cost $9.90, and a nine-room house in Morristown, New Jersey, cost $2,500.[16] One hundred years hence, butter now sells for $4 per pound (an increase of 1,081 percent), men's suits for $600 (6,060 percent increase), and the median house price in Morristown, New Jersey is $431,900 (17,276 percent increase).

Yes, we have inflation to thank for these price increases. But, no, it has not always been this way. One hundred years prior to 1913, butter, suits, and houses were not 1,000, 6,000, and 17,000 percent cheaper. In 1813 the price of a pound of butter was 25 cents, a mere 12 cents less. And for the preceding two centuries the price of butter barely fluctuated more than a dime. As far back as 1633, the price of butter was a remarkably constant 12 cents per pound.[17]

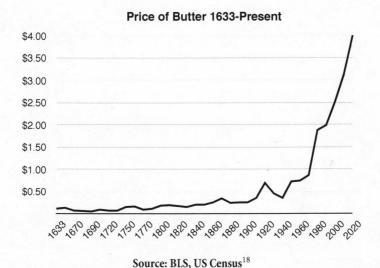

Price of Butter 1633-Present

Source: BLS, US Census[18]

Why have prices skyrocketed only in the last century, after several centuries of relative stability? The answer lies in a pivotal event that occurred in 1913: the passage of the Federal Reserve Act by Congress, and the establishment of a privately-owned central bank, granting the Federal Reserve the exclusive power to issue money. Each quarter the Federal Reserve Board

16. *The Daily Record*, "Historical Prices: 1913."

17. Bureau of Labor Statistics, *History of Wages*, 20.

18. Bureau of Labor Statistics, *History of Wages*, 20; Mass. Bureau of Statistics of Labor, *Comparative Wages*, 86–87; *Report on the Statistics of Wages*, 44; Bureau of the Census, *Historical Statistics of the United States*, 213; BLS, "Series Report: Butter."

meets and decides whether to raise or lower the rate at which it lends money to other banks. Its stated objective is to achieve 2 percent inflation in consumer prices every year. When inflation falls below 2 percent, the Fed drops interest rates, encouraging more borrowing and spending.

Why target 2 percent inflation and not 0 percent? It is the Federal Reserve's belief that inflation encourages spending, and spending, rather than saving, drives the economy. Over time, the cumulative effect of *intentional inflation* through credit expansion is the chief reason for the dramatic price increases we have today.

Concerns about these matters were widely known and openly debated in Congress prior to the passage of the Federal Reserve Act. U.S. Senator Henry Cabot Lodge, Sr., warned in 1913, "The powers vested in the Federal Reserve Board seem to me highly dangerous especially when there is political control of the Board. . . . The [Federal Reserve] bill as it stands seems to me to open the way to a vast inflation of the currency. . . . I do not like to think that any law can be passed that will make it possible to submerge the gold standard in a flood of irredeemable paper currency."[19]

Since 1913, through intentional inflation, the U.S. Dollar has lost 97 percent of its purchasing power. Jefferson was right when he said, "Paper is poverty. It is only the ghost of money, and not money itself."[20]

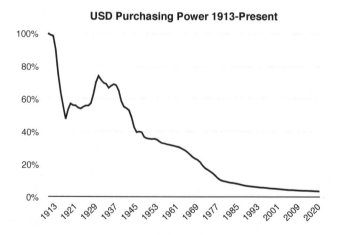

USD Purchasing Power 1913-Present

Source: BLS Consumer Price Index

19. Sen. Lodge, letter to Sen. Weeks, December 17, 1913.
20. Jefferson, letter to Edward Carrington, May 27, 1788.

So why is devaluation of the currency a crack in the foundation? First, nearly all civilizations experience times of devaluation of their official currency. Sometimes these are due to external factors such as war, sustained natural disasters, or trade imbalances. Sometimes these are due to internal factors, such as intentional inflation by their central banks. Historically, governments do not debase their currencies except as a last resort to avoid defaulting on their debts. In other words, inflation can be a precursor to collapse. Examples include hyper-inflationary Weimar Republic in Germany following World War I, Hungary in 1946, and Zimbabwe in 2008, where prices doubled every 24 hours.

As of this writing, the Venezuelan currency is also in free-fall, the government having truncated five zeros from the value of the bolivar in 2018. The hyperinflation in Venezuela now supersedes the oft-cited "extreme" example of 1923 Weimar Republic.[21]

The Western Roman Empire provides one of the most well-documented cases of currency debasement. The denarius, containing 4.5 grams of pure silver, was the coin of the realm for hundreds of years. Over the years, in order to keep up with expanding deficits, the government reduced the silver content of the denarius, replacing it with cheaper metals until eventually the coins contained only 3 percent silver—a 97 percent loss of purchasing power. Sound familiar?

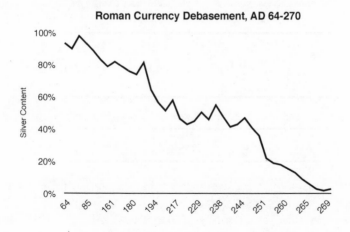

Source: Kenneth W. Harl, Tulane University[22]

21. Durden, "Venezuela Slashes 5 Zeros From Currency."
22. Harl, "The Later Roman Empire."

"One of the things that had happened in the course of this third-century inflation," says Joseph Peden, "was that the government found that when it paid its troops in token coinage, or even debased silver coins, prices immediately rose. Every time the silver value of the denarius dropped, prices naturally rose."[23] It's hard to miss the parallels between ancient Rome and our country today: America stopped circulating silver coins in 1965.

Observers note that "debasement and inflation helped lead to the demise of the Western Roman Empire, which collapsed by 476 A.D."[24] But the freedom of Roman citizens evaporated long before that. The fifth-century Christian priest Salvian of Marseille wrote that "the Roman people, the mass of the population, had but one wish after being captured by the barbarians: to never again fall under the rule of the Roman bureaucracy."[25]

The second reason devaluation of a nation's currency represents a serious crack in the foundation is that the longer a society resorts to devaluation, the fewer "tools" it has to cope with the inevitable consequences of debt accumulation and market fluctuations. Since the Great Recession of 2008, the Federal Reserve has been attempting more and more risky maneuvers to avoid sinking back into recession, including lowering interest rates to 0 percent and printing $4 trillion worth of "stimulus" spending. Eventually, if there is not a return to a sound currency, there will be no more options left. As former Federal Reserve Chairman Ben Bernanke said in 2012, "If the fiscal cliff isn't addressed, as I've said, I don't think our tools are strong enough to offset the effects of a major fiscal shock."[26]

The Robots are Coming

The Industrial Revolution kicked off two centuries of relentless automation, and the pace has not abated since. Professions that once endured for generations—being passed from parents to children to grandchildren—now last only a few years. According to the Bureau of Labor Statistics, the average worker will change jobs every 2.5 years.[27]

In the past decade we have seen revolutions in warfare with unmanned aerial drones, in spaceflight with self-launching and self-landing autonomous rockets, in transportation with the first self-driving vehicles hitting

23. Peden, "Inflation and the Fall of the Roman Empire," para. 27.

24. Desjardins, "How Currency Debasement Contributed to the Fall of Rome," infographic.

25. Peden, "Inflation and the Fall of the Roman Empire," para. 92.

26. Irwin, "If we go off the fiscal cliff, the Fed can't save us."

27. BLS, *National Longitudinal Surveys*, "Number of Jobs Held in a Lifetime."

the roads, and in farming with unmanned tractors and harvesters. According to *The New York Times*, forthcoming innovations that will "Change Your Tomorrow" include electric clothing which can harness temperature differentials in your body to charge your cellphone, the elimination of highway traffic through adaptive cruise control, more potent sleeping pills, and blood-tests to measure depression and anxiety.[28] Innovation, it appears, is increasingly attempting to solve problems created by previous innovations.

Killer Toasters

And this brings us to the darker side of automation. The more we come to rely on advanced technologies, the more vulnerable we become to their disruption. A stark example of this was the widespread Internet outage in 2016. A hacking group was able to bring down major Internet platforms and hundreds of high-profile websites across a wide swath of Europe and North America by leveraging millions of Internet-connected devices—WiFi routers, digital video recorders, even baby monitors—to attack a single target of computer servers that route Internet traffic.

The hacked devices—Internet-of-Things (IoT), as it is known—shut down such notable websites as Twitter, Netflix, and Amazon.com. The payment sites PayPal and Visa, and such news sites *The New York Times*, CNN, and *The Wall Street Journal* were also unavailable. "The attack broke the tools we use to monitor attacks," reported one observer.[29] Communications and commerce at affected sites were unavailable for the duration of the outage. This episode raised serious concerns as to the underlying vulnerability of the Internet, which up to that point was assumed to be resilient. Following the incident, one security professional wrote, "we've taken a system built to resist destruction by nuclear weapons and made it vulnerable to toasters."[30]

Other disturbing developments include the rapid increase and potency of computer viruses. Ransomware—a virus that blocks access to the infected computer unless a payment is made—has skyrocketed in recent years and is responsible for shutting down services at numerous hospitals around the world, with patients literally being turned away until systems could be restored.[31]

28. Koerth-Baker, "32 Innovations That Will Change Your Tomorrow."

29. Ali, "Toasters are breaking the Internet."

30. Jarmoc, Twitter post, October 21, 2016.

31. Rayome, "Report: Ransomware attacks grew 600%."; Lawless and Parra, "World cyberattack cripples UK hospitals."

As a result of increasing reliance on Internet-based technologies, all modern nations have been ramping up their cyber defensive—and offensive—capabilities, and many credible observers believe it is only a matter of time before a major cyber war erupts, causing widespread and prolonged disruption—up to and even including shutting down electric power grids.[32] In an ironic twist, it is the highly automated nations that are most vulnerable to cyber-attack.

Stealing Your Attention

Another dark side of innovation is the impact that excessive screen time is having on our increasingly digitized society. Americans now spend nearly 11 hours a day in front of screens.[33] Dads spend five hours a day watching television but only 34 minutes "caring for household children."[34] Studies continue to be released linking screen time and social media usage to depression, anxiety, and a host of other mental health issues, especially among children.

In late 2017 Facebook publicly acknowledged that social media can be bad for you, citing multiple studies that indicate a correlation between Facebook usage and mental health.[35] But this was not news to insiders. A recent string of investors, employees, and even co-founders have come forward denouncing the technology they helped create. Chamath Palihapitiya, former vice-president for user-growth at Facebook admitted he feels "tremendous guilt" over the company he helped to build. "I think we have created tools that are ripping apart the social fabric of how society works," he said.[36]

Sean Parker, a co-founder and the first president of Facebook, says that social media is "exploiting a vulnerability in human psychology." Parker explained that when building Facebook the company's thought process was "how do we consume as much of your time and conscious attention as possible?"[37]

Timothy Cook, CEO of Apple, told reporters he would not let his nephew on social media, and Palihapitiya also "tries to use Facebook as little

32. Koppel, *Lights Out*, 8–10.

33. Howard, "Americans devote more than 10 hours a day to screen time."

34. Hinckley, "Average American watches 5 hours of TV per day."; Bureau of Labor Statistics, "American Time Use Survey Summary," Table 9.

35. Facebook, "Hard Questions."

36. Vincent, "Former Facebook exec says social media is ripping apart society," para. 3.

37. Ong, "Sean Parker on Facebook," para. 2–3.

as possible" and does not allow his children to use it.[38] With a user base approaching two billion on Facebook alone, we must ask the obvious question: what do these Silicon Valley insiders know that the rest of us do not?

"The largest supercomputers in the world are inside of two companies—Google and Facebook—and where are we pointing them?" asks former Google design ethicist Tristan Harris. "We're pointing them at people's brains, at children."[39] Harris, along with other former employees at Google and Facebook, formed the Center for Humane Technology, which seeks to change the way people use technology and challenge the companies that they themselves helped create.

To be successful, social media platforms must vie for every moment of their users' attention. To choose not to adopt a manipulative feature would put one platform at a competitive disadvantage. So every day thousands of social media engineers are working to make their platform more addictive than the competition in order to "consume as much of your time and conscious attention as possible." Harris calls this a "race to the bottom of the brain stem."[40]

"As an example," Tristan explains, "the CEO of Netflix recently said the biggest competitors to Netflix weren't other video [rental] sites; the biggest competitors to Netflix were Facebook, YouTube, and sleep."[41]

Despite this string of admissions and detractors, Facebook has since launched Messenger Kids, a social media app aimed at pre-teens and children as young as six. The release was met with immediate opposition from child welfare experts, who urged Facebook CEO Mark Zuckerberg to discontinue Messenger Kids:

> At a time when there is mounting concern about how social media use affect adolescents' wellbeing, it is particularly irresponsible to encourage children as young as preschoolers to start using a Facebook product.[42]

Whether Facebook will heed the warning of concerned parents and teachers remains to be seen—a quick search online reveals that Facebook is currently hiring for over 300 positions in psychology-related fields.

Harris registers his overriding concern this way: "Never before in history have the decisions of a handful of designers working at 3

38. Gibbs, "Apple's Tim Cook: 'I don't want my nephew on a social network.'"; Vincent, "Former Facebook exec," para. 1.

39. Bowles, "Early Facebook and Google Employees Form Coalition," para. 6.

40. Bosker, "The Binge Breaker," para. 5.

41. Harris, "The Eyeball Economy."

42. Campaign for a Commercial-Free Childhood, "Open letter to Mark Zuckerberg."

companies"—Google, Apple, and Facebook—"had so much impact on how
millions of people around the world spend their attention."[43]

Summoning the Demon

An often disputed but no less threatening impact of technology is the rise
of Artificial Intelligence, or A.I. In 2015, outspoken tech titan Elon Musk
made headlines when he donated $10 million to kickstart research into
averting human extinction caused by Artificial Intelligence. This is not just
the imaginings of science fiction writers. Musk believes artificial super intelligence run-amok is humanity's "biggest existential threat."[44] And Elon is
not alone in his concerns. Microsoft co-founder Bill Gates wrote, "I am in
the camp that is concerned about super intelligence . . . I agree with Elon
Musk and some others on this and don't understand why some people are
not concerned."[45]

The late theoretical physicist Stephen Hawking shared similar senti-
ments: "the development of full artificial intelligence could spell the end of
the human race."[46] Musk and Hawking are among 3,700 prominent signa-
tories of an open letter by the Future of Life Institute calling for a ban on
offensive autonomous weapons. The letter explains:

> Unlike nuclear weapons, [autonomous weapons] require no
> costly or hard-to-obtain raw materials, so they will become
> ubiquitous and cheap for all significant military powers to mass-
> produce. It will only be a matter of time until they appear on the
> black market and in the hands of terrorists [and] dictators wish-
> ing to better control their populace. . . . Autonomous weapons
> are ideal for tasks such as assassinations, destabilizing nations,
> subduing populations and selectively killing a particular ethnic
> group. We therefore believe that a military AI arms race would
> not be beneficial for humanity.[47]

In the mad dash for automation, open letters cautioning against the use of
robot weaponry seem like too little, too late. For all the opportunity A.I.
presents, Musk assumes a more foreboding posture. He warns, "With artificial intelligence, we are summoning the demon."

43. Bosker, "The Binge Breaker," para. 16.

44. Musk, "Centennial Symposium."

45. Gates, "Ask Me Anything."

46. Cellan-Jones, "Stephen Hawking warns artificial intelligence could end
mankind."

47. Future of Life Institute, "Autonomous Weapons," para. 2.

Understanding the Exponential

Perhaps the most visible impact of automation is the staggering number of jobs that are being lost to advances in robotics. One study predicts that 47 percent of all U.S. jobs will be automated within the next 15 years.[48] There is a tendency to dismiss concerns over job loss due to automation because such concerns have always been a false alarm. Until now, automation has led to more jobs rather than fewer. But experts say this time is different.

"Craftspeople were an important group," says employment researcher Chris Tilly, referring to artisanal jobs that have been lost over time due to machine automation. "But they were not the majority of society. Now when we talk about machines taking the jobs of the great, great majority of working adults, it's a different level of distress than it was in 1800."[49]

A recent study from McKinsey Global Institute predicts that up to 800 million people will be displaced by the coming robotic revolution in the next 10 years.[50] This includes 375 million full-time workers and 38.6 million Americans—one-third of the employed workforce—that will need to find new jobs by 2030.

And it's not just the low-wage manufacturing jobs that are at risk. Many knowledge-worker jobs are highly susceptible to the coming disruption. In many cases, the more highly specialized the profession—and therefore more highly paid—the more likely it is to become a target for automation. Doctors, lawyers, and IT professionals are just a few of the hundreds of professions that will be impacted. One researcher notes: "When high paid white collar jobs dealing with information processing can be replaced by software, the situation becomes more acute."[51]

"It's been said that the greatest failing of the human mind is the inability to understand the exponential," says Erik Brynjolfsson, professor at MIT. At first, changes from computerization come slowly and appear manageable to humans who think linearly. But soon the changes outpace our ability to deal with them. Many believe we are now approaching "escape velocity," when machines will rapidly displace humans in virtually all categories of labor. According to author and technologist Ray Kurzweil, by 2025, one computer will have the capacity of one brain. By 2050, one computer will have the capacity of all brains.

48. Frey and Osborne, "The Future of Employment," 1.
49. *Automation and the Future of Jobs.*
50. Manyika et al., "Jobs Lost, Jobs Gained," 8.
51. *Automation and the Future of Jobs.*

The coming innovations and automation, as in technological revolutions of the past, will no doubt bring great advancements in efficiency and standards of living. Also, like past innovations they will be eagerly adopted with little consideration for their displacing effects on families and communities. Machine automation has little time for the *inefficiency* of human relationships.

Measuring Morality

Pointing to an over-dependence on vulnerable global systems, some claim we are on the brink of societal collapse. Others argue that such claims are exaggerated and that collapse is not inevitable. But by examining a different set of metrics one could conclude that collapse is neither imminent nor far off. It has already happened.

When Tainter describes collapse as "the rapid loss of complexity in a society" he's referring to complex *systems* on which societies depend. The rapid decline of *social institutions* that undergird our way of life and make prosperity possible is nothing other than a national catastrophe—if instead of measuring material wealth we measure moral impoverishment.

The Incredible Shrinking Family

"For millennials currently aged 18 to 30, just 20 percent are married, compared with nearly 60 percent of 18- to 30-year-olds in 1962," according to research published by Gallup.[52] As a group, 59 percent of millennials have never married, compared to 10 percent of their grandparents. Why bother with divorce statistics when couples aren't getting married in the first place?

Out of wedlock births have increased to 57 percent of births, up from 5.3 percent in 1960.[53] That's a 10-fold increase in two generations. Delaying and avoiding marriage has also coincided—and likely caused—a collapse in childbearing. Birth rates over the same period have halved, from 3.7 births per woman in 1960 to 1.8 today.[54] According to the CDC, the birthrate "has generally been below replacement since 1971."[55]

---

52. Flemming, "Gallup Analysis: Millennials, Marriage and Family," para. 5.

53. Cherlin et al., "Changing Fertility Regimes," 8; CDC, "Number and Percent of Births to Unmarried Women," Table 1–17.

54. World Bank, "Fertility rate, total."

55. Hamilton, et al., "Births: Provisional Data for 2017," 2.

In summary, Americans are abandoning marriage and child-rearing. The children they do have are not growing up in two-parent households. In other words, Americans are not starting families anymore. But this is hardly an American phenomenon. The UN's *World's Population Prospects* states that "during 2010–2015, fertility was below the replacement level in 83 countries comprising 46 percent of the world's population."[56] According to Procter & Gamble, adult diapers will outsell baby diapers within the next decade.[57] Around the world, all industrialized nations and many developing countries have seen radical demographic shifts in birth rates, marriage, and family composition over the last 60 years.

Losing Our Religion

Religious adherence has also seen a precipitous decline. According to Gallup, church membership in America hovered around 70 percent since Gallup started taking measurements in 1937, and it remained at that level until 2000. Since then, the number has rapidly declined to an all-time low of 50 percent in 2018.[58] Another study showed that the number of self-identified Christians in America fell a staggering 8 percent between 2007 and 2014—a loss of 25 million Christians in seven years.[59] Meanwhile, the number of atheists and agnostics rose to an all-time high of 23 percent.

Those still attending church are not passing their faith on to their children. Various studies indicate that the vast majority of youth abandon the faith of their parents after leaving high school.[60] For some denominations the situation is more dire: a report by the Southern Baptist Council on Family Life in 2002 found that 88 percent of children from evangelical homes leave the church within two years of graduating from high school.[61] Add to that the rapidly declining number of practicing parents, and it isn't difficult to predict the implosion of traditional religion in America within a relatively short time.

Theological debates aside, the church has served as the central hub of social life since America's founding. For centuries after the collapse of Rome and the rise of Christianity, pagan temples were torn down and churches

56. United Nations, "World Population Prospects: The 2017 Revision," para. 11.

57. *Toronto Sun,* "Adult diapers expected to outsell baby diapers soon."

58. Jones, "U.S. Church Membership Down Sharply in Past Two Decades."

59. Pew Research Center, "America's Changing Religious Landscape."

60. Lifeway Research puts the dropout rate at 70 percent, Barna puts the rate at 59 percent.

61. Walker, "Family Life Council says it's time to bring family back to life," para. 2.

built in their place. In the last 50 years we have seen a dramatic reversal. "For a thousand years, cities in the Western world built cathedrals to bring glory to God and civic pride to their communities," writes one journalist commenting on a recently built $1-billion football stadium. "At the dawn of the third millennium, we build stadiums."[62] Media mogul Rupert Murdock agrees. "It's the true religion of America: sports. That's what we love, and we are religious about it."[63]

Rise of Neopaganism

Concomitant with the decline of orthodox Christianity there has been a renewed interest in pagan religions in America and abroad. Halloween is the fastest-growing "holiday" in the U.S., and Wicca is the fastest-growing religion.[64] Estimates of the number of practicing witches in America now number in the millions.[65]

With the rise of neopaganism comes the re-emergence of pagan practices. One of the ways historians trace the spread of Christianity through the Western world is by identifying when laws banning infanticide were enacted. Infanticide was practiced in virtually every pagan culture. In Iceland infanticide was banned shortly after AD 1000 when Christianity was adopted following the arrival of missionaries from Norway. The legalization of abortion in modern times is viewed by many (this author included) as the re-introduction of infanticide. Pagan cultures routinely exterminated children deemed to be unfit. Iceland legalized abortion in 1975 and is "on pace to virtually eliminate Down syndrome through abortion."[66] It should come as no surprise that Iceland recently finished construction on its first pagan temple in 1,000 years.[67] "The worship of Odin, Thor, Freya and the other gods of the old Norse pantheon became an officially recognized religion exactly 973 years after Iceland's official conversion to Christianity."[68]

62. Geisendorfer-Lindgren, "Stadiums, cathedrals: Marks of their eras," para. 1.

63. Zahn, "'The true religion of America,'" para. 7.

64. According to the National Retail Federation, consumer spending on Halloween has increased 90 percent since 2009 while Christmas spending has increased 35 percent; Kimball, "Wicca Experts Encourage Christians to Engage America's 'Fastest-Growing' Religion."

65. Fearnow, "Number of Witches Rises Dramatically," para. 2.

66. Desanctis, "Iceland Eliminates People with Down Syndrome," para. 4.

67. *Iceland Monitor*, "Iceland's first pagan temple in 1000 years."

68. Olsen, "A Norse temple for the 21st century," para. 2.

America re-introduced infanticide in 1973, a few years prior to Iceland, with the Supreme Court ruling on *Roe v Wade*. Abortion is now legal on request in nearly all Western nations. The World Health Organization estimates that up to 50 million babies are aborted annually, over 135,000 per day—or 95 per minute. Over the last 45 years, two billion abortions have been performed, roughly a quarter of the planet's population.[69] Those who hold to a materialistic view may take no issue with the wanton destruction of human life. They may even, under pretenses of population control, wish these numbers to be higher. But those who hold to a traditional religious view see these numbers as an unbearable manifestation of a culture that has lost its way.

Liberty or Libertine?

Other pagan practices have re-emerged in recent decades as well. Sexual promiscuity, as evidenced by rampant increase in sexually-transmitted diseases, as well as the mainstreaming of every form of sexual libertinism is not in fact a modern idea.[70] Homosexuality, pedophilia, and polygamy are in fact old practices; ancient. These practices fell under intense condemnation following the collapse of Rome and the rise of Christianity in the West. Only in the last generation has opinion been overturned. The landmark 2015 Supreme Court ruling on *Obergefell v Hodges*, codifying homosexual marriage into national law, was in hindsight a predictable conclusion to the dissipating trend of traditional Christian understanding of marriage, family, and life in America.

Is collapse imminent, far off, or has it already happened? Looking at stock market rallies, technological breakthroughs, and ever-increasing material abundance, it would seem unlikely that collapse has already occurred. But material abundance, along with its sister decadence, is a lagging indicator. The institutions and social contracts that have supported our way of life for centuries—marriage, family, faith, community and morality—have been utterly decimated. While it is true modern efficiencies continue to increase, the stock that maintains it has been depleted. As Rod Dreher has said,

> The West has lost the golden thread that binds us to God, Creation, and each other. Unless we find it again, there is no hope of halting our dissolution. . . . The shadow of the Enlightenment's

69. Approximately 43 million abortions per year, worldwide: Boquet, "1.72 billion abortions worldwide in the last 40 years."

70. CDC, "STDs at record high."

failure to replace God with reason has engulfed the West and plunged us into a new Dark Age.[71]

So how did we get here? What or who cracked the foundation? While there are many causes, people, events, and philosophies that we could point to over a period of several centuries, there is only one that cannot be ignored. It's what historians call the "watershed event in human history": the Industrial Revolution.

---

71. Dreher, *The Benedict Option*, 46–47.

2

The Industrial Revolution

Then and Now

Technology is not morally neutral.

—ROD DREHER

IN 1972, NEARLY 200 years after the French Revolution, Chinese Premiere Zhou Enlai was asked about its significance to world events. He responded: "It is too soon to say."

The same year as the French Revolution, two other world-reverberating developments were underway: the establishment of a new nation called the United States of America, and the emergence of a new order of manufacture in the Western world that came to be known as the Industrial Revolution. Historians have called the Industrial Revolution "the most important event in the history of humanity since the domestication of animals and plants, perhaps the most important since the invention of language."[1] Of its significance and full extent of impact to world events, one could rightly conclude: it is too soon to say.

1. McCloskey, Review of *The Cambridge Economic History of Modern Britain*, para. 14.

'Irresistible Though a Slowly Coming Tide'

Starting near the close of the eighteenth century, the Industrial Revolution marks a 50-year period from roughly 1790 to 1840 during which "production of goods moved from home businesses, where products were generally crafted by hand, to machine-aided production in factories."[2] During this period, entire industries were born, overturned, or put to rest. It is difficult to imagine the upheaval families experienced during this period when thousands of years of custom were upended in a single generation. Much of the advance was welcome. Families saw financial abundance like they had never known, as individual members could seek profitable employment in factories. Women and even children could work for wages with little or no prior skill due to the specialization of labor and standardization of parts.

For others the changes were most unwelcome. Mass production depressed prices of commodities everywhere, forcing subsistence farmers and artisans into factories simply to survive. Farms ceased to operate as they had for centuries. Families that divided into factory labor no longer educated and mentored their children at home. Dependence on the family and community was replaced with dependence on the employer.

As one historian records, prior to the introduction of machinery:

> The typical shoemaker had long been his own master. He worked in his little shop at home as he pleased, doing perhaps farm work or engaging in some other occupation a part of the year. He objected to serving any other master than himself, and believed that obedience to a foreman was a surrender of his personal rights and liberties. He was reluctant to submit to factory hours, from seven o'clock in the morning until six at night, and to exacting factory regulations. He opposed in the like manner the introduction of labor-saving machinery. The general industrial growth of communities was, however, an irresistible though a slowly coming tide. Progressive methods of employment and the introduction of machinery gradually broke down all opposition.[3]

Urbanization & Crime

The centralization of the factory system drove millions away from rural settings and into populated cities. Prior to the Industrial Revolution, only

2. Library of Congress, "The Industrial Revolution," 1.
3. Allen, *The Shoe Industry*, 21.

200,000 Americans lived in cities. By 1850, that number jumped to 3.6 million. About this time we see the first police departments being organized in American cities, further evidence of the erosion of community integrity and social responsibility. For hundreds for years prior to the Industrial Revolution, decentralized communities policed themselves and maintained order primarily through strong social bonds and shared values. This all came to an end by the late 1830s as crime became untenable in the rapidly urbanizing cities. Author Dr. Gary Potter points out in *The History of Policing in the United States:*

> The key question, of course, is what was it about the United States in the 1830s that necessitated the development of local, centralized, bureaucratic police forces? One answer is that cities were growing. The United States was no longer a collection of small cities and rural hamlets. Urbanization was occurring at an ever-quickening pace and [the] old informal watch and constable system was no longer adequate to control disorder. Anecdotal accounts suggest increasing crime and vice in urban centers. . . . Public disorder, mostly public drunkenness and sometimes prostitution, was more visible and less easily controlled in growing urban centers than it had been in rural villages.[4]

By 1920, the majority of Americans lived in cities, and the number is well above 80 percent today.[5] The effects of urbanization is "one of the defining and most lasting features of the Industrial Revolution."[6]

Factory Schools

Concurrent with the flight to cities and the rise of mass-production was the emergence of a factory of another sort: public education. In *Comparative Wages, Prices and Cost of Living* the Massachusetts Bureau of Statistics of Labor records that following 1820:

> We shall hereafter see that the revival of education in Massachusetts, as in other States, was contemporaneous with the inception of the factory system and the introduction of machinery as an industrial force.[7]

4. Potter, "History of Policing," para. 7.
5. US Census, "New Census Data."
6. Cleary, "Effects of the Industrial Revolution," para. 16.
7. Mass. Bureau of Statistics of Labor, *Comparative Wages*, 10.

Public schooling was a tool for the industrialists, by which they intended to mass-produce "workers" in the same way they mass-produced wool. However, initial experiments in free, state-run schools were not altogether successful. The citizens of Massachusetts overwhelmingly rejected public schooling, perceiving it as violating their personal liberties and parental rights.[8]

The solution, therefore was coercion. The first compulsory education attendance laws were passed in Massachusetts in 1852. For the first time since freedom-seeking pilgrims settled on American shores, it became illegal to educate one's own children in the home. Non-compliant parents faced imprisonment, and many towns were "militarized when they refused to take their children out of their locally-run schools or home-schools and place them in the state-run, state-controlled institutions."[9] In 1858 it took an invasion by the state militia to force the last holdouts in Barnstable, Massachusetts, to capitulate and release their children, who were then marched to school under armed guard.[10] Within 40 years nearly every state in the union had enacted compulsory attendance laws.

Addressing a New York teacher's association in 1909, soon-to-be-president Woodrow Wilson touted the progressive vision for public education in America:

> For we want to do two things in modern society. We want one class of persons to have a liberal education, and we want another class of persons, a very much larger class, of necessity, in every society, to forego the privileges of a liberal education and fit themselves to perform specific difficult manual tasks.[11]

In 1850, two years prior to the enactment of compulsory attendance laws, the literacy rate in Massachusetts was 97 percent. In the rest of New England it was even higher, exceeding 99 percent in several states. Girls in particular in colonial New England had higher literacy rates than girls anywhere else in the world.[12] Twenty years following the introduction of state-run education, the literacy rate in Massachusetts dropped to 93 percent and stands still lower today.[13] Public education was never intended to

---

8. Turtel, *Public Schools, Public Menace*, 29–30.

9. Hartmann, "Good German Schools Come to America," para. 32.

10. Gatto, *The Underground History of American Education*, 142.

11. Wilson, "The Meaning of a Liberal Education," para. 10.

12. Selcer, *Civil War America*, 301.

13. Selcer, *Civil War America*, 304.

increase the nation's literacy but to create compliant laborers able to satiate the demands of the growing industrial behemoth.

Fractured Families

The dissolution of parental education was one of many collateral effects caused by the Industrial Revolution on eighteenth- and nineteenth-century families. As factories arose, individual family members separated to find employment. No longer were days spent on the family's farm, its members working alongside each other towards a common purpose.

> Under factory production [textile] work was still carried on largely by women and children. Their employment was looked upon then as an unqualified good which made possible the development of manufacture without taking men from agriculture, while at the same time it made women and children, to quote Alexander Hamilton, "more useful than they otherwise would be."[14]

So pervasive was the mindset of the factory system that even motherhood was denounced by American leaders as "less useful" than the mass-production of cloth. Breaking apart the family was deemed an "unqualified good" for the sake of industrial efficiency.

Factory production also meant the end of the apprenticeship system— the primary method of skill transfer for thousands of years—and with it the opportunities for mentorship and discipleship. Prior to the Industrial Revolution,

> The apprentice system was in vogue, and all parts of a trade were then taught where it is now usual and needful to teach but a single branch. The youth who aspired to become a shoemaker might, for instance, during his period of apprenticeship, acquire knowledge of every step from the tanning of the leather to its embodiment in the finished shoe.[15]

The statisticians of 1885 record that this apprenticeship system "permitted a more intimate relation between employer and employed than is usual today." Work was no longer a context for older generations to transmit faith, culture and values to the next generation. It was an impersonal, at times de-humanizing, endeavor that existed solely to make stuff.

14. Bureau of Labor Statistics, *History of Wages*, 85.
15. Mass. Bureau of Statistics of Labor, *Comparative Wages,* 10.

As urbanization increased, younger generations saw greater opportunity in the city and abandoned the rural existence in favor of a better life elsewhere, breaking family continuity with the land. Allan C. Carlson writes,

> The most socially disruptive effect of the industrial revolution was the way it severed the place where adults work from the place where adults live. Most of our current family questions— from loud disputes over gender roles to child care to low fertility—derive from this great disruption.[16]

The working conditions during this period were notoriously bad. The unsanitary, often dangerous, conditions resulting from the demanding pace "extended from five o'clock in the morning until seven in the evening, with one-half hour for breakfast and dinner. . . . It was not until 1842 that the hours of labor for children under twelve years of age were limited to ten per day."[17] At least laborers had Saturday to look forward to: "Saturday was often, perhaps generally, shorter by at least two hours than the other working-days."[18]

The Trapper Boys: 13-year old Willie Bryden's sole job was opening a door for the mule cart, "waiting all alone in the dark for a trip to come through," relates the

16. Carlson, "The Family-Centered Economy," para. 16.

17. Robinson, *Loom and Spindle*, 13.

18. Robinson, *Loom and Spindle*, 90.

photographer. "It was so damp that Willie said he had to be doctoring all the time for his cough. . . . Willie had been working here for four months, 500 feet down the shaft, and a quarter of a mile underground from there." (Photo: Lewis Hine/Library of Congress)

Maintaining a homestead was not easy work and perhaps required not fewer hours in total. But joined together as a family, colonial Americans did just that for 200 years. The work was varied and rewarding—sowing, cultivating, harvesting—not a singular task performed 14 hours a day, six days a week.

The abandonment of a rural, agrarian manner of living meant the abandonment of the family as the source of provision. During the Industrial Revolution, a whole new class of society arose—"factory folk." While most families still stayed together, sometimes living and working in tenements constructed by employers, the family members now depended on an employer for their sustenance rather than on each other. Writing of the early cotton manufacture industry, nineteenth-century historian Samuel Batchelder records:

> It was the custom, instead of making payments in money, to establish what was called a Factory Store, from which the families were furnished with provisions and other articles in payment for their labor, which resulted in a sort of dependence upon their employers.[19]

Implications of this demographic shift were enormous. Prior to being dependent on employers, American's were mostly self-sufficient:

> Nearly every article in domestic use that is now made by the help of machinery was then 'done by hand.' It was, with few exceptions, a rural population, and the material for clothing was grown on the homefarm, and spun and woven by the women. . . . Every household was a self-producing and self-sustaining community.[20]

Thomas Jefferson spoke fondly of the self-sufficient family farm, referring to "those who labor in the earth" as "the chosen people of God, if ever he had a chosen people, whose breasts he has made his peculiar deposit for substantial and genuine virtue." Of the budding industrial landscape, however, Jefferson also warned: "Dependence begets subservience and

19. Batchelder, *Introduction and Early Progress of Cotton Manufacture*, 74–75.
20. Robinson, *Loom and Spindle*, 2.

venality, suffocates the germ of virtue, and prepares fit tools for the designs of ambition."[21]

Replacing Religion

As the traditional agrarian family began its decline, so did role of religion in society. Absent the close connection to the land and rhythms of nature, with its continual witness of rebirth and renewal, the nation's accompanying "firm reliance on Divine Providence" began to wane. In his book *The Fourth Civilization*, Sutcliffe explains that many people began to sever their connection to organized religion following the initial upheavals of the Industrial Revolution. Migrations from rural landscapes to the cities with their artificial environs led to a loss of confidence in the institutionalized church, which relied on "traditional authorities to explain the physical world and its workings."

> The Bible (and by association God) came to be seen as a limited creation of the institutional church. What was created by humans could eventually be seen as flawed, and then discarded. At the same time, the increasing availability of consumer goods helped to promote a materialism that separated people from the spiritual roots of traditional morality.[22]

Materialism and unprecedented abundance gave credence to a host of emerging philosophies at odds with traditional Christian understanding of nature and man's place in it. In view of the material abundance spawned by the Industrial Revolution, new ideologies emerged to compete with long-held Christian beliefs.

> People came to place their religious-like faith in the philosophies of science (scientism), reason (rationalism), progress (progressivism), the state (statism), or humankind (humanism) as the measure and end of all things.[23]

The idea of an all-powerful God who created and sustains the universe fell into disrepute, and many discarded the outward forms of religion. "Over time, religion ceased to be part of the glue that held society together."

Sutcliffe points out that while religion has not vanished altogether from modern life, it "seems to have had little influence upon intellectuals or

21. Jefferson, *Notes on the State of Virginia*, 176.
22. Sutcliffe, *The Fourth Civilization*, para. 22.
23. Sutcliffe, *The Fourth Civilization*, para. 23.

upon the leading institutions in Western society in the Industrial age, and this fact alone would set off the last century-and-a-half as unique among all periods of history."

Seeds of the Revolution

To understand why people so willingly surrendered tried and true methods of the past to the promises of material abundance, it can help to assess the prevailing mindsets and ideologies of the time. The Industrial Revolution was not merely a revolution of technological progress. It was, as all revolutions are, a revolution of ideas first and foremost. It was a revolution in the way people thought about work, family, community, God and creation. It was the triumph of humanism—man over nature, man over God—that brought down the levees and let loose the flood of modernity.

Our forebears did not think of work as modern Americans do today. The famed "Puritan work ethic" shared by early settlers was real. To them, work was a form of worship, and vocation a divine calling—not something to be avoided through labor-saving devices. Puritan author and preacher Thomas Watson, wrote: "Let us walk as the children of God, in our labors. We must be diligent in our calling. Religion does not seal warrants to idleness . . . 'Six days shall you labor'. God sets all His children to work. . . . Heaven indeed is a place of rest . . . but while we are here, we must labor in a calling. God will Bless our diligence, not our laziness."[24]

According to Watson and the Puritans, work *was* worship: "Whatever you do, work heartily, as for the Lord and not for men, knowing that from the Lord you will receive the inheritance as your reward. You are serving the Lord Christ."[25] The biblical idea of work as worship had to be undone before people were ready to submit to the idea of leisure, comfort, and wealth as acceptable pursuits in and of themselves.

The second revolution in thought came through the gradual breaking down of the family and relationships. As previously mentioned, inventors did not suddenly appear on the scene in 1790. Human history is nothing if not a story of innovation. What made this period unique was the combination of ability through manpower and natural resources, and the relaxing of moral restraints that, heretofore in Christian communities at least, channeled the currents of man's ambition. It is no secret that every invention has the potential to displace radically those working in an industry or a community, or even to change how individual families live in their homes.

24. Watson, *The Beatitudes.*
25. Col 3:23–24

Under Capitalism this is known (lately) as "creative destruction." In highly interdependent relational towns and villages, where the brick layer depends on the carpenter, and the carpenter depends on the blacksmith, and they both depend on the farmers, there is careful consideration of the impact that new technologies have on each others' ways of life and on the community as a whole. As towns grew into crowded cities, relationships devolved, and consideration shifted away from community impact toward individual gain. Inventions that would never see the light of day in small villages could germinate and grow in cities of strangers.

We have become so accustomed to the unequivocal "good" of technology, because of the labor it saves and material abundance it contributes, that it can be difficult to comprehend why it would be avoided in previous eras. But consider a family context: a devoted father is not likely to pursue an invention that will put his own son out of a job. Neither is he likely to open a competing franchise in the same town as his daughter's boutique. He is not likely to sell his rural acreage to a real estate developer when his children are seeking land on which to build homes. This is the natural boundary of a healthy family. Even if the father stands to make a fortune—even if the invention or lower prices will benefit the masses—he is not likely to place his personal ambitions above the well-being of his own family.

The same natural restraints are present in close-knit communities where members have an active interest in the well-being of one another. John Winthrop preached to a congregation of Puritan settlers in 1630: "We must delight in each other, make others conditions our own, rejoice together, mourn together, labor and suffer together, always having before our eyes our commission and community in the work, our community as members of the same body."[26] In my church there is a woman who sells eggs from her farm to the congregation. Her husband was badly injured in a car accident several years ago and has been unable to work since. Selling eggs is one of the means by which they subsist. Our family also farms, and the opportunity exists for us to sell eggs to the congregation. But because of our love for Becky and her family, we do not entertain the idea of competing with her to make a buck when we have other means by which to earn an income. During the Industrial Revolution, it is precisely these kinds of relationships that had to be broken down before the natural restraint on "creative destruction" could be lifted.

To be sure, technology was not rejected wholesale by our pilgrim ancestors. Many clever agricultural implements were in widespread use by the founding of our country. However, technology was not treated, as

26. Winthrop, "A Model of Christian Charity."

Rod Dreher puts it, as morally neutral. Before accepting a new invention, its displacing effects and impacts on the family and community were carefully considered. Saving labor was not the final assessment of whether a new technology should be adopted.[27]

So it was not the genius of any particular invention that spawned a thousand years of innovation in a single generation. It was neither Eli Whitney and his cotton gin nor Samuel Slater and his mechanized mill. It was the collapse of cultural boundaries combined with the ascendancy of humanist thought about the nature of work that unleashed the amoral, and immoral, use of technology.

Real Wealth

Proponents of industrialism will no doubt point to the "hockey stick of human prosperity" beginning in the nineteenth century. For centuries, per-capita GDP held steady at less than $2 per day. By 1900, that figure rose fivefold to $11 per day.[28] The problem with this statistic, however, is that self-sufficiency doesn't require money.

Milk from the cow, eggs from the chicken, pork from the hog, fresh fruits and vegetables from the orchard and garden, wide open spaces and fresh country air—such amenities would demand a high income today. It is nearly impossible to buy food from the store, organic or otherwise, that has not already been dead for weeks. Indeed, grocery store eggs are over 30 days old on average and can be up to 60 days old by the time they are placed in your cart. But healthy, living food was the normal way of things for subsistence farmers of the 17th and 18th centuries. And none of it required the exchange of money.

Anthropologist Hugh Brody writes of the family-centered lives and economy that was common in this era, before industrialism "rescued" subsistence farmers from their poverty:

> A family is busy in the countryside. Mother is making bread, churning butter, attending to hens and ducks that live in the yards and pens beside the house, preparing food for everyone. Father is in the fields, ploughing the soil, cutting wood, fixing walls, providing sustenance. Children explore and play and help and sit at the family table. Grandma or Grandpa sits in a chair by the fire. Every day is long and filled with the activities

27. We find the same approach to technology still in use today in Amish, Mennonite and Hutterite communities in North America.

28. Maddison, "Statistics on World Population," 28:A–CN.

of this family. And the activities are contained, given purpose and comfort, by a piece of countryside at the centre of which is home. . . . The family in its farm is the family where it belongs.[29]

Families who lived on farms during the Great Depression would often relate that they never knew they were in a depression. Their pantries were stocked, their homes were heated, they still had jobs. Their wealth was standing in the barn, in the fields, and in the accumulated knowledge of generations. Irresponsible speculation in the markets did not collapse their stock.

By contrast, paper currency and imported goods are not the surest forms of wealth. The Great Depression of the 1930s revealed who had true wealth, when in the span of four days, trillions of dollars in today's equivalent were lost and entire life savings wiped out. Banks were shuttered, and, when re-opened, depositors were given ten cents on the dollar. "The thud of falling bodies" could be heard in the streets off Wall Street.[30]

Real wealth, it must be admitted, cannot be accurately measured by per-capita income.

To be sure, even accounting for these benefits, we are still vastly richer today. But at what cost? Free-market economist John Ikerd writes bluntly about the dilemma we face:

> Capitalistic economies gain their efficient advantage by using people to do work, while doing nothing to restore the social capital needed to sustain positive personal relationships within society. There is no economic incentive for capitalists to invest in families, communities, or society for the benefit for future generations.[31]

It can take centuries for the earth to naturally form an inch of topsoil, but only a single season to deplete it through industrial agricultural methods. Food is cheap and abundant right now, but it may not always be so if we continue to deplete our soils. Similarly, we are discovering that through over-reliance on efficiency we have enriched ourselves at the cost of depleting our social capital. Perhaps this is why, 230 years after Slater's mechanized cotton mill, we are beginning to see a reversal of industrial trends in certain aspects of life, namely, education, food, and fertility.

29. Brody, "Nomads and Settlers," 3.
30. Lowenthal, "The Jumpers of '29," para. 1.
31. Ikerd, "Is Sustainable Capitalism Possible?" 4.

The Unrevolution

As recently as 1980, homeschooling was "treated as a crime in nearly every state."[32] "Hundreds [of parents] were imprisoned for seeking to reclaim this pre-modern family task."[33] Today, the number of homeschoolers approaches three million, and home education is legal in all 50 states.[34] Moreover, the last few decades have seen a surge not only in homeschooling but in other home-based methods of production: gardening, small-scale livestock, home births, and natural fertility.

The United States saw an increase of four million home gardens and two million community gardens from 2007 to 2013, as more and more people pull up the sod to plant tomatoes. Farmer's markets, co-ops and community-supported agriculture (CSAs), once obscure enterprises, have exploded across the country and can be found, sometimes by the dozens, in nearly every city. Farmer's markets increased from fewer than 1,800 in 1994 to over 8,000 by 2013. Even chickens and honeybees have found their way into the backyards of urban dwellers. In *Letter to a Young Farmer*, Gene Logsdon refers to this "unrevolution in progress" as the "economic decentralization of nearly everything":

> There is clearly something new and invigorating going on in the food production world as artisanal garden farms multiply and large-scale industrial farming fades into the fog of crushing cost overruns and faltering prices. The new economy understands that farming is a biological process, one to be handled with careful love and very gentle agronomy and husbandry, not industrial production that concentrates on cramming more and more animals under one roof to lower the per unit cost of production, or growing corn on hillsides and prairies that nature never meant for industrial cultivation.[35]

People from all walks of life, political persuasions, and faiths are desiring a more stable, more meaningful, more connected way to live than industrial efficiency has delivered, with its promises of greater material wealth. Perhaps we will see a return to durable trades as well.

Wendell Berry eloquently addresses the fractured life we now live and what must be done about it:

32. Somerville, "The Politics of Survival: Home Schoolers and the Law," 1.
33. Carlson, "Sweden and the Failure of European Family Policy," 19.
34. Carlson, "The Family-Centered Economy."
35. Logsdon, *Letter to a Young Farmer*, 28.

If we are to hope to correct our abuses of each other and of other races and of our land . . . then we are going to have to go far beyond public protest and political action. We are going to have to rebuild the substance and the integrity of private life in this country. We are going to have to gather up the fragments of knowledge and responsibility that we have parceled out to the bureaus and the corporations and the specialists, and we are going to have to put those fragments back together again in our own minds and in our families and households and neighborhoods. We need better government, no doubt about it. But we also need better minds, better friendships, better marriages, better communities. We need persons and households that do not have to wait upon organizations, but can make necessary changes in themselves, on their own.[36]

36. Berry, *The Art of the Commonplace*, 86.

3

Defining Durable

The butcher, baker, and candlestick maker have been around a lot longer than supermarkets and Walmart.

—JOEL SALATIN

WHAT SHOULD OUR RESPONSE be to brittle systems and future (and present) challenges? How do families build their houses on the rock in a time of shifting sands? What will last and what will crumble under its own weight?

These are the very questions I originally set out to answer—for my own family first, and then for the benefit of others who "see danger coming and (want to) take refuge." The process has been illuminating, both in identifying the causes of decline in historical family-based businesses and in discovering why some family-centered economies have stood the test of time.

In short, there are no easy answers. But there are lessons from the past. We are not the first society to face these problems, and we will not be the last. In the pages that follow, I present my solutions to the brittle systems outlined above: Durable Trades. My hope is that this research will in some way contribute to the stability and prosperity of other families in the years to come.

What is Durable?

Defining "durable" has not been easy. I wanted to know which types of businesses have been the least affected by external factors throughout history, place, governments, economic cycles, invention, and social upheaval. Which trades have endured for centuries and still exist today? Which trades are the most family-centric? And, of course, which trades do all this and still provide a living? Conversely, which trades are overly dependent on brittle systems and are therefore not likely to withstand economic, societal, or technological upheaval?

The scope of this study is limited to the minimum range of time and place that could answer these questions and still bear relevance to us today, and therefore it centers on trades that existed during the earliest periods of American history—prior to the Industrial Revolution (c. 1790)—and are still thriving today. Trades during this 230-year period have survived revolution, civil war, world wars, transitional governments, currency devaluation and hyperinflation, recessions, depression, industrial revolutions, and machine automation. Sources include period literature, statistical abstracts, historical works, and personal interviews. In some cases, I even went to work in the trade to test my assumptions—I spent three months working at a meat locker to learn more about butchering.

A Few Caveats

With any such project there are obvious limitations. First, many viable trades today were merely domestic functions in colonial America. For example, 'Veterinarian' did not become a dedicated profession in the U.S. until after 1850. Prior to that, all shepherds handled their own animals' healthcare. Second, some trades have the potential of being very durable but do not have a long enough history to make this list—plumber and electrician come to mind (indoor plumbing did not come into usage until the mid-nineteenth century, and electricity until the early-twentieth century). To be included, professions must have been in existence by America's founding. Third, new professions are being classified all the time: biomedical engineer, solar voltaic installer, search engine optimizer. Some of these may endure. Most will not. The Industrial Revolution spawned an abundance of specialty trades that at the time seemed durable, only to disappear from history a short time later.

In truth the Industrial Revolution never ended. It is still ongoing today, and significant marketplace distortions exist because of it. In periods of low growth—considered normal throughout history—many modern industries would simply cease to exist. Take sports medicine, for example. Today it represents a rapidly growing $23-billion industry, part of the $46-billion professional sports industry—itself part of the much larger $270-billion entertainment industry.[1] But professional sports as we know it only recently came into existence, following the Civil War. Prior to that, one would have to go all the way back to the fourth century AD to find professional athletes—a 1,500 year gap. What will happen to supporting industries like sports medicine during periods of severe economic contraction? While it is impossible to predict exactly what the future holds, considering the long view of history helps to identify those industries and occupations that have more lasting power than others.

Finally, research revealed that the most successful family economies over history involved a mix of trades rather than just one. The village blacksmith also farmed his own land. Our first president was also a distinguished orchardist. Ben Franklin was a courier, author, publisher, statesman, and inventor. So it will be today. Successful, enduring family economies will most likely need to be diversified and cross a range of durable trades.

Scoring Trades

After examining hundreds of occupations spanning the past four centuries, I developed a scoring system to rank trades according to their merits. All trades covered in this book made the list because they are durable. Regardless of how they rank against each other, every trade has survived for at least 230 years, and in most cases several thousand years. But the goal of this research was to determine the *most* durable, *most* family-centered economies.

In all, five categories and 20 sub-categories were determined and used to score each trade objectively, with weighted averages to favor certain aspects.[2] They are as follows:

1. **Historical Stability (20 percent of total score).** How much have the core products, methods, tools, and clientele changed since the trade was practiced two hundred years ago?

2. **Resiliency (15 percent).** How vulnerable is the trade to short-term disruptions in supply or demand? How long is the supply chain and how sustainable are the inputs? Finally, how resistant is the trade to technological automation?

1. *IBISWorld*, "Sports Medicine."; US Census, "Number of Firms."
2. A detailed breakdown of scoring is provided in the Appendix.

Jobs that depend on high-tech materials manufactured in countries on the other side of the world are heavily impacted by disruptions to the global supply chain. On the other hand, trades that rely on
locally-sourced raw materials, on human or animal power, or organically grown products are less likely to be disrupted by international
disturbances.

3. **Family-centeredness (35 percent).** How much time is spent together
for family members working in this trade? Are there roles for children
and the elderly? Husband and wife? Can the trade be practiced from
home or only off-site? And, finally, does the business generate tangible
assets that can be passed down through generations?

4. **Income (20 percent).** Does the trade provide enough income to support a family? It should be noted that more is not necessarily better
here. The most durable trades—those that experience the least amount
of turnover and best withstand economic cycles—are those producing
close to the median wage. On the other hand, highly specialized trades
that generate high incomes—double or triple the median wage—are
more likely to experience upheaval during economic turbulence and/
or become targets for automation. It should also be noted that some
trades, such as farming, offset lower incomes by producing at home
what currently requires purchasing outside the home.

Income has been scored according to the Federal Poverty Guidelines (FPG), a standardized cost-of-living reference. In 2019, a family
of six with an annual income of $34,590 would be at 100 percent of
the Federal Poverty Guidelines, sometimes referred to as "the poverty
line." Median household income in the U.S. is just under $60,000, or
about 175 percent of FPG for a family of six.[3]

Income Scoring		
FPG	Annual Income	Score
100%	$34,590 or below	20%
150%	up to $51,885	40%
200%	up to $69,180	60%
250%	up to $86,475	80%
300%	up to $103,770 or more	100%

3. US Census, "Real Median Household Income in the United States."

5. **Ease of Entry (10 percent)**. How expensive is it to start a business in the trade? How fierce is the competition? How heavily regulated is the industry? What are the near-term projections of growth? And how much formal education is required to work in the field?

As a general rule, multi-generational durability tends to favor professions that can be passed down through apprenticeships rather than through protracted accreditation programs. But this is not mandatory. Many generations of lawyers and physicians began their education under their parents and finished with obtaining the necessary credentials. The general rule, however, is this: the fewer obstacles, the better.

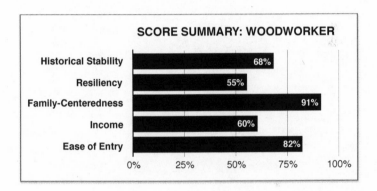

Example score for Woodworker

In all, 61 trades are ranked according to these criteria and an in-depth summary is provided for the top-scoring occupations, with a brief synopsis written about the rest. Each of the trades is named for its original title, but they may be known by other names today. For example, the Watchman of yesteryear became our Policeman today.

It should also be noted that not all of these professions will be around 200 years from now. Some of them may not even be around 20 years from now. However, the goal of this research is not to predict which professions will last indefinitely but which have survived to this point. Projections of near-term growth accounts for a very small portion of the overall score. Readers are encouraged to take inventory of both the history and future challenges facing each industry and draw their own conclusions. Further discussion, research, and reflection is encouraged before jumping into any new venture.

While it is impossible to convey accurately the real working conditions of every trade, since every business within a trade is unique, my hope is that this book can serve as a starting point for those searching for another way forward.

PART II

Durable Trades

They keep stable the fabric of the world, and their prayer is in the practice of their trade.

—YESHUA BEN SIRA, *ECCLESIASTICUS* (175 BC)

1

Key Findings

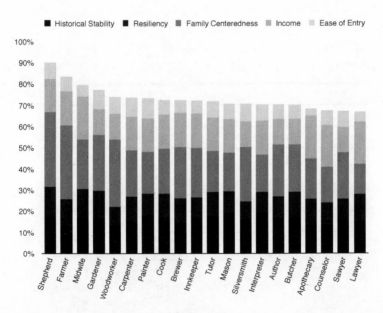

■ Historical Stability ■ Resiliency ■ Family Centeredness ▨ Income ▨ Ease of Entry

The Top 20

SEVERAL FACTORS INFLUENCE THE success of family-based businesses. Some are general themes that apply to a wide range of trades. Others are specific factors that differentiate successful businesses within a trade. In the pages that follow I present key findings that most indicated success for family-centered economies over the last two centuries.

Food, Fiber and Shelter

One of the most persistent themes in this study is the number of trades concerned with providing basic necessities—food, fiber and shelter. Four of the top five trades are directly involved with food and housing, and 12 of the top 20 are connected to food, housing, or clothing. On the other end of the spectrum, only one in twenty of the lowest-scoring trades are involved with providing basic necessities. The research confirms that trades catering to core human needs are not only the most stable over time; they are also the most family-centric.

Currently, spending on basic necessities consumes only one-half of household budgets in the U.S. But it didn't always used to be this way. Without the support of government subsidies and extreme societal complexity, the true cost of many heretofore cheap products would become exorbitantly expensive. Conversely, luxuries considered expensive today would appear cheap by comparison if basic commodities were ever to become scarce. This is not a bold prediction, nor should it come as a surprise. It is easy to look back and see how Americans historically apportioned their budgets.

In 1901 the average U.S. household allocated 80 percent of its budget to basic necessities. One hundred years later that number had fallen to 50 percent. And the number would in fact be much lower if the necessities did not also include "luxuries" such as dining out or vacation homes.

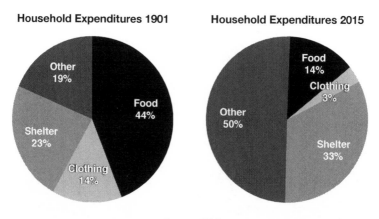

Source: BLS

Inspecting the numbers more closely we see that Americans spent three times more on food and four times more on clothing a century ago than they do today. Even accounting for modern industrial efficiencies, without government subsidies the price of a gallon of milk would be over

$8 today.[1] Historically, as a percentage of household expenditures, the real cost of milk is closer to $20 per gallon in today's dollars. I am not suggesting that we will see grocery stores stocked with $20-per-gallon milk anytime soon. I am, however, suggesting that the prices we see today for many basic necessities are unsustainably low.

The possibility of price reversals plays a significant factor when predicting which trades will remain viable in the years ahead. If we see a reversion to historical pricing as unsustainable supports are removed, there will likewise be a resurgence in trades catering to these core human needs. Those same trades that are looked down upon today as dirty, dead-end jobs will in fact be highly-sought-after—not unlike the butchers in fourteenth-century Europe after farmland reverted to pasture following the Black Death, or medieval masons who were held in such high regard during the castle-building era that they did not need to bow to their monarchs, or blacksmiths in colonial America who were awarded free land in exchange for setting up a village smithy. Should the prevailing economic supports ever falter, those possessing skills in producing food, clothing, and shelter will again be in a position to prosper greatly.

Success Factors

The difficulty with ranking trades is that there is such a wide range of business approaches within each trade. Even if a particular trade is highly resilient, there is no guarantee of success. There are, however, several factors that emerge. These factors, taken together, offer the best opportunity of achieving success, regardless of which trade a family chooses to undertake:

1. **Have a passion for the work.** Successful owners are passionate about what they do. There is an inner drive that propels them forward, which is essential during the demanding startup phase and inevitable rough patches every business experiences. To such owners, money is a secondary concern. There must be enough income to pay the bills, of course. But turning their vision into a reality is a much stronger draw than potential financial benefits.

2. **Seek mentors.** Find people who are doing what you want to be doing and learn from them. Books, workshops and instructional videos are a step in the right direction, but there is no substitute for working in the trade to truly learn it. Volunteer your time, if necessary, to learn from a master before striking out on your own. Master gardener and

---

1. Khimm, "A gallon of milk could cost $8."

arborist Paul Gautschi said it best: "Throughout history, everywhere in the world, people who were successful learned from masters. It's always been that way."[2]

3. **Work toward ownership.** Individuals or families who own the businesses in which they work are able to command much higher incomes than when utilizing the same skillset as wage-earning employees. Over and over the data show historical professions becoming sub-divided, standardized, and commoditized over time, leading to low-wage employees who cannot support a family, or the trade becoming obsolete through automation. More often, family-owned-and-operated businesses have been able to resist these pressures and remain viable.

4. **Avoid debt.** Successful owners do not accumulate debt. They vigorously avoid it. They do not buy big shiny trucks or expensive equipment on credit. They do not go back to school to get a second degree. Instead they take drastic measures to get out of debt—such as selling their houses and moving into smaller ones—because they know that unaccountable debt will kill their businesses faster than anything else.

5. **Build trust, one customer at a time.** In every business the real product is *trust*. No matter how good the product or valuable the service, customers will not buy from someone they do not trust. Successful businesses grow slowly, one customer at a time. Successful owners have face-to-face relationships with their customers and know them by name.

6. **Let your work speak for itself.** Despite what experts say, marketing is not the key to success. The most successful owners I spoke to do not advertise their businesses at all. Their work is their advertisement. Virtually all of their customers come by word of mouth. In his book *You Can Farm*, Joel Salatin tells aspiring entrepreneurs not to worry about getting customers (plural). "Really, the question boils down to a more basic, simpler one: 'How do you get your first customer?'" In other words, if you produce a quality product and are trustworthy, your customers will take care of advertising for you.

7. **Focus on repeat business.** It has been said that it's 25 times more expensive to acquire a new customer than to keep an existing one.[3] Successful businesses have more repeat business from fewer clients.

2. Paul Gautschi, interview with author, September 3, 2018.

3. Gallo, "The Value of Keeping the Right Customers."

8. **Practice multiple, overlapping trades.** Many skillsets can be applied to multiple trades. Carpenters are also woodworkers. Shepherds are also farmers. Often the same skillsets and property can be leveraged across multiple, related trades, and the burden of earning a living from any one trade is greatly reduced. Further, a family enjoys greater resilience when exposure to a single trade's vulnerabilities is minimized.

9. **Think generationally.** Design your business around your family, not the other way around. Instead of asking, "What am I good at?" ask "What are *we* good at?" Children should be involved from an early age. Elderly adults should participate for as long as possible. At every age people need to know they are needed and provide a meaningful contribution to the family economy. Successful enterprises—especially those that continue from parents to children—must have people in them who think generationally.

2

1. Shepherd

Rancher, Livestock Farmer, Dairyman

Now Abel kept flocks . . .

—GENESIS 4:2 (4000 BC)

THE KEEPING OF ANIMALS surpasses even farming as the most historically durable trade. While animal husbandry has undergone many changes in the last century, it has not seen the extent of commoditization and technological change that crop farming has. Aside from industrial-scale confinement operations, keeping animals today on open pasture remains largely the same as it was thousands of years ago. Shepherding and its modern counterparts comprise all aspects of animal husbandry—the raising of animals for food, fiber, and productive labor. There are 1,004,564 livestock farms in the United States today generating $184 billion annually.[1]

In Genesis we see the first division of labor when Adam's sons, Cain and Abel, become farmer and shepherd, respectively. But it is common today to see these two trades combined in order to achieve the overlapping benefits of labor, fertilizer, and meat production. It is worth mentioning that the eating of animals was prohibited until after the Flood in Noah's time, so likely Abel was keeping flocks for the animal byproducts of dairy, wool, and leather garments, as well as sacrifices for sin.[2]

1. USDA, "2012 Census of Agriculture," Table 2.
2. "Everything that lives and moves about will be food for you. Just as I gave you the

Historical Stability: 88 percent

The kinship between man and beast dates back to the earliest records of civilization. In the Bible, God tasks Adam with naming His creatures shortly after creation. The ancient Egyptians considered certain animals to be sacred and worshipped them as gods. Regardless of the source one consults, animals have been integral to human societies since records began.

Animal husbandry, as with any trade, has diversified into numerous specialties. In addition to keeping cattle, hogs, sheep and goats, people also keep alpacas and bees, and maintain hunting farms and aquaculture. Poultry has enjoyed a renaissance in recent years as municipalities have begun loosening codes to allow citizens to keep "backyard chickens."

Through all of the changes, the core product—animals—and methods for raising animals have remained nearly identical for hundreds of years. Advances in genetics have improved yields and sizes, particularly in cattle, but heirloom breeds are still highly sought after for their proven reliability and hardiness. Although most supermarket meat comes from animal feedlots, the increasing demand for grass-fed meat has created many opportunities for family-scale farms to raise animals the old-fashioned way, and do so quite lucratively.

Resiliency: 93 percent

Since food, and meat in particular, is the backbone of the nation's food supply, shepherding is a highly resilient trade. In a grass-fed operation, virtually all the inputs are local, on-farm—even replacement stock. Demand for locally grown food means that most customers can be local as well. Worldwide demand for meat continues to increase, and healthier, organic options have held up well during past recessions:

> While Americans economized on their food purchases during the 2007–09 recession, including purchases of organic products, growth in demand for organic products rebounded quickly following the recession. . . . Industry data suggest that the market share of organic sales held by various food categories has been remarkably stable over the last decade.[3]

---

green plants, I now give you everything." Gen 9:3

3. Greene, "Growth Patterns in the U.S. Organic Industry," para. 1–2; See also Kadlec, "Organic Food Sales Remain Strong."

Finally, the unpredictable nature of working with animals limits the risk of automation. Humans rather than robots make the best shepherds.

Family-Centeredness: 100 percent

Animal husbandry and farming are the most family-centered of all trades. From collecting eggs to hauling water, to milking, to mending fences, to cheesemaking, and even the dreaded manure-pitching, there is an endless variety of chores suited to all ages, both men and women. Children can work with farm animals from a very young age. At county fairs it is not uncommon to find children as young as eight showing animals in the 4-H program. This is an important aspect of the trade: children are taught from a young age where their food comes from; they are also taught many essential life skills. Moreover, families who raise animals as a primary vocation will spend most of their time together, with ample opportunity to mentor children in developing a traditional religious consciousness, as anyone familiar with the Bible—especially the history of Israel and the parables of Jesus—knows.

It almost goes without saying that livestock farming is a home-based business. Animals need care throughout the day and, during birthing season, often through the night. It makes the most sense for caretakers to live on-site. In truth, well-fenced, well-sheltered animals do not need constant care. It's the unpredictable situations that require shepherds always to be "on-call." It can also be difficult to leave a farm with animals. Neighbors may be willing to feed your dog, but less willing to milk your cow. But with a little planning and generous neighbors, family vacations are still a possibility.

Shepherds leave behind significant tangible assets to their heirs. Not only are land, buildings, and durable equipment involved, but animals have a tendency to multiply all on their own. Twins are even triplets are common in many breeds of sheep and goats. A starter herd of four ewes purchased for $1,500 can multiply to 60 breeding ewes within five years, and you can sell the male lambs along the way for $37,000.[4] Try to beat that return in the stock market!

Naturally, shepherds will seek to improve the genetic lines of their animals to achieve higher quality offspring: more disease resistance, higher productivity, and better temperaments with every generation. The resulting stock over several decades can be extraordinary and often extremely

---

4. Assumes twin births and selling rams for meat at $5 per pound hanging weight, 60-pound average.

valuable. Children who follow their parents into animal husbandry stand to reap tremendous benefits.

Income: 80 percent

Livestock farmers can earn above average pay, but actual salary depends on a wide range of factors. According to the Bureau of Labor Statistics, a Farm Manager's median pay is $69,620 per year, but that number is skewed by the number of corporate farming operations. Meat production, dairy, wool and fiber, and specialty breeding are all products of animal husbandry, and each can earn vastly different sums depending on the animal, breed, environment, and scale. Although they are the mainstay of American meat production, confined animal feeding operations, or CAFOs, are capital-intensive and heavily dependent on large buyers who have all the bargaining power. These operations do not require much land, but zoning and regulations are more strict.

On the other end of the spectrum, grass-fed meat requires much more land per animal, relies almost entirely on on-farm inputs, and follows a direct-to-consumer model. As a result, the price of pastured meat is often double the price of feedlot meat, sometimes more.

Demand for locally grown, free-range chicken has never been higher. Compared to $1.20-per-pound grocery store chicken, locally raised organic chicken sells for $5 to $6 per pound. Open-pastured, grass-fed lamb sells for $12 to $16 per pound, compared to $7-per-pound feedlot lambs. Healthier, organic milk, which comes from cows grazing on pasture rather than confined animals fed only grain, costs $6.50 per gallon as compared to $3.30 for regular, non-organic milk.[5] And, of course, raising animals on one's own land bestows the additional benefit of supplying the owner with a stable supply of the freshest, healthiest food available.

Ease of Entry: 74 percent

Animal husbandry is not an altogether expensive trade in which to get started. Some land is required, but not nearly as much as is needed for crop farming. Animals do not need lavish accommodations. A wind break, water source, and open pasture or other food source is all that is needed, even in cold winters. They are much hardier than most people realize.

---

5. Tuttle, "Is Organic Milk Worth the Extra Money?"

It can take a several years to build a loyal customer base or breed enough stock to generate a decent income. But, as mentioned, locally grown meat is in high demand, and it doesn't take long before respected growers have a waiting list.

Although raising animals requires no formal education, its greatest barrier to entry is the steep learning curve. If you did not grow up handling animals breaking into the industry can be difficult—from finding breeders and sources of feed to building adequate shelter and fencing, from administering vaccines and assisting with births to finding customers or livestock auctions at which to sell your finished stock. For new livestock farmers, all of this can be overwhelming. The best option is to learn as much as possible from an experienced handler, such as the one from which you purchase your starter herd.

The Bureau of Labor Statistics projects demand for livestock managers will essentially stay constant through 2028.

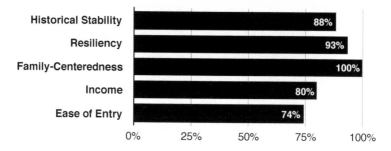

SCORE SUMMARY: SHEPHERD

Historical Stability	88%
Resiliency	93%
Family-Centeredness	100%
Income	80%
Ease of Entry	74%

Profile: KRK Katahdins

Sheep breeder Karen Kenagy has been raising sheep for over 50 years. She started when she was just 12 years old when a neighbor gave her an orphaned lamb to bottle-feed. Her family moved out to the country, and she started participating in 4-H and learning how to raise sheep. With the help of her husband, Karen now manages 125 breeding ewes on her livestock farm in Oregon and sells prize-winning lambs all over the country.

KRK Katahdins, the company named after the specialty breed of sheep Karen raises, is unique and differs from other breeders. She performs intensive disease testing, selecting for parasite resistance. Her sheep are also raised to perform well on pasture and forage rather than in barn stalls. As a result of many years of selective breeding, Karen's lambs are bigger and hardier, they have few parasite and disease problems, and the mothers are more attentive to their young. But don't take her word for it. Karen's lambs won Overall Supreme Champion over all breeds at several fairs in recent years.

A typical day for Karen involves filling up feeders and spreading fresh bedding. In the winter, when fresh pasture isn't available, Karen buys hay and alfalfa from local providers. She also spends a lot of time on paper-work—filling out registration and transfer forms so customers can receive pedigree papers when they purchase from her. She spends time answering questions for customers and educating the public at fairs. "There's getting to be a big gap between the farmer and consumer," she says. "People haven't thought past the grocery store." She asks them, "Do you know where your meat comes from? What kind of life did it have?"

The biggest challenge for Karen is the steep learning curve. "Being able to look at sheep and know when they're starting to get sick" can be very difficult. "Being a prey animal they don't show weaknesses. It's a lot of learn-ing." But she enjoys the work. "I like how calm and mellow they are," she says. As a former nurse, Karen used to come home after a stressful day and find peace in the barn. "You walk out there in the field with them and they all gather around you. It's just calming."

Karen's family has been actively involved in raising sheep. Her four children, now grown, helped from a young age. "Finding something they like to do with the farm is important," she says. "Just getting them out when they're young, and teaching them." Her husband, who is self-employed as a machinist and welder, helps with the heavy lifting and anything that needs to be constructed. Her niece and nephew also help. "It's good to have some help when you really need it."

Karen has seen the overall population of sheep decline in the U.S. since she's been involved, something she attributes to farmers getting older and no one stepping in to replace them. She also points to the accumulating laws that make it harder for livestock farmers to do their jobs. But Karen expects the industry to continue growing slowly in the future. "There's a big demand," she says. "They ship a lot of sheep from Australia and New Zealand to fill the market."

Her advice for those interested in becoming livestock farmers is to find someone in their area who is raising animals and learn from them. "Finding a mentor is a good thing," she says.

Additional Resources

- *Back to Basics: A Complete Guide to Traditional Skills* edited by Abigail Gehring (Skyhorse, 2008); Provides summaries for raising a wide range of livestock along with many other farming and homesteading topics.

- *The Shepherds Life: Modern Dispatches from an Ancient Landscape* by James Rebanks (Flatiron, 2015).

- *The Practical Beekeeper: Beekeeping Naturally* by Michael Bush (http://bushfarms.com/bees.htm).

3

2. Farmer

... and Cain worked the soil.

—GENESIS 4:2 (4000 BC)

FARMING IS THE TRADE upon which all others depend. It is one of human-ity's oldest trades, emerging early in human history and forming the basis of civilization. Up until the last two or three generations, virtually all humans were farmers to one degree or another. Even highly sought-after blacksmiths of the seventeenth century—the high-tech professionals of their day—were expected to farm their own plots to provide for their basic subsistence rather than rely solely on wages paid to them.[1] Historian Allan C. Carlson writes:

> A most striking, yet commonly forgotten, attribute of the Pu-ritan settlers in seventeenth-century Massachusetts was that all were farmers. Even pastors, shopkeepers, and artisans spent a substantial portion of their time tilling the soil and tending animals. When asked to identify their vocations, most chose "yeoman" or "husbandman." This meant, in turn, that they lived by nature's clock.[2]

1. "As early as 1635 [the town of] Lynn voted to admit a landless blacksmith, and later granted him 20 acres of land, thus keeping both the blacksmith and the letter of the law requiring that residents be landholders." BLS, *History of Wages,* 8.

2. Carlson, *Family Cycles,* 5.

For the purposes of this study, farmers include those who "work the soil" for crop production. There are 860,710 crop farmers in the U.S. today, generating $172 billion in revenues annually.[3] This includes the large mono-crop farms growing corn, wheat or soybeans over thousands of acres as well as small CSAs growing a wide variety of vegetables on a relatively small plot for direct sale to consumers. While it is true that farming as a profession has plummeted as a percentage of the population over the last century, it still employs nearly 2.5 million people, and remains the irreplaceable foundation of the $3-trillion-dollar agribusiness sector in America.

Historical Stability: 68 percent

It has been said there can be a post-industrial culture, a postmodern culture, even a post-Christian culture, but there will never be a post-*agri*culture. Agriculture is the oldest and most central activity in human history. In the past century massive changes to scale, efficiency, and quality have occurred, but the same basic product is still being produced. And for the most part the methods are the same: cultivating, fertilizing, planting and harvesting. The most dramatic change to crop production has been in tooling—that is, mechanization. In a very short span of time, tractors and associated implements have replaced animal labor in virtually all farm operations, from the largest commercial farm to the smallest CSA.

Resiliency: 80 percent

As the underpinning of the nation's food system, farming is generally re-silient. But this depends on the individual characteristics of each farm. Is it heavily dependent on off-farm inputs (seed and fertilizer)? Or does the farmer utilize saved seed and animal fertilizers? Is the operation over-leveraged or debt-free? Does the farm grow only one crop or a wide variety of grains and vegetables? Are products sold to middlemen or directly to consumers? Factors such as these determine individual resiliency against the whims of market forces.[4]

Despite its inherent stability, crop farming has undergone many revolutions and will continue to do so. In 2017, the first ever completely automated

3. USDA, "2012 Census of Agriculture," Table 2. (Not including orchards and nurseries.)

4. Industrial systems have historically favored specialization in farming. The "get big or get out" mantra of the 1960's pushed many farmers into untenable debt positions, only to be followed by massive waves of farm failures in subsequent recessions.

seed-to-harvest farm experiment was completed using drone tractors.[5] But while technology will continue to evolve, demand for food will never disappear, nor will the need for people who understand how to grow it.

Family-Centeredness: 100 percent

Farming is uniquely suited to families and people of all ages. From pitching hay to transplanting seedlings, the sheer magnitude of little tasks is well suited to multi-generational cooperation, which is why the term "family farm" came into being. The vast majority of farms are home-based, and families who work them spend most of their time working together.

As farming industrialized during the twentieth-century, economies of scale demanded that farms consolidate activities, specializing in one or two things with maximum efficiency. It was more cost effective to take animals off the land and raise only a single crop. With single-function farming, machines replaced people, family sizes fell, and children began leaving multi-century farms. Eventually most family farms became corporate farms where few if any of the original family members were actively involved. However, there remain today many genuine family farms, not merely privately-owned but actively worked by all family members.

Farmers, if they have not accumulated too much debt, leave behind a significant amount of tangible assets including land, equipment, structures, and of course vital knowledge.

Income: 80 percent

Inasmuch as farming is the most pervasive profession in history, one would assume data on wages paid would be easy to find. But the records are mostly silent on farming wages up until about 1840, when the Industrial Revolution was in full swing. Indeed, the *Statistical Abstract of the United States, 1885 Edition* doesn't even list farming as an occupation. The missing data bespeaks more than it conceals: farmers rarely had need of money, because they produced almost everything they needed. It's hard to put a price on self-sufficiency.

The Bureau of Labor Statistics lists a Farm Manager's median pay at $69,620 per year. But a lot more goes into farming than management. A family-run farm can earn above average income. And depending on the size or specialty, earnings can go much higher. However, the more specialized or

5. Feingold, "Field of machines."

leveraged a farm becomes to maximize profitability, the more susceptible it becomes to macro-economic impacts.

When it comes to wages, today's farmers generally fall into a few categories. Conventional farmers' wages depend entirely on the acreage under cultivation and its yield. At current market prices, on very good land, it would take roughly 300 acres to match the median household income in the U.S.,[6] and that doesn't include the cost of land, machinery or outbuildings, which would require initial outlays of $1.5 to $2 million. This is why, aside from inheritance, it is virtually impossible to get into conventional farming today. This is also why roughly 90 percent of farms, even large ones, rely on off-farm income and why the agricultural industry as a whole is so heavily subsidized.[7]

Organic farmers, whose products are purchased directly by customers participating in Community Supported Agriculture (CSAs) or from local co-ops or restaurants favoring locally-grown food can earn a comfortable living and are growing in number. But organic farming, like its industrialized cousin, is not a high-wage venture.

Ease of Entry: 68 percent

As already discussed, conventional farming is a highly capital-intensive business. Land, the single biggest expense, averages $3,000 to $5,000 per acre, with prime land exceeding $10,000 per acre in some parts of the country. That's $1.5 million on average for a 300-acre farm. Barns, silos, tractors, implements, and harvesters can also run into the hundreds of thousands in short order.

Direct-sale farms, such as CSAs, can be started for much less. Thanks to demand for organic, locally-grown foods, restaurants are paying (and charging) top-dollar for farm-to-table fare, which can be profitably grown on much smaller plots of land. The USDA Farm to School Census reports that 42 percent of public school districts in the U.S. participated in farm-to-school activities and spent a combined $790 million on locally-grown food

---

6. Based on yield of 200 bushels of corn per acre selling at $3.50 per bushel, with 50 percent direct costs and 20 percent overhead; According to the US Census Bureau, median household income was $61,937 in 2018.

7. "By 1970, more than half of farms had off-farm income, and by 2000, 93 percent of farms earned off-farm income." Dmitri et al., "The 20th Century Transformation," 2–3.

in 2014.[8] One 10-acre organic farm in our community holds a $250,000 contract to provide salad greens to Minneapolis public schools.

But competition is fierce, particularly in commoditized products, and direct-sale farmers will have to spend several years developing a loyal customer base. While no formal education is required to farm, the learning curve is steep. Most farms are multi-generational, the farmers passing down knowledge through a lifetime of participation. It is difficult, but not impossible, to break into farming, and many first-generation farmers are doing just that—leaving the cubicle to find fulfillment on the land.

SCORE SUMMARY: FARMER

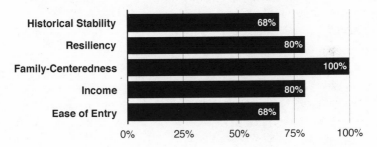

Historical Stability	68%
Resiliency	80%
Family-Centeredness	100%
Income	80%
Ease of Entry	68%

0%   25%   50%   75%   100%

Profile: Jagodzinske Farm

Fifth-Generation Farmer Sarah Jagodzinske Rohman with her family
(Photo: Sarah Rohman)

8. "Census data indicate that schools purchased nearly $790 million in local food from farmers, ranchers, fishermen, food processors, and manufacturers in school year 2013—2014." USDA, "Farm to School Census."

Sarah Jagodzinske Rohman is a fifth-generation farmer currently in the process of taking over her parents' farming operation in southern Minnesota. The Jagodzinske Farm dates back to 1891 when the claim was filed by Sarah's great-great-grandfather. In addition to taking over the family business, Sarah and her husband Brooks are raising five children, ages four to twelve.

Sarah began exploring the possibility of taking over the family farm after moving back to the area with her husband and first child. "For me personally, farming was not on my radar," Sarah says. Initially, Sarah farmed with her dad for a year to see if it would be a fit, while husband Brooks worked in town as a chiropractor, helping as much as he could with farming activities. "I really enjoyed it, and so did Brooks."

Sarah and her dad began a transition plan whereby Sarah and Brooks would rent more land each year to farm independently. This arrangement allowed Sarah gradually to take on more responsibility while still working alongside her dad. "I've always been very comfortable working with my dad and receiving his wisdom from his lifetime of farming," Sarah says. This ongoing mentorship also allows Sarah to grow more comfortable with the demands of farming as she learns the business. "When I first moved back," Sarah explains, "I did everything I do today. I was just way less comfortable."

Speaking on the challenges of farming, Sarah notes the steep learning curve. "There are so many things we are not in control of," she says. "You definitely need to have a lot of patience and faith that things are going to work out." Also, managing all the elements of the farm—the bookwork, cashflow, purchasing, marketing, and long-range planning—is just as important as the manual labor, she says.

Deciding when to sell the end-product is always a major challenge. Fluctuations in market pricing means farmers often have to sell their crop at a loss. "The market has dropped so significantly," Sarah laments of current soybean prices, "every time we take a truckload in [to the grain elevator] we're losing $1,800."

Finally, staying abreast of industry changes can be a challenge. Keeping up with changes to machinery, soil amendments, and seed and fertilizer traits can be daunting. "You have to be continuously learning and improving your own knowledge." To help, Sarah surrounds herself with a good team of advisors.

For Sarah, the greatest joys of farming involve family. "The family-business aspect is really special," she says. "I know how much work and effort are involved. I'm thankful for every generation that has worked so hard to make this an opportunity for us."

Family has always been at the center of the Jagodzinske Farm. Working with her family on a daily basis is an opportunity Sarah does not take for granted. "It is special that I get to see my parents every day and work side-by-side. And what's even more important is to watch my kids do that." Even Sarah's two-year-old is in on the action. "He's is truly a farm baby," she says. "The tractor is where he would spend his whole day if he could." Since Brooks opened his own practice closer to home, he has the opportunity to join Sarah in more of the day-to-day farming activities.

There is a high degree of flexibility on a farm, which allows family members to be together more often. "I don't think there are many professions where you are able to have your children with you side-by-side," Sarah says. "It's just a different way of life." For example, bringing meals and having a picnic on the side of the field during harvest is one way Sarah's children stay involved, even during the busiest of seasons.

Sarah has seen vast changes to farming since she grew up. She points out the technologies and different products available to modern farmers that weren't around a generation ago. "When I was growing up, we walked beans," she says, referring to weeding fields by hand just 15 years ago. Today, most farmers rely on chemical herbicides to do the same job.

Soon after beginning on her family's farm, Sarah introduced GPS guidance systems. GPS allows tractors to follow an exact route when planting, spraying, or harvesting crops to within a one-inch tolerance. The goal is to fit more rows per acre, thereby increasing yield, as well as pinpoint areas of lower yields where more fertilizer is needed. The machinery is always getting better, Sarah says, but "with technology comes price tags, and more things that can go wrong."

Sarah sees big changes coming to the industry, including fully-autonomous tractors, with people "sitting in an office somewhere watching screens" rather than working in the fields. "From my experience, people farm because they love farming," Sarah says. "I don't know where this technology leaves the people who are not farming 10,000 to 20,000-acre and larger farms." At the same time, Sarah is excited to see advancements and improvements in technology that will make her operations more efficient. "My hope is that we can keep up with the changes and be able to bless our kids if they want to choose this profession."

Sarah's advice to would-be farmers is to be open-minded and not let your own pride get in the way. "It's important to listen to the people who have done it before you," she says. In farming, there is always more to learn. "Every year is a learning experience. If you can find a mentor who will help, that's priceless." For Sarah, finding that mentor was never in doubt: "I'm very lucky. I have my dad."

Additional Resources

- *You Can Farm: The Entrepreneur's Guide to Start & Succeed in a Farming Enterprise* by Joel Salatin (Polyface, 1998).

- *Letter to a Young Farmer: How to Live Richly without Wealth on the New Garden Farm* by Gene Logsdon (Chelsea Green, 2017).

4

3. Midwife

I am the son of a midwife and have myself a midwife's gifts.

—SOCRATES, IN PLATO'S *THEAETETUS* (369 BC)

MIDWIVES ARE MAKING A comeback. After several decades of disrepute, natural birth has enjoyed a renaissance in America. After reaching a low point in 2004, by 2016 home births had increased 80 percent and out-of-hospital births by 90 percent. Today one in ten births in America is attended by a midwife rather than a doctor—a 300 percent increase since 1989.[1]

But the resurgence is not without its detractors. Legal battles continue to be fought over the right to practice midwifery in many states, and licensing laws are changing the nature of the industry. Still, demand for natural birth continues to grow, and as a result midwifery is one of the fastest growing professions in America. There are approximately 15,000 midwives in America today earning a combined $1.7 billion annually.[2]

1. According to the CDC, home and out-of-hospital births were recorded at 0.56 percent and 0.84 percent respectively in 2004, and 1 percent and 1.6 percent in 2016. Midwives attended 3.3 percent of births in 1989 and 9.6 percent of births in 2016. See CDC, "Births: Final Data for 2016," Tables 13 and I-4; CDC, "Trends in Out-of-Hospital Births."; Declercq, "Midwife-attended births."

2. MANA, "Midwives & the Law," para. 1; Revenue estimates based on number of midwife-attended deliveries in 2016 (378,594 according to the CDC) and average cost of services ($4,500).

Historical Stability: 84 percent

Midwifery as an independent profession has been around for a very long time (the earliest recorded reference is around 1900 BC).[3] And as long as people keep having babies, the profession will always be around. Although midwifery is common in most developed nations, midwives in America have faced significant challenges from the conventional medical establishment. According to Midwives Alliance of North America, an advocacy group,

> Midwives safely and effectively attended the vast majority of births in the United States until the 1930s when the place of birth was moved from home to the hospital, and midwives were replaced with physician birth attendants. The United States is unique in the developed world in criminalizing the practice of midwifery.[4]

But since 2004, midwifery has been rebounding in America with surging interest in natural birth and rising concerns over unnecessary medical interventions and drugs in the hospital delivery process.

There have been some changes to the practice and tools of midwifery, but overall it remains a highly stable profession. In most respects the trade is practiced the same today as it was thousands of years ago.

Resiliency: 91 percent

Midwifery is nearly impervious to economic cycles, and may even see an increase during recessions. The average cost of a midwife-attended delivery ranges from $3,000 to $6,000, a fraction of the cost of hospital births, which can exceed $20,000 for routine deliveries.

Attending roughly 10 percent of total U.S. births, midwives are able to find plenty of customers in their own cities and even in rural locations. Traditional midwives do not depend on sophisticated equipment or long supply chains to provide services. Moreover, automation poses virtually no risk of making this industry obsolete. If women are leaving the hospital to have babies at home, it will be a long time before they let robots into the nursery.

---

3. Gen 35:17
4. MANA, "Legal Status of U.S. Midwives," para. 1.

Family-Centeredness: 67 percent

Midwifery affords a high degree of family-centeredness for those who wish to practice it. If daughters are interested and capable, they make for excellent doulas and assistants. Many midwives operate the business from home, where much of client-interaction takes place, such as pre-natal appointments and postpartum check-ups. The actual time spent off-site for delivery can range from two hours to two days, depending on the birth. Midwives can also adjust their workload up or down based on family demands. Very few trades offer the level of flexibility, particularly for mothers, as midwifery does.

That having been said, being a professional midwife means always having to be on-call. Babies do not respect holidays, birthdays or family vacations. To avoid burn out, midwives need to learn their capacity quickly and plan very long-range schedules that include ample time off. A further drawback is that there are very limited roles for husbands and sons, and midwifery does not generate any tangible assets besides loyal customers and essential knowledge.

Income: 100 percent

Full-time midwives are among the highest-paid professionals today. A midwife starting out can expect to earn $3,000 per birth. Experienced midwives can earn $6,000 or more per birth. Full-time midwives handling six to nine births per month can earn well above $300,000 per year. Depending on workload (number of deliveries per month), midwives can surpass even physicians in net take-home pay.

Furthermore, overhead is quite low, since midwives often base their practice at home. Assistants typically come in the form of apprenticing doulas rather than full-time wage-earning employees. And because they are not practicing medicine, midwives are not required to carry costly medical malpractice insurance.

Ease of Entry: 56 percent

There are typically two tracks for entering midwifery. Direct-entry midwives often start as doulas and apprentice under another midwife before starting their own practice. These midwives may or may not register as Certified Professional Midwives (CPM) through licensing agencies. Direct-entry midwives more closely resemble historical midwives. The more medically-oriented Certified Nurse Midwife (CNM) is an advanced-practice registered nurse and requires many years of schooling and advanced degrees.

While formal education requirements are low, traditional midwives face difficult legal barriers. Depending on one's state, midwifery can be either lightly regulated or outlawed entirely. Direct-entry midwives are legally authorized to practice in only 30 states. Although legislation is planned or pending in an additional 15 states, midwives are "at risk of criminal prosecution for practicing medicine or nursing without a license" in the other 20 states.[5] Certified Nurse Midwives (CNM) are able to practice in all 50 states, but not always without physician supervision.

Despite the legal hurdles, midwifery is the fastest growing durable trade. The Bureau of Labor Statistics projects a 26 percent increase through 2028, while the average for all other trades is 5 percent. However, following the trajectory of a 300 percent increase in midwife-attended deliveries over the past 30 years, it is possible that the profession will grow much faster, even doubling over the next decade.

SCORE SUMMARY: MIDWIFE

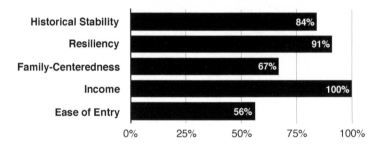

Historical Stability — 84%
Resiliency — 91%
Family-Centeredness — 67%
Income — 100%
Ease of Entry — 56%

Profile: Helping Hands Birth Services

Nickie Kerrigan, a Certified Professional Midwife, is owner of Helping Hands Birth Services and has been actively involved in midwifery for 25 years.

Nickie, who has three grown children and 12 grandchildren, started training as a midwife when her children were teenagers. "I was planning to home birth my second child when my midwife backed out two weeks prior to the due date," recounts Nickie. "This was a time when midwives were being prosecuted, and my midwife's friend had been sent to jail. She told me

5. MANA, "Legal Status of U.S. Midwives," para. 6.

she couldn't risk it for her family's sake. It was during that time that I felt impressed by God that someday, somehow I would help women give birth wherever they wanted to give birth."

During her career Nickie has assisted with over 3,300 pregnancies, attending 500 births herself. Nickie has also mentored numerous apprentices into the profession.

The greatest challenge, according to Nickie, is managing family time. "Babies don't know it's Christmas, Easter, or somebody's birthday," she says. To take time off, Nickie blocks out two weeks before and two weeks after planned vacations, because babies can come early or late. But she takes burnout very seriously. "The average career span of midwives is seven years, mainly due to burnout." For Nickie, the sacrifices are worth it. "Those first breaths, those first cries. Not many people get to witness that. It will never get old."

Nickie sees changes coming to the industry. "There is a push to make the profession seem more legitimate by trying to get all states to require midwives to be licensed," she says. "In doing so, it makes the requirements for midwives become more medical, so the state of traditional midwifery is becoming more medical."

Nickie's advice to those interested in becoming midwives: "Don't go it alone." If something goes off-plan and both mom and baby need help, you can't help both. "Another midwife or well-trained assistants can be the helping hands that you need."

Additional Resources

- *Guide to Childbirth* by Ina May Gaskins (Bantam, 2008).
- *Midwives Alliance of North America.* Advocacy group (https://mana. org/).
- *Midwifery Today.* Magazine and website (https://midwiferytoday. com).
- *Christian Heritage Academy of Midwifery.* Training programs (https:// christianheritagemidwifery.org).

5

4. Gardener

Arborist, Vinedresser, Landscaper, Flower Farmer

Man was lost and saved in a garden.

—PASCAL (1650)

Gardeners comprise those professionals who work the soil but do not as a general rule rely on heavy machinery. As distinguished from farmers, they tend established crops, such as orchards, tree farms, and vineyards, as well as start plantings from seed for sale in nurseries. Historian Walter Duckat writes, "In biblical times, a garden evidently meant variously a vineyard, an orchard, a kitchen garden, or a royal garden."[1]

There are over 100,000 gardening-related businesses today generating $78 billion annually, and the profession is projected to grow well above average over the next decade.[2]

Historical Stability: 84 percent

George Washington is well reputed for his beloved apple orchard, and Thomas Jefferson for his magnificent gardens at Monticello. But gardening

1. Duckat, *Beggar to King,* 92.
2. US Census, "Number of Firms."; BLS, *Occupational Outlook,* "Grounds Mainte-nance Workers."

as a vocation goes back much further than colonial times. Gardening is the first profession cited in the Bible. Even before Eve was created, Adam was instructed to take care of Eden, the garden planted by God. The Hanging Gardens of Babylon in 600 BC were one of the Seven Wonders of the (Ancient) World and would have required legions of gardeners to construct and maintain.

Overall there has been little change to the practice of gardening since antiquity. While there is ongoing specialization to meet consumer tastes, such as the vast almond groves of California, this is nothing new. Fig and olive orchards date back to biblical times—Noah planted a vineyard soon after stepping off the ark.[3] Chainsaws, chemicals, and harvesting equipment have come onto the scene since then. But generally, gardening tools and methods have remained the same for generations. The biggest shift has come in terms of clientele, where garden centers and hardware stores now act as middlemen to the actual growers, although this trend has not altogether taken over; independent nurseries and "u-pick" orchards selling directly to consumers remain a staple in the industry.

Resiliency: 85 percent

Gardening is generally resistant to short-term disruptions. The supply chain and customers are typically local, and food is still a necessity in any recession. Trees continue to grow in all economic environments and need continual tending. And the irregular requirements of gardening make it resistant to automation. However, certain specialties such as floriculture and ornamentals are more discretionary and likely to be affected by tightening budgets during a recession.

Family-Centeredness: 76 percent

Family members who pursue gardening as a profession will spend most of their time together. There are ample opportunities for young and old to participate in a meaningful way. Even six-year-olds can weed. There are suitable tasks for both men and women, boys and girls. We humans are naturally equipped to tend gardens, even if we claim not to have a "green-thumb." We were in fact created for this very purpose.

A successful home-based gardening business is more difficult to achieve. Ample land for nursery products and/or retail space for customers

3. Gen 9:21

are needed. Professional arborists do not require land, but need to travel to stay employed. Nursery centers are most commonly located in cities, near buyers. Certain specialists such as vinedressers and flower farmers may be able to grow enough product on small acreages to sustain a living.

Gardening does not generate many inheritable assets apart from land, which may be owned for growing crops or commercial property for retailing. But many gardening-related professions do not require anything more than some skill and a trusty pair of shears.

Income: 60 percent

Gardening-related professions rank in the middle of the pack when it comes to income. Individuals working as landscapers earn $14 per hour on average, or about $28,000 per year. A certified arborist averages double that amount, $60,000 per year.[4] Nurseries and garden centers vary widely in income, aligning more with retail trends. As with other trades, a family-owned gardening business should be able to generate enough income to provide a modest living—and stay in business for a long time.

Ease of Entry: 90 percent

Gardening has one of the lowest barriers to entry of the trades listed. Competition and regulation is low, as are educational requirements. And the trade is projected to grow 9 percent through 2028.[5] While it can take many years to become a proficient arborist, tools of the trade are relatively cheap. Likewise, seeds, pots, and dirt are inexpensive to acquire. Time, sunshine and occasional watering is all it takes to turn these inexpensive ingredients into profitable products. Orchards would be the exception, where much more land and time is required to produce salable products. But on the continuum of agricultural commodities, fruit is one of the highest margin crops farmers can grow. For orchardists, a little land goes a long way.

---

4. Payscale, "Salary for Certification: ISA Certified Arborist."
5. BLS, *Occupational Outlook*, "Grounds Maintenance Workers."

SCORE SUMMARY: GARDENER

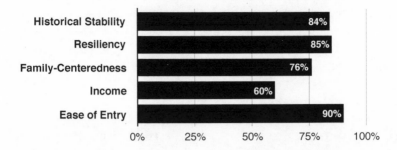

Historical Stability	84%
Resiliency	85%
Family-Centeredness	76%
Income	60%
Ease of Entry	90%

0%   25%   50%   75%   100%

Profile: Paul Gautschi

Master Gardener Paul Gautschi (Photo: Rory Groves)

Paul Gautschi is a master arborist and gardener in the Olympic Peninsula of Washington. Paul is world-renowned for pioneering the organic gardening method known as "Back to Eden" gardening. A documentary was made about Paul in 2011 and has been viewed over 50 million times in 228 countries. During the summer months people from all over the world flock to Paul's backyard to "taste and see" his gardens and hear his inspired wisdom.

Paul started his tree-care company after coming back from the Vietnam War. "The whole country was so against that war and they so ostracized veterans," remembers Paul. "I couldn't get any work." Every time Paul would submit a job application, the employer would see 'U.S. Army' as his previous employer and say there were no openings. The only way Paul could earn any income was to work for himself, so he began to work as an arborist. "It was the pressure of life that pushed me into this wonderful career," says Paul, who has been gainfully self-employed ever since, for 48 years.

Paul, a devout Christian, calls his company Vinedresser after the verse in St. John, chapter 15: "I am the true vine, and my Father is the vinedresser, and every branch that does bear fruit He prunes, that it may bear more fruit."

"I love it!" says Paul, "My Father God is an arborist!"

Paul uses a unique Japanese method of pruning trees, where the pruning takes place from the inside out. The goal is to make the tree look like it grew into the finished shape. Paul had no formal training or schooling. He learned everything by observing masters of the trade. "Let me tell you something about credentials," Paul says, "Throughout history, people learned from masters. That was their credential." Paul's method of pruning rather than trimming continues to attract attention and steady customers. "Because my work stands out and looks good, everybody wants it," he says. "My work is my advertisement."

The work can be challenging, however, especially if you are afraid of heights. When Paul first started, he pruned some 140-ft eucalyptus trees. "Everything after that was easy," he says. "It's important to meet challenges up front so you gain confidence."

The greatest advantage of being an arborist, according to Paul, is permanent work. "Every time you prune something it comes back," he says. "When people accuse me of creating more work for myself, I say it's not intentional; that's just the natural response." As a result, a good arborist has continual work. "When someone builds a house, they're done. But when you start doing tree work, you keep improving for decades."

Vinedresser has always been a family business. While Paul and his wife Carol were raising and homeschooling their kids, Paul would often bring them to work. His kids would pick up and dispose of prunings and help with simple, repetitive tasks. "In doing that they learned, were connected, and felt needed," Paul says. "When you take your kids to work with you, they think, 'I'm needed, I'm a necessary part of this family.' That is powerful!"

To those seeking to become arborists—or enter any profession for that matter, Paul offers this advice: "Find a master. Moses mentored Joshua. Jesus mentored the twelve disciples. Paul mentored Timothy and Titus. Throughout history, everywhere in the world, people who were successful learned from masters. It's always been that way."

Additional Resources

- *Back to Eden Film* (video documentary) featuring Paul Gautschi (backtoedenfilm.com).

- *The Apple Grower: A Guide for the Organic Orchardist* by Michael Phillips (Chelsea Green, 2005).

6

5. Woodworker

Cabinetmaker, Finish Carpenter

The inside of the temple was cedar, carved with gourds and open flowers. Everything was cedar; no stone was to be seen.

—1 Kings 6:18 (1000 BC)

WOODWORKERS PRODUCE A VARIETY of products by cutting, shaping, and assembling wood. Demand for custom interiors in homes, such as built-in bookshelves, wardrobes, staircases, and cabinets has only increased over the last few hundred years. Woodworkers may also manufacture wood-based products for sale, such as furniture and artistic pieces. It is common to see woodworking overlap with carpentry, the difference being that in rough carpentry dimensions and cuts can be off by a little. With woodworking, they must be exact.

The craft of woodworking has been around for thousands of years but did not always provide full-time employment. "Cabinetmakers in colonial Virginia produced fine furniture, but neither England nor the colonies could support full-time furniture producers until the last half of the 17th century."[1] It wasn't until 1722 that the first documented cabinetmaker appeared in Williamsburg, Virginia. But since that time cabinetmaking and professional woodworking has proven to be an enduring profession in America and around the world.

Cabinetmaking is a $54 billion industry, with over 13,000 companies specializing in cabinets and household furniture. However that number does not account for the thousands of self-employed woodworkers who build custom products for homeowners. Including these, the actual number of woodworking shops is closer to 100,000.[2]

Historical Stability: 68 percent

As mentioned, custom cabinetry came into fashion centuries ago and continues to this day. Even in the post-industrial age, there will always be a need for professional woodworkers to create one-of-a-kind furnishings. Tools of woodworking have changed substantially over the years, especially with the advent of power tools. However, these changes are mostly improvements in efficiency rather than fundamentally new approaches to woodworking. The largest change to method would involve the use of CNC machines, computer-controlled machinery, that automatically cuts and carves wood into a desired shape according to predefined computerized, or CAD, drawings. While CNC continues to make inroads, it is by no means the dominant approach, nor is it a pre-requisite to get started in woodworking.[3]

Master cabinetmakers today share a unique link with the past. In a time when home furnishings are increasingly standardized, cabinetmakers possess the ability to make each piece of furniture special and give it personality. "Eighteenth-century furniture was artistically and structurally more refined than in any period previously or subsequently," says Mack Headley, Jr., head of interpretive and craft efforts at Colonial Williamsburg's cabinetmaking shop.[4]

While handmade furniture virtually disappeared during the Industrial Revolution, the demand for wood-based products has dramatically increased since the colonial period, and today, as with organic farming, there is a resurgence of interest in handmade, finely-crafted pieces.

1. Colonial Williamsburg, "Cabinetmaker," para. 2.

2. US Census, "Number of Firms."; BLS, *Occupational Outlook*, "Woodworkers."

3. More than half of all cabinetry shops have no CNC capability: Hoffman, "Time is on your side," para. 8.

4. Crews, "Plain and Neat," para. 4.

Resiliency: 55 percent

Professional woodworking is less resilient when compared to other durable trades. Cabinetry closely follows the housing industry. When construction is booming, so is custom cabinetry. But in recessions, cabinetmakers can take a big hit. Resilience to economic cycles can be improved by diversifying into more products that appeal to different markets rather than focusing solely on homeowners and remodelers.

Some woodworkers take resiliency a step further by acquiring wooded property and sourcing lumber from their own land. This insulates the business from increasing material costs and supply disruptions, not to mention increases the uniqueness and profitability of the end-product.

To the degree that cabinetmakers rely on increasingly complex, foreign-made tools such as CNC machines, they increase the risk of disruption to their business from outside sources. Efficiencies gained by the use of such tools must be carefully weighed against the total cost of ownership, which includes training, replacement parts, and loss of trade expertise. Craftsmen with a chisel and hammer need not worry about long supply chains.

Finally, while the fine woodworking industry has generally resisted automation, CNC machines will almost certainly continue to increase in usage, particularly as they come down in price. This will reduce the number of jobs available to woodworkers, particularly in larger manufacturing enterprises.

Family Centeredness: 91 percent

Woodworking scores its highest marks in family-centeredness. Ample opportunity exists for family members to work together, both at home, making custom products in the workshop, and away from home installing or finishing cabinetry. There are roles for both young and old, from keeping a tidy shop to sanding, painting and working with customers. Although power tools and complex machinery would be handled by adults, there are still many woodworking tools in use, such as sandpaper, that are safe and easy for children to use.

Cabinetmakers leave behind tangible assets such as tools and facilities in which to work. In some cases, if managing their own woodlots well, they leave behind land.

Income: 60 percent

Woodworkers score about average for income, ranging from $30,000 to $60,000 per year. With low cost tools the trade is easy to get started in, but it can be difficult to stand out from the competition. As with other trades, the more customized the work, the better the pay. Working on a factory floor for a large furniture-maker will net the least amount of pay. Building custom furniture for individual clients will yield the most. However, high-end buyers expect high-level skill, which can take many years to master.

Ease of Entry: 82 percent

The same disadvantages that work against higher incomes work in favor of those wanting to get started in the trade. The cost of tools is generally low, there are no formal education requirements, and industry regulations are practically non-existent for the small woodworking shop. At the same time, there is intense competition. But for dedicated craftsmen who build a loyal clientele, the work can be steady and long-term.

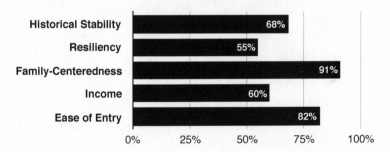

Profile: Signature Woods

Brad started his woodworking business while he was still in college. Following an opportunity to harvest barn wood for a hobby woodworking project, Brad discovered he could earn more money selling reclaimed lumber than working a job using his degree in mechanical engineering. After graduating, Brad's between-semesters side job turned into a full-time venture for him and his wife Lauren. Signature Woods is now a premiere supplier of reclaimed lumber and high-end finished pieces, including sliding barn doors, beam fireplace mantles, and reclaimed-wood wall paneling.

Initially, Brad found raw material by driving country roads and approaching farm owners directly. Old, dilapidated farm buildings can be hazardous and expensive to remove. Brad was able to solve the problem by dismantling the buildings for free in exchange for keeping the materials to sell. Brad knew he was on to something from the very beginning. "I couldn't answer the phone fast enough," he recalls after listing his excess reclaimed lumber online for sale. "I didn't realize how much value was there until we started selling it." Lauren was with him right from the beginning, tearing apart barn siding and pulling nails. Over the first year or two Brad and Lauren took down ten buildings.

As the business grew, Brad started hiring crews to dismantle buildings while he and Lauren focused more on the business. They soon learned how much profit-potential was available in finishing the raw materials themselves. Reclaimed wood can sell for ten times the price if finished properly, according to Brad. Original hand-hewn, reclaimed beams finished as fireplace mantles run anywhere from $300 to $600 retail.

But turning reclaimed lumber into living room centerpieces is not as simple as it sounds. To source the raw material, first they must find a building, negotiate with the owner, dismantle the building, transport the material, cut sections to length, clean and prepare the piece for finishing, then apply stain or coatings to customer specifications. "A lot of times people don't see that," Brad says, "but the point is we're adding value to the material."

Brad prides himself on quality of craftsmanship and the culture of the business. "We only do three products," he says, referring to barn doors, fireplace mantles, and wall paneling, "and we do them exceptionally well." The ability to create a consistently high-quality product from inconsistent material is what sets Signature Woods apart from the competition.

There is no typical day, according to Brad. Since implementing strict step-by-step processes and working on orders in batches, Brad and Lauren have freed up a significant amount of time in their daily activities. What used to take 40 to 50 hours per week working on start-to-finish orders now requires only 20 hours per week following a standardized approach and working on several orders at the same time.

Over the years, Brad and Lauren have learned to work together, delegating tasks according to strengths. That means Lauren spends more time with customers and pitching to distributors. She also handles most of the finishing—staining, coating, and painting. Brad handles the product assembly as well as back office tasks like bookkeeping and taxes. Although Brad has employed additional help in the past, the ambitious husband-and-wife team are currently the only employees running the entire operation.

Brad enjoys the freedom he has as a business owner and seeing the direct rewards of his own work. "There's a sense of ownership and pride in doing what I'm good at," he says. Brad also enjoys the real-life education he receives through starting and growing a business. "What I've learned in the first two years running this business trumps any MBA."

Marketing and understanding sales channels has been the biggest challenge for Brad. "Not being able to scale beyond where we are is very frustrating," he says. Another challenge for Brad and Lauren is learning how to separate personal and business demands. "We've had to work at our relationship and really define what is business and what is personal."

Since Brad first started his business he has seen the reclaimed lumber industry swell, both in prices and demand. He also has seen competition come and go. Brad likens the industry to a gold rush, where people see the high margins and are quick to rush in but do not have the staying power or business savvy to create an enduring business.

Reclaimed lumber is a "very large trend" that Brad does not see going away anytime soon. The demand for high-quality, recycled, old-growth wood is only getting stronger every year as it continues to evolve into different uses. And there is no shortage of supply. "There is so much reclaimed wood in this country, you wouldn't believe the volume," he says. Brad cites a single wooden granary in Duluth, Minnesota, which contains six million board-feet of reclaimed nineteenth-century lumber. "That's just one of hundreds of thousands of buildings built at the turn of the century," he says.

Brad's professional advice to those entering woodworking is, first, to determine whether you are interested in woodworking as a hobby or as a trade. "A lot of trades are also hobbies," Brad says. "Something happens when you take a hobby and make it a business, and you have to make sure you're ready for that transition." His other piece of advice is to find a niche. "Woodworking is such a wide gamut because you have everything from fine finished cabinets to wall paneling." Finding a profitable niche that fits your passion, says Brad, is key to building a successful company.

Additional Resources

- *The Essential Woodworker* by Robert Wearing (Lost Art, 1988).

- *Mastercrafts: Green Woodcraft.* Video documentary (BBC, 2010).

- Woodshop News. Magazine and website (https://www.woodshop-news.com).

7

6. Carpenter

Is not this the carpenter, the son of Mary and brother
of James and Joses and Judas and Simon?

—MARK 6:3 (AD 29)

CARPENTRY, THE BUILDING OF structures from wood, is truly one of the oldest and most durable of trades. Wood is particularly adept for building: easy to harvest and shape, sturdy, and renewable. Moreover, well-maintained wooden structures can last centuries. Coffins of ancient Egyptian pharaohs were often made of wood, and furniture found in tombs survives to this day. The earliest recorded reference to building structures from wood is in Genesis, when about 4,600 years ago God told Noah to build an ark.[1] Most assuredly carpentry was around long before Noah and will survive—through boom and bust—far into the future.

Residential construction and remodeling is a $340 billion industry with 170,890 carpentry firms in operation today.[2] While the housing and remodeling industry is highly cyclical, the profession is projected to grow faster than average over the next decade.

1. "Make yourself an ark of gopher wood. Make rooms in the ark, and cover it inside and out with pitch." Gen 6:14
2. US Census, "Number of Firms."

Historical Stability: 76 percent

Undoubtedly, the most famous carpenter in history was Jesus. Apprenticed by his own father, he practiced the trade 2,000 years ago, and it is likely many of the same tools in Jesus' hands are still in use by carpenters today. Writing in AD 79, Pliny the Elder states that "Daedalus invented carpentry, and with it the saw, axe, plumb-line, drill, glue and isinglass; but Theodorus of Samos discovered the square, plummet, lathe, and lever."[3] That such tools can be found at every construction site still today is a testament to the stability of this trade.

As building materials have evolved, so have the methods for installing them. Plywood sheeting replaced plank flooring, drywall replaced plank walls. More recently, poured concrete forms are replacing block concrete foundations, and composite materials are replacing even wood. With each iteration in materials, carpenters must adapt; however, the overall profession today remains remarkably similar to what it was in generations past.

Resiliency: 78 percent

With one notable exception, carpentry is a highly resilient trade. The vast majority of work for carpenters comes through residential construction and remodeling, and that industry is highly affected by recessions. But these are temporary setbacks: building will never cease entirely. As with other tradesmen, professionals with good reputations and well-managed businesses that are not overly in debt can weather short-term disruptions and even come out stronger as the competition thins.

Subtracting for housing-industry vulnerabilities, carpenters do not need a large, geographically dispersed customer base to stay employed. Many carpenters cannot keep up with demand in their own city. This localized relationship with customers, and the frequency of repeat business gives carpenters a buffer against external forces. Also, the nature of the work— always custom to some degree—means the likelihood of robotic take-over is small.

Family Centeredness: 62 percent

For one of the top durable trades, carpentry ranks lower for family-oriented work. While it is common to see adult-age relatives working together, the

---

3. Stewart, *One Hundred Greek Sculptors*, 2.1.1.

strength required, tooling, and dangerous working environments prevent younger children from joining in. The same goes for wives, who may help with administrative work but are generally not seen on job sites with their husbands. A further disadvantage is that most carpentry work is by nature off-site, away from home. In terms of inheritable assets, carpenters do leave many tangible ones behind, including valuable equipment and such structures as woodworking shops, vehicles, and trailers.

Income: 80 percent

Depending on their specialty and years in business, carpenters can earn a very good income. Rates for independent carpenters range from $25 to $75 per hour, not including profit and overhead, which are customary line-items for general contractors. Those at the higher end of the range, who are in high demand, have plenty of work and can be highly selective about taking jobs. During good economic times, carpenters can have waiting lists of jobs that are six to twelve months out.

Ease of Entry: 92 percent

Carpentry has one of the lowest barriers to entry of all trades. For those with aptitude, an initial outlay of a few hundred dollars can buy a basic set of tools. There is no formal education required other than obtaining licensing if working independently as a general contractor. While competition is stiff, especially during recessions, it is common for seasoned carpenters to turn down work.

Carpentry is expected to grow rapidly in the years to come. The Bureau of Labor Statistics projects an 8 percent increase by 2028, while other estimates are even higher. The McKinsey Global Institute predicts that while clerical and administrative jobs are being eliminated through computer automation, building trades will soar by 35 percent by 2030.[4]

---

4. Manyika et al., "Jobs Lost, Jobs Gained."

SCORE SUMMARY: CARPENTER

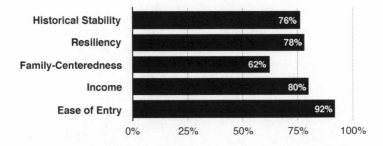

Category	Score
Historical Stability	76%
Resiliency	78%
Family-Centeredness	62%
Income	80%
Ease of Entry	92%

Profile: Voight Home Improvement

Fourth-Generation Carpenter Nathan Voight (Photo: Rory Groves)

Nathan Voight is a fourth-generation carpenter. He started his business Voight Home Improvement over a decade ago after working with his dad for several years. Nathan and his wife Amy have four children, ages eight to eighteen.

One of the ways Voight Home Improvement differs from other building contractors is that Nate is a proprietor who also does all the work, rather than subcontracting the work to others. In doing this, Nate has built tremendous trust and loyalty with his customers, who provide him with years of repeat business. Nate has never spent money on advertising; all his work comes by word-of-mouth. On average he has several weeks of work lined up, but during busy seasons that can expand to six to twelve months.

Nate focuses most of his time on residential remodeling projects. "It's less cut-throat than new construction," he says. And it pays better, too. The going rate for remodeling projects is currently $65 to $75 per hour, plus profit and overhead, an additional 20 percent. Even working in a small town of 20,000 residents, Nate can afford to be selective in which jobs he takes. When asked if customers ever balk at seeing a profit line-item on their estimate Nate said, "If they don't want me to make a profit, I usually don't want to work with them."

On a typical day, Nate is at the job site by 8 a.m. and stays until 4 p.m. His activities may include remodeling kitchens or bathrooms, hanging drywall, repairing roofs or installing siding. "It runs the gamut," Nate says. "It's everything related to residential housing." At least one night a week Nate meets with prospective clients, lining up future projects well into the evening.

Since Nate does most of the work by himself, he doesn't face as many challenges as other builders do, namely, finding competent workers. But he is challenged with juggling family obligations and other priorities while working off-site. For example, Nate tries to be at his kids' sports games whenever he can. Despite the scheduling challenges, being self-employed gives Nate a lot more flexibility than he would otherwise have. He also loves the work. "Doing the work myself is the part I enjoy the most," says Nate, who chooses not to grow his business because he doesn't want to give up that aspect of the job. "It's why I chose this profession," he says.

As for family involvement, Nate says, "if you set it up right, it's a business your kids can really help you in." Kids as young as eight can help with demolition, according to Nate. (The Fair Labor Standards Act exempts parents who employ their own children from minimum working-age requirements in most professions.) Nate says carpenters can work into their 80s, but in general there is a fast decline after age 60, and owners need to plan accordingly.

The recession of 2008 weeded out a lot of builders, says Nate, who was just getting his business off the ground at the time. During the multi-year recession, 40 percent of Minnesota contractor licenses were not renewed. "I did work part-time delivering pizza during those years," he recalls. "But I had a huge advantage at that time because I had no debt." Consequently, Nate was able to weather the recession and come out ahead. "If you're debt-free you can weather almost anything."

Nate's advice to anyone choosing carpentry as a profession is to learn the work before going into business. "Work for somebody who does what you want to do for about five years," he says. "So the work becomes second-nature. Then go into business."

Additional Resources

- "So You Want My Trade: Carpenter." *The Art of Manliness* (https://www.artofmanliness.com/articles/so-you-want-my-trade-carpenter).

- *Fine Homebuilding*. Magazine (https://www.finehomebuilding.com).

- *General Contractor Licensing Guide.* Website and licensing directory (https://generalcontractorlicenseguide.com).

8

7. Painter

Siding Contractor, Wall Covering Specialist

*There are extant in the temples at Ardea, at this day,
paintings of greater antiquity than Rome itself; in
which, in my opinion, nothing is more marvelous,
than that they should have remained so long unpro-
tected by a roof, and yet preserving their freshness.*

—PLINY THE ELDER, *NATURAL HISTORIES* (AD 79)

A surprisingly steady trade, interior and exterior wall-painting and wall-
coverings have endured for thousands of years. During colonial America,
linseed oil, copper, and iron oxide pigments were used for creating cream,
green, and red paint hues.[1] While the materials and tools have changed
somewhat since then, at its core, painting is still very much the same profession it was hundreds of years ago.

Painting is also a booming business, with projections of solid growth.
There are currently 43,209 painting and siding businesses in the U.S. earning
a combined $32 billion annually.[2] Further, due to its customized nature,
painting resists the automation that is creeping into other building trades.

1. Aron, "Paint the Town."
2. US Census, "Number of Firms."

Historical Stability: 88 percent

There has been little change to the core service of painting in the last 250 years. While function played a larger role than form in centuries past, the necessity of protecting walls from the elements while providing an aesthetic appeal has always been in demand. As mentioned, tools have changed slightly. For example, the composition and durability of paints have improved tremendously in recent years, and pressurized sprayers afford a higher degree of efficiency. But brushes are still an indispensable tool in every painter's toolbelt.

Through the years, a painter's clientele has also remained steady. The vast majority of residential painting contractors are working directly with homeowners, just as they did centuries ago.

Resiliency: 71 percent

Painting closely follows the construction industry. When construction is expanding, so is demand for painters. But painters and wall-covering specialists stay in demand long after the structures have been built and the carpenters have gone home. Depending on region and sun exposure, a wood or stucco home needs to be repainted every five to fifteen years. Vinyl siding lasts much longer but still requires maintenance and repair. So while painting follows the construction industry, the ongoing repeat-demand for painters creates a durability that far outlasts the initial construction phase and that can help a tradesman weather the down cycles.

In addition, demand for painting is local. Even the smallest towns with a few hundred homes require assistance from professional painters. Only in areas where there are no dwellings will demand for painters disappear.

A painter's primary supply-chain vulnerability is in the wall covering components themselves. As the ingredients in paints and other materials become more sophisticated, the supply chain becomes more vulnerable to disruption. Paint manufacturers are widespread in most countries, vinyl and steel siding manufacturers less so.

Finally, the customized nature of painting and wall coverings resists machine automation, which generally targets repetitive jobs. Painters need to work closely with the homeowner to determine goals and must utilize a wide variety of techniques to paint each structure competently in accordance with its specific requirements. In painting, every job is one-of-a-kind.

Family-Centeredness: 56 percent

Painting contractors are able to base their operations from home, and certainly most do. However, as with other building trades there is no getting around the fact that most of the time working is spent away from home. Still, there are opportunities for young people to be involved, and many family-owned-and-operated painting franchises exist. The physical demands of painting or siding tend to favor men; however, there are many opportunities for women to be involved in the business, including painting themselves.

There are some tangibles, such as tools, that can be passed on to children. However, the majority of value comes in the form of loyal customers.

Income: 80 percent

Income for painters is very strong. The Bureau of Labor Statistics puts the median income for all painters at around $20 per hour. But self-employed painting contractors can earn much more than that—up to $80 per hour. Besides building a base of happy customers, becoming the "go-to guy" for building contractors can mean a steady supply of new jobs for many years.

Ease of Entry: 94 percent

Painters and wall-covering specialists enjoy very few barriers to entry. There are no educational requirements aside from basic proficiency, which can be learned on the job. Regulations are minimal, and startup costs are extremely low, with most of the costs coming from materials used on the job and therefore covered by the customer. Due to the low barriers, competition in this industry should be higher than it actually is. But this is simply not the case. Currently, reliable and competent painters find no shortage of work. And in the near term, employment in the painting trade is projected to increase by 6 percent.[3]

3. BLS, *Occupational Outlook*, "Painters."

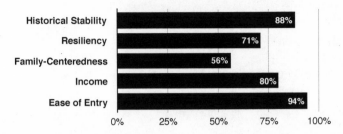

Profile: Severson Painting

Adam Severson grew up around the trades. His mom ran a painting and wallpapering business for 40 years. Although Adam would work with his mom when he was younger and then between jobs as an adult, he initially pursued a different career path, which included joining the Army and a tour in Iraq in 2008. When Adam returned home he worked a series of jobs in the corporate world, from high-tech data storage to transportation. But Adam found the cubicle-style job in front of a computer unfulfilling and began to seek out other alternatives. After researching the trades and median wages of people who are self-employed, Adam and his wife Christina decided to strike out on their own.

Severson Painting, which focuses on exterior custom painting, has been a great success. "We took a hit that first year," Adam recounted. "But what made it work was becoming debt-free." Prior to starting their business, Adam and Christina sold their house and moved into a smaller one, paying off debts in the process. Since the first year, the business has grown rapidly. With bill rates ranging from $50 to $80 per hour, Adam now earns more than he did in his director-level corporate jobs.

Adam starts his day around 6:30 a.m. He may spend eight to twelve hours a day on the job, depending on which activities he's engaged in. "Painting is about 90 percent prep," Adam says. If a project is already prepped and underway, he and Christina may put in a longer day to get everything finished. "Once you're fully prepped, the painting is easy."

Being an owner-operator, Adam needs to guard against overextending himself. "Everything that comes your way you try to take on," he says, "But you have to be smart." Balancing the job with home life is not easy. "I'm putting in ten-hour days, and when I come home I may still have three bids to work up." But despite the long hours and juggling bids, Adam finds the work fulfilling. "You can actually see the progress as you're going," he says. His greatest joy is "the gratification of seeing our work come to life for the customer, and seeing their reaction. It's pretty neat."

Painting has always been a family-centered business for Adam, who worked off and on with his mom through the years. Because of the increased income they now enjoy, Christina can stay home with their two daughters, and she also works in the business as a bookkeeper. They see the business as a way to build up an inheritance for their children. "My ultimate goal would be to build this business and have one of the kids take it, and run with it," he says.

Adam sees the tide turning for all trades in the future, including painting. "Kids are getting sick of leaving college with a degree and $60,000 of debt," he says. "The job they get is paying $20 per hour. It's not what they were promised." Adam sees first-hand every day the opportunity in trades. "Bill rates in all trades are going up, across the board," he says. "And so are the wages."

Adam also anticipates steady work from painting, even during recessions. "If you look historically, painting usually stays steady," he says. Even if construction activities are curtailed during recessions, painting is still needed in the smallest remodel. Machine automation does not pose an imminent threat, either. Adam's brother, who works for a large government contractor on advanced weapons systems, has expressed concerns about the possibility of technology eliminating his job. He once told Adam, "A.I. is not going to take over custom exterior painting."

Adam's advice for those interested in a career in painting is to try to avoid debt when starting out. "Don't go take out a loan and buy a big shiny truck," he says. "Customers get turned off by that." Instead, he recommends starting organically and having a passion for the work. "Let that be what sells your job."

Additional Resources

- *inPAINT*. Magazine (http://inpaintmag.com).
- *Paint Talk*. Painting contractor's online forum (https://www.painttalk.com).

9

8. Cook

Chef, Caterer, Restaurateur

*Every investigation which is guided by principles of
nature fixes its ultimate aim entirely on gratifying the
stomach.*

—ATHENAEUS, *DEIPNOSOPHISTAE* (AD 200)

EVERYBODY EATS. BUT NOT everybody cooks. That is why restaurant and catering industries in America are booming. While restaurants certainly feel
the impact of economic cycles, the reality is that people love to eat out and
are doing so more than ever. According to the Bureau of Labor Statistics,
Americans currently spend 44 percent of their food budget dining out, a 50
percent increase over the previous generation.[1]

While the majority of food is still prepared at home, not everyone
has the ability or desire to create gourmet meals. This is what chefs and
professional cooks do. Some serve in fine dining establishment, others in
coffeehouses. Some cooks prefer the flexibility of catering, preparing meals
en-masse for special occasions. Often professional cooking is a mix of both.

---

1. BLS, "Consumer Expenditures."; Kumco and Okrent, "Methodology for the
Quarterly Food-Away-from-Home," 7.

The food service industry is massive, with over 600,000 restaurants and catering businesses in the U.S. generating $665 billion annually.[2] Demand for cooking professionals is expected to grow rapidly in the near term.

Historical Stability: 84 percent

Independent eateries have always been around, mostly for the weary traveler. In the Acts of the Apostles, Paul speaks of meeting up with other believers at the Three Taverns, an eating establishment outside Rome.[3]

But until recent history there were no local diners catering to people on their lunch breaks, since virtually all food was prepared at home. As recently as 1910, 90 percent of food was consumed at home—and much of it *grown* at home.[4] The vast increases in dining establishments that appeared in the Western world coincided with cultural shifts that increasingly took people out of the home, namely, transportation and wage-labor. Leisure travel has also had a significant impact on dining out. However, tourism as an industry did not much exist prior to the twentieth century and did not include the masses until after 1960.

Although modern incarnations and frequency of restaurants is relatively new, the trade itself is highly durable. The core product—prepared meals—has not changed. And while the methods and tools of the trade have changed somewhat with modern equipment, the trade is still very hands-on, with repeat customers making up the core of the business.

Resiliency: 75 percent

Today it is difficult to find a town in America, no matter how small, that does not have at least one restaurant, and often dozens. But while increased prevalence makes for fierce competition, it also means that to be self-supporting restaurants do not require large populations.

Unfortunately, the food industry is highly dependent on disposable incomes. When recessions hit, people tend to cut their dining-out budgets first. A further disadvantage is the long supply-chain. As ingredients are sourced from many miles, sometimes countries, away, cooks and caterers can experience disruptions to their business if that supply is interrupted. In 2018, international fast-food giant KFC made headlines when it was forced

2. US Census, "Number of Firms."

3. Acts 28:15

4. USDA, "Food and alcoholic beverages: Total expenditures," Table 1.

to close two-thirds of its 900 restaurants in the United Kingdom for several days after it ran out of chicken.[5]

Because of this, as well as health concerns, there is a move towards locally-sourced food that bypasses the industrialized food transport system altogether. Chefs are purchasing ingredients directly from local farms instead of from middlemen to improve not only quality but also resilience.

Family Centeredness: 61 percent

Cooking, while naturally home-based and family-oriented, ranks a bit lower on family-centeredness, because cooking as a profession almost always requires facilities away from home. Also, aside from restaurant property, if owned at all, the trade does not leave much in the way of tangible assets to inherit. But, on the positive side, family members engaged in this business full-time will spend most of their time together. And there are many roles for both men and women, young and old.

Income: 80 percent

Restaurant owners are often the hardest-working, lowest-paid staff members. Unlike tradesmen other trades, they do not get to charge customers by the hour. But the long hours and dedication can pay off. As the business grows, owners are able to hire out more of the work—often to family members—and spend more time working on the business rather than in it.

Median income for cooks and head chefs is $45,950 per year, according to the Bureau of Labor Statistics, with those in the upper percentiles earning close to double that. Successful restaurateurs in a bustling city may earn $150,000 or more. But for every restaurant that succeeds, many will go broke.

Ease of Entry: 72 percent

Cooking requires no special certifications or education. Professional chefs seeking employment in fine restaurants may undergo intensive training to master their trade, but it is by no means mandatory in order to work in the food industry. Ultimately, satisfied customers will determine a restaurant's success—and the competency of its chef.

5. *Financial Times*, "KFC runs out of chicken."

Startup costs for food professionals depend entirely on the business' specialty. Caterers using rented kitchens do not need deep pockets to get started. Restaurateurs, on the other hand, do. Buying, constructing, or re-modeling a space to host patrons and serve food can easily range into the six-figures. And as previously mentioned, competition is fierce for dining establishments. Even with careful planning, most restaurants will fail in their first five years due to insolvency—it's not just about the food.

Even so, the Bureau of Labor statistics projects that demand for cooks and head chefs will increase by 11 percent over the next several years—much faster than the average for all occupations.

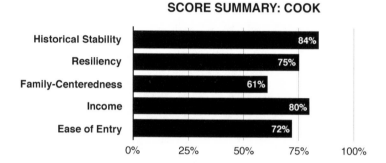

SCORE SUMMARY: COOK

Historical Stability	84%
Resiliency	75%
Family-Centeredness	61%
Income	80%
Ease of Entry	72%

Profile: The James Gang Coffeehouse & Eatery

Nate and Tanya Mollenhauer acquired The James Gang in 2015, a cof-feehouse and eatery on the outskirts of Northfield, Minnesota. Named in honor of the local legend of town heroes who ran the notorious Jesse James Gang out of town, The James Gang is one of several businesses Nate and Tanya operate together. Married for 23 years with three children, the entrepreneurial couple had no prior restaurant experience. They saw the coffeehouse as an opportunity to use their gifts of hospitality.

"It's a way to serve the community," says Nate who acts as the general manager, overseeing the financial and marketing aspects as well as casting the vision. Tanya is much more involved with the day-to-day operations, including hiring, training, and managing staff, preparing food, cleaning and keeping supplies stocked. Many days you will find Tanya behind the cash register as she welcomes customers into the shop by name.

"I love hospitality," Tanya says. "Here, I get to do that." Engaging with customers and staff is a key aspect of the business. "Each day is different, de-pending on who comes in," says Tanya. Nate confirms that the atmosphere is unique. "Customers feel something is different here," he says.

Excellent service, quality food, and a welcoming environment is what sets The James Gang apart. "We see this as an extension of our living room," says Nate of the relaxed, family-like atmosphere. One of Nate's greatest joys is connecting with customers who treat The James Gang as a second home. Tanya enjoys serving people and seeing their responses. "Just knowing you made their day because you listened to them or they got great food," she says.

This trade comes with an incredibly demanding schedule, so it is important for families who work in it to set boundaries. "Owning your own business can consume your life if you let it," says Nate, "You have to set boundaries around it." Nate and Tanya meet weekly to discuss important topics but are engaged in ongoing conversations throughout the week. Nate's goal is not to let the business become a burden to his family but instead to let it become part of who they are. Initially there was concern their kids might be disruptive if they were involved with the work. But later Nate and Tanya decided to incorporate them into the business. "This is our place," says Nate. "We're going to be who we are, and not conform to the community, but more so the community can conform to who we are."

Their three children embraced the opportunity and are now invested in many aspects of the business. Nate and Tanya's 13-year old daughter works the counter, taking orders and preparing sandwiches and drinks. Their 10-year old daughter can be found engaging with customers in the dining area.

Looking ahead, Nate sees the industry becoming more focused on quality. "Coffee has definitely become like the beer or wine-connoisseur industry," he says. "Staying true to organic farming and fair trade, having a good variety of different roasts is going to be key."

Those looking to start their own restaurants need to be prepared for long hours. "You've got to be all-in," says Nate. "It's an industry with a lot of moving parts." There's a lot that goes into building a sandwich and pouring a cup of coffee, from sourcing ingredients to maintaining equipment to keeping track of profit margins on every component. Someone needs to keep a watchful eye on all of this. Starting from scratch, Nate estimates, you will need $150,000 in capital to cover initial expenses and to get through the first three to six months of operation.

Tanya recommends shadowing other business owners. "Go and experience the specific industry you plan to go into," she says. "It's not going to be identical, but you will learn things you didn't think about." And in order to succeed you must have a passion for the people you are serving and for your staff. "Those two pieces are what keep it moving," Tanya says. "The rest of it will fall into place."

Additional Resources

- "How to Start a Restaurant." *Entrepreneur* (https://www.entrepreneur. com/article/73384).

- *A Chef's Life*. Reality documentary series (PBS).

10

9. Brewer

Winemaker, Distiller

Eat the food, Enkidu, it is the way one lives. Drink the beer, as is the custom of the land.

— *Epic of Gilgamesh* (1800 BC)

For nearly as long as there has been food, there has been drink. In all times and cultures, fermented beverages have been synonymous with celebration and revelry—as well as debauchery and excess. In antiquity, at a time when sources of clean drinking water were hard to come by, beer and wine were sought as much for their health benefits as their spiriting effects. Consequently, the brewer, winemaker and distiller are among the oldest and most stable of professionals, and have strong family ties. Some family-run wineries in Europe have succeeded for over 30 generations, operating continuously since the tenth century AD.

    With relaxing laws and surging demand, alcohol is a booming industry.[1] There are currently over 7,500 breweries, wineries and distilleries

---

1. Many states have recently repealed so-called Blue Laws which restrict the sale of alcohol on Sundays and loosened regulations over venues where alcohol can be purchased.

in the U.S. that manufacture $74 billion worth of products annually.[2] In America, total expenditures on alcoholic beverages have surpassed $217 billion—more than doubling since the year 2000.[3] While this is good for business, it is not necessarily good for public health. The CDC reports that one in six drinkers is a binge drinker, and binge-drinking leads to 88,000 deaths per year. The total cost resulting from alcohol abuse to federal, state, and local governments amounted to $249 billion in 2010—over $2 dollars in economic impact for every drink served.[4]

Historical Stability: 72 percent

Despite its long run as a stable profession, distilling has changed much over the centuries. The core product is still the same, but equipment and distribution have seen significant changes, and the whole enterprise is highly-regulated by federal, state, and local agencies. Concocting a homemade brew to share among friends is one thing; earning a living from the manufacture of alcohol is entirely different.

Mass production has made its mark on this industry: breaking even generally requires large-scale manufacture and distribution. Still, tastes are changing in beverages as they are in food. Consumers are beginning to favor small-scale breweries and locally-run wineries over national brands. Craft beers are hugely popular, and smaller, local breweries known as microbreweries have driven rapid growth in the alcohol industry. "The number of breweries in the United States increased more than fivefold from 2010 to 2016," reports the Bureau of Labor Statistics, and now account for 25 percent of employment in the entire beverage industry.[5]

Resiliency: 77 percent

In almost every city in America one can find a microbrewery, and often several. A brewer's customers need not be widespread, unless he is working exclusively through distributors instead of selling locally. Even then, regional sales can usually sustain locally-made beverages.

Liquor sales are generally resilient, in good times and bad. However, if the model of distribution is through restaurants and microbreweries,

2. US Census, "Number of Firms."
3. USDA, "Nominal food and alcohol expenditures."
4. CDC, "Excessive Drinking."
5. Delainey and Haines, "Industry on Tap: Breweries."

sales will follow dining trends and be severely impacted during recessions. The supply chain need not be extensive after initial purchase of equipment. Locally-sourced ingredients are possible and often preferable when it comes to craft beers. For wineries, the entire operation from vine to bottle can be accomplished onsite. That having been said, alcohol ingredients are commodities that are subject to the same shortages and weather disruptions that threaten other food. "The availability and cost of raw materials is a major concern for the craft brewing industry overall," according one source.[6]

The main threat of automation comes in the form of mass production, which is already mature and beginning to lose market share to smaller-scale alternatives—not dissimilar from the organic revolution in food. People want more control over their food (and beverage) choices, and are willing to pay for them. Nevertheless, both automated and craft breweries will be with us for a long time to come.

Family-Centeredness: 69 percent

Distilling has traditionally been a very strong family-oriented business. Accounts of family-run wineries lasting for many centuries are not uncommon. If strict but essential age-related laws did not exist, distilling would have scored much higher in this category: children can participate in nearly all stages of beverage production, with the exception of drinking it legally.

How much time family members spend together depends largely on how the business is structured. Families growing vineyards and making wine in a home-based operation are at an advantage here. Families operating a microbrewery more closely resemble restaurateurs and will spend more of their time away from rather than at home.

The manufacture of alcoholic beverages has the potential to generate tremendous assets for family inheritance. In the case of wineries, not only is land an asset, but the end-product increases in value with age.

Income: 80 percent

Because there are so many ways to structure a business involved in alcohol production, it is difficult to put an exact price on income. The median salary for a brewmaster in 2017 was slightly less than $50,000. This could be much higher—at a national brewery—or much lower, at a fledgling microbrewery.

---

6. Godard, "The Economics of Craft Beer," para. 5.

Those rare and hugely successful breweries can earn millions, similar to successful restaurants.

There are other ways to be peripherally involved as well that do not directly involve the manufacture of alcohol. Specializing in growing ingredients used in manufacture, such as grapes, barley, and hops, can be a lucrative venture. According to a Michigan State University study, hops—an essential ingredient in beer—can generate gross revenues in excess of $20,000 per acre.[7] Two families I spoke with from rural acreages in Minnesota are growing specialty varieties of barely to sell to local microbreweries.

Ease of Entry: 64 percent

Starting a brewery, winery, or distillery will be cost-prohibitive to most, with startup costs ranging from $100,000 to $1 million for necessary equipment alone.[8] Buildings to house a brewery or pub, or land to grow a vineyard, would cost extra.

No formal education is needed, but regulations are strict. Licensing is required in all 50 states and can amount to $14,000 total in licensing fees.

> In the United States, each state has the authority to regulate the production, sale, and distribution of alcohol within its borders. This means state and local jurisdictions may have their own requirements in addition to federal requirements.[9]

Competition is also fierce, with nearly one thousand new microbreweries and hundreds of new wineries opening annually.[10] However, thus far the swelling demand for craft beer and regional wineries is more than enough to offset the competition.

7. Sirrine et al., "Estimated Costs of Producing Hops," Table 2.

8. Gitlen, "How Much Does It Cost to Start a Brewery?"

9. US Dept. of Treasury, "Alcohol Beverage Authorities," para. 1.

10. "In 2012, there were 2,420 craft breweries in the United States. By 2017, that number had jumped to 6,266, plus a large increase in the number of microbreweries." Gitlen, "How Much Does It Cost to Start a Brewery?"; The number of wineries in North America grew from 8,391 in 2014 to 9,872 in 2017. *Wines & Vines*, "Number of Wineries Grows," and "North American Winery Count."

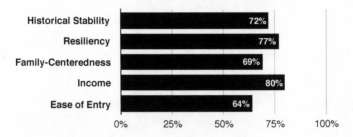

SCORE SUMMARY: BREWER

Historical Stability	72%
Resiliency	77%
Family-Centeredness	69%
Income	80%
Ease of Entry	64%

Profile: Old Nation Brewing Co.

Travis Fritts did not set out to become a brewer; he just wanted to see the world. After studying abroad through a high school student exchange program, he was recruited into the brewmaster program at VLB Berlin, a prestigious research and education institute serving the brewing industry. During his time there, Travis worked at breweries across Europe. "I was working with as many masters as I could, because that's the way they still do trades in Germany," he recalls. Travis returned to the States a certified brewmaster.

After working for several years as a consultant to failing breweries run by businessmen rather than brewmasters, Travis became frustrated with the lack of expertise and dedication to the craft. His big opportunity came in 2015 when Travis and with his wife Camilla, along with a brewing part-ner, opened their own brewery in Williamston, Michigan. "We bought a building, redid the floors, rigged the tanks . . . and started making beer that nobody cared about."

Travis was determined to bring back the traditional styles of beer he was trained in making. But he was having trouble selling them: "We were not dying," he recalls, "but not far away from it." Travis decided to make an unorthodox move: seeking input from craft beer enthusiasts in online forums. "You don't talk to these guys," he confided. "Their whole hobby is sitting online and tearing apart whatever brewery they are talking about." But Travis was well received and the conversations led to the creation of a new beer based on their feedback. Travis then invited the enthusiasts to his brewery to sample the new brew. "They came and drank it all and asked, 'where's the next batch?'"

That was the genesis of M-43, an English IPA that has become a runaway success. "We went from 7 barrels every other week to 120 barrels a week within eight months." Over the ensuing 18 months, his company increased production from 1,500 barrels a year to 17,000 a year. "You never know what you're capable of until you have no other choice," Travis says. "It took me 16 years to become an overnight success."

The work is varied for a brewer. "You're always wet," says Travis, referring to the steady contact with liquids, ingredients, and steam a brewer must contend with every day. Also, the job can be physically strenuous: pulling 100-foot hoses, dumping 55-pound bags of grain into mills, moving 200-pound kegs, and stirring 800 gallons of porridge. "That's what brewing is like," he says. "The romance in brewing is thinking of creative recipes, and how to name the beers," Travis explains. "But all of that is one and a half percent of your actual job."

Sustaining the energy and motivation required to create and market a successful brand is difficult for Travis. With 20,000 barrels in production each year, 13 beers on tap, and five in distribution, "keeping it up is the challenge now." Travis also talks about *Schlimmbesserung*, a German word that can be translated as "negative improvement." There is a point in every project where it can no longer be improved, after which the optimum result begins to worsen. The same applies to crafting beer. Knowing when to stop is extremely challenging.

The true joy of brewing cannot be found in money or prestige, according to Travis. "Winning awards is cool," he says, "but the shine wears off real quick." But a good day's work with a dedicated team is always rewarding. "When you leave at the end of the day, when the tanks are full . . . when everything is fine and will be fine in the morning, that is a true joy," he says. "The shine never wears off."

Old Nation Brewing Company is a true family business. Travis runs the production facility and his wife runs the restaurant. His three sons, ages four to ten, are also involved: working in the kitchen, waiting on tables, cleaning. "They're starting off like apprentices always have. That's how everybody started in every trade."

Since Travis has been involved with the industry, he's seen a big shift in the types of people entering the profession. Formerly the purview of "rough and tumble" brewmasters well suited to the work, brewing has become populated with business professionals with little knowledge of the craft or respect for masters who have been working in the trade for decades. "The field of brewing is littered with bodies like that," he says. Going forward, Travis expects trust to become a critical factor again for brewers. "People are much more loyal to breweries than they were five years ago," he says.

Those who are not capable and dedicated will be winnowed out as customers increasingly seek out brewers they can trust.

For those going into the trade Travis warns, "There's no such thing as an easy path. You have to work for it. If you make a home brew that your buddies like that doesn't make you a master brewer." It takes many years of trial-and-error but, Travis says, "Stick with it. There are rewards: emotionally, financially, and in the community."

Additional Resources

- *Designing Great Beers: The Ultimate Guide to Brewing Classic Beer Styles* by Ray Daniels (Brewers Publications, 1998).
- *Technology Brewing and Malting* by Wolfgang Kunze (VLB Berlin, 2014).

11

10. Innkeeper

Hotelier

And she gave birth to her firstborn son and wrapped him in swaddling cloths and laid him in a manger, because there was no place for them in the inn.

—LUKE 2:7 (5 BC)

LEISURE TOURISM HAS A sporadic history. Mass tourism as we know it today only came into existence about 50 years ago, with the advent of air travel and rising discretionary incomes following World War II. Industrialization of the 19th and 20th centuries created surplus incomes and idle time, as well as fewer attachments to home, permitting some degree of movement and leisure. Prior to that, leisure travel was restricted to the affluent, the sick seeking healthier climes, or the religious making pilgrimages.

You'd have to go all the way back to first-century Rome to find tourism somewhat on the scale that we see today, with citizens spending their summers away from the city, in coastal villages and the countryside. For the majority of the last 2,000 years, travel was simply too expensive, too time-consuming, and too dangerous.

Today, tourism is a strong and robust segment of every economy, from small seaside fishing villages to the Waldorf Astoria in downtown New

York. Not only is tourism booming, but business travel continues to expand. Lodging is a $257 billion industry in the U.S., with 47,385 hotels, motels, and B&Bs currently in operation.[1]

Historical Stability: 84 percent

The core service is much the same today as it was 250 years ago. If it weren't for the irregular history of lodging, innkeeping would score much higher in historical stability. Methods of hoteliers have certainly changed, but mostly in response to competitive demands. Number of rooms, swimming pools, and proximity to attractions all play a larger factor now than they did in the past.

Computerized bookkeeping and reservation management systems have changed the tools of the trade, if they can be called that. But one thing hasn't changed: weary travelers needing a place to rest.

Resiliency: 63 percent

Lodging depends on travelers, and travelers depend on discretionary income. That is why innkeeping is so vulnerable to recessions as compared to other trades. But with the majority of the U.S. population living in cities, almost every small town has some form of lodging.

The supply chain for locally-owned inns is not extensive or long, the primary requirement being labor. However, lodging does depend on larger geographic areas—represented by travelers—rather than on local consumers to sustain itself. Automation will continue to increase in administrative work, such as in booking and reservation systems, but it will not be able to fully replace people any time soon.

Family-Centeredness: 67 percent

There are definite opportunities for family-based businesses in lodging, particularly in B&Bs and VRBOs. From an early age, children are capable of many housekeeping chores, and so are elderly adults. Tasks required for hosting guests complement both men and women. At its best, a B&B could be an ideal opportunity for family members to live together, work together, and serve others while building a lasting inheritance.

On the other hand, hotel-type operations requiring large staff and dozens or hundreds of rooms are much less family-friendly. However, the

1. US Census, "Number of Firms."

increased occupancy of hotels provides an income that B&Bs cannot match. In both cases, significant tangible assets are generated in this trade both in buildings and land.

The Cott Inn at Cott, Dartington, Devon, UK dates from AD 1320 and is still in operation today. (Source: Totnesmartin/Wikimedia)

Income: 80 percent

Lodging managers earned a median pay of $53,390 in 2018, according to the Bureau of Labor Statistics. For those running their own operations, the rewards can be much greater. The average rate for a B&B is around $150 per night. With an industry average of six rooms and 43 percent occupancy, this adds up to over $140,000 per year, before expenses.[2]

At similar prices and occupancy, hotels averaging 90 rooms could gross up to $2 million annually.[3] However, with higher debt loads, this is an industry in which it takes a long time to turn a profit. And there is no guarantee that "if you build it they will come."

Ease of Entry: 64 percent

With an average size of six rooms and 5,700 square feet, a B&B property suitable for business is not easy to acquire. In the U.S., the median price for a house

2. PAII, "About The Industry."

3. 54,200 properties nationwide with five million guest rooms. American Hotel & Lodging Association, "Frequently Asked Questions."

this size is about $850,000.[4] Hotels, on the other hand are truly a capital-intensive endeavor. One source reports that those wishing to open and operate a hotel as a franchisee should expect initial outlays of $7 to $10 million.[5]

While no formal education is required to operate an inn, the competition is fierce, and regulations can be restrictive depending on one's state and municipality. According to the Bureau of Labor Statistics, employment in the trade is expected to remain steady through 2028.

SCORE SUMMARY: INNKEEPER

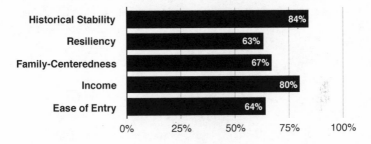

Profile: Ross Hospitality

Jeff and Linda Ross outside their B&B in Louisville, Kentucky

In the course of raising a family and hosting company for many years, Jeff and Linda Ross discovered the joy of hospitality. "We just love having

4. Median home price in the U.S. is $153 per square foot. Zillow, "United States Home Prices & Values."

5. FranchiseHelp, "Courtyard by Marriott Franchise."

people in our home," Jeff says. In 2016 they purchased a 3-story house in the historic district of Louisville, Kentucky, with hopes of turning their passion into an income-producing livelihood. After moving, the Ross's furnished the third floor of their house and a carriage house above their garage and listed them on AirBNB as private rentals. Within 18 months, the rentals were producing enough income to cover mortgage, insurance, taxes, and utilities. "And it has stayed there ever since," according to Ross.

The Ross's approach to innkeeping is unique. "It's not really about the income for us," Jeff says. "It's about being the best hosts we can be." Jeff and Linda's goal is to make the guest experience as good as possible, and it shows. To date, the Ross's have received over 130 five-star reviews on AirBNB.

Since most rentals occur over the weekends, operating a B&B is not a full-time commitment for Jeff and Linda. A typical day involves communicating with guests prior to arrival. Jeff likes to arrange his schedule to personally greet guests when they arrive. He leaves to the guests how much interaction they want while staying. Some guests prefer to be left alone; others enjoy socializing with their hosts. Between stays, Jeff and Linda share the duties of cleaning and restocking.

Hosting strangers can be challenging at times, Jeff acknowledges. "You have to be open to any kind of person from any walk of life," he says. The Ross's have hosted guests from dozens of states and several countries. Another challenge, cites Ross, is the increasing regulatory environment surrounding home-sharing. "When we purchased the house, there were no regulations for short-term rentals," he says. Since that time legislation has been passed in Louisville requiring B&B operators to obtain conditional use permits and gain permission from neighbors and zoning committees. "That can be a very lengthy process," Jeff says.

Despite the challenges, the experience has been overwhelmingly positive for Jeff and Linda. "We have met such a variety of wonderful people that we would never in a million years have met otherwise," he says. "That has been the greatest joy." The Ross's have also been able to use their space to provide hospitality to people in need.

The Ross's view this as a family-based business. Jeff and Linda share duties of cleaning, restocking, and laundry. One of their grown children who lives in town fills in as a backup host when needed and likes to assist with repairs and handiwork around the house. He also designed the carriage house built atop the garage. Grandkids also help with setting out a room and restocking the refrigerator.

Jeff sees the popularity of B&Bs and home-sharing continuing to grow. But with that comes increased regulation and competition from the hotel industry. Jeff mentions that there is always "an effort by hotels to undermine

B&Bs and promote as many horror stories as they can find." Going forward, Jeff expects home-sharing hosts will have to become more professional. "A lot of guests are demanding it, expecting a hotel-type experience," he says.

For anyone considering this type of business, Jeff recommends doing your homework. "Talk with experienced hosts and guests," he says. "Get both perspectives." He suggests staying at other B&Bs to find out what pleased you and what didn't. Also, "know your city's and state's rules before you embark." You can be subject to expensive fines by violating rules depending on where you live. But don't let the obstacles deter you. "People are going to keep traveling and needing a place to stay and will be inclined to this kind of setup."

Additional Resources

- *AirBNB.com.* Home-sharing platform (https://airbnb.com/host/).

- *Airbnb: How To Make Money On Airbnb and Easily Earn Up to $10,000 A Month* by Mark Thomas (Createspace, 2016).

- *STR (Short-term Rental) University.* Youtube channel.

- *Airbnb Homeshare Hosts.* Facebook group.

12

11. Tutor

Private Instructor, Coach

The mind is not a vessel to be filled, but a fire to be kindled.

—PLUTARCH (AD 100)

BEFORE THERE WAS MASS education, there were tutors. Centuries before Roman schools existed, the philosopher-king Solomon wrote: "'Look,' says the Teacher, 'this is what I have discovered: Adding one thing to another to discover the scheme of things . . .'"[1] Tutors are anyone who provide private instruction to students seeking specific skill development. They are different from school teachers, in that they typically work one-on-one with individual students. Tutors may travel to the student's home or may teach in their own homes, offices, or workshops. In some cases, tutors work online, recording and selling video lectures, or using videoconferencing software to teach their students.

An alternate form of tutoring is informal education, in which private instructors host workshops for adults, focusing on specific skills. In many cities it is common to find "Community Education" workshops, with topics

1. Ecc 7:27

covering arts and crafts, hobbies, language, home and garden, and health and fitness.

Some operators have taken this a step further to provide year-round programming, offering training on unique skillsets that are hard to find in formal institutions. North House Folk School in northern Minnesota provides workshops on traditional crafts. Courses include blacksmithing, timber framing, boat building, wood-fired baking, fiber arts, carving, and outdoor skills. Every year North House attracts thousands of students from all over the world who are interested in learning lost arts and methods practiced by past generations.

A more recent incarnation of tutor is the coach. A coach is someone who both instructs and holds his or her students accountable to desired outcomes. The most common form is a sports coach, but in recent years other variations have appeared. These include the business coach who works with executives and business owners, and the life coach who assists clients with personal goals.

Altogether, private instruction generates at around $25 billion annually in the U.S., with more than 400,000 private tutors, instructors, and coaches in business today.[2]

Historical Stability: 88 percent

Private instruction is a highly stable profession in that it is essentially unchanged after thousands of years. There have been changes to methods and tools, but the core service provided by tutors is the same today as it was centuries ago, as is the direct connection with clients. Alternate forms of education have arisen over the last 150 years reducing the demand for private tutors, particularly with compulsory education in the nineteenth century and today with online learning. However, these forms of mass education cannot replace the need for individualized attention by students who fall outside the one-size-fits-all approach of public schooling.

Resiliency: 75 percent

People value education if they can afford it. Vulnerability to economic downswings depends on the subjects being taught and the students being served. Speech therapists helping students with learning disabilities are akin

2. Not including professional sports; US Census, "Number of Firms."

to medical practitioners and unlikely to be affected by recessions. Instructors specializing in basket weaving might need to diversify.

Generally speaking, customers for private instruction can be found locally, or at least regionally. Outside of a few educational aids, there are no extended supply chains or raw materials that tutors depend on; the service is entirely relational.

Finally, while there are inroads being made in computer-based training that may help some students who were formerly assisted by private tutors, overall this is a highly customized industry with every student being treated as unique. Some subjects are too complex or hard to grasp from a book or video. Therefore, it is improbable that machine automation will eliminate the need for people in this industry.

Family-Centeredness: 55 percent

Tutors score about average on family-centeredness. Due to the wide variations in this profession, there are opportunities to spend much time with family or little. Private tutors who travel to their students' homes or schools will spend most of their time away from their own family. However, they can still base their business from home. Private instructors or tutors who have the meeting space may host workshops or sessions on their own property and therefore spend nearly all of their time with family.

There is limited opportunity for children to be involved, as tutors and instructors are expected to be experts themselves. However, for this same reason private instruction favors the elderly who can draw not only from formal education but life experiences as well. Roles exist for both men and women and can complement each other's strengths. For example, workshops teaching prenatal health are well-suited to female instructors, while tree-felling workshops are better suited to men.

Unfortunately private instruction does not generate any tangible assets for future generations.

Income: 80 percent

Incomes in private instruction can be quite high. As with family-centeredness, the specialty chosen within this trade largely determines the result. Special education tutors earned a median pay of $59,780 in 2018, according to the Bureau of Labor Statistics. Licensed business coaches may earn double or triple that amount depending on workload. Private instructors teaching an occasional Community-Ed workshop will not approach this figure.

Ease of Entry: 76 percent

Private instructors do not need college degrees if they have the life experience required to teach. In fact, it is more preferable to learn from an accomplished professional than from someone who is merely accredited without the accompanying life experience. Professional tutors, on the other hand, are going to find it difficult to become licensed or find employment without advanced degrees. Therefore, startup costs as well as formal education requirements largely depend on the type of instruction one is pursuing.

Besides licensing requirements for certain specialties, there are minimal regulations involved with private instruction, and competition is lower than average. Demand for tutors and private instructors is expected to increase by 6 percent over the next decade according to the Bureau of Labor Statistics.

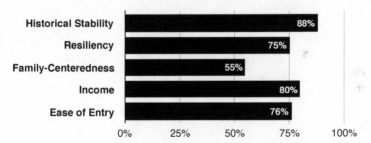

SCORE SUMMARY: TUTOR

Historical Stability	88%
Resiliency	75%
Family-Centeredness	55%
Income	80%
Ease of Entry	76%

Profile: Victoria Stanley

Victoria Stanley began teaching art over 30 years ago to her own children. As a homeschooling mother of five with a degree in Art Education, Victoria saw an opportunity to enrich her children's education with a deeper study of art. Other homeschooling parents began sending their kids to Victoria's house to join in, and soon her career as a private instructor was underway. "It's a very joy-filled job," says Victoria. "I get to work with a subject I love and its really fun working with children."

The business has always ebbed and flowed, according to Victoria. "There are lean years and bumper crop years and you never know," she says. Over the decades Victoria has built her business from teaching her own children at home to teaching 150 to 200 kids in multiple cities and home-school cooperatives. She could handle more students, but family has always been her priority. "For me it was more a quality-of-life aspect," Victoria says. "I wanted time with my kids and grandkids."

When Victoria's husband died unexpectedly in 2006, and with children still at home, teaching became an important source of income for her family. Since then her business has continued to grow, almost exclusively through word-of-mouth. Much of Victoria's success can be attributed to her warm and friendly demeanor, as is evident to anyone who has met her. "Parents like to know their kids are in a place where the teacher really cares about them," she says.

Much preparation goes into a single day of teaching. The curriculum is planned and materials ordered months before classes begin. The day before a class is held Victoria prepares a lesson plan and sample. Classes are usually held in a church or community building, where she will teach multiple 90-minute sessions back-to-back for different ages. In the class, which may be attended by 8 to 24 students, she begins by teaching concepts and history, then explains the project or teaches in steps.

The biggest challenge for Victoria is coming up with unique curriculum year after year. Unlike public school teachers who teach a single grade, Victoria may teach the same child from kindergarten through 10th or 11th grade. Even after 30 years, Victoria struggles with developing new lessons that kids—and parents—will like.

But for Victoria, teaching art is a job with lasting value. "I'm enriching a child's life in an area where some parents cannot." Moreover, learning art develops cognitive abilities affecting many other areas of a child's life. "Art is a subject where there is not always a right and wrong answer," Victoria explains. "That is really good for minds, to learn to be problem-solvers when there is not one right answer." As a Christian, Victoria also feels blessed to be able to integrate faith with learning, such as starting classes with prayer and talking about God freely in the classroom.

Victoria's teaching has periodically involved her family. In addition to teaching her own kids and grandkids, Victoria's children have served as art-room assistants. Two of her grown children are actively involved in art-related professions. According to Victoria, a family pursuing this trade could train multiple members as art instructors and have many more locations under one business, teaching the same lessons at each location so as not to reinvent the wheel.

Victoria hasn't seen much change to her industry in 30 years. "Families are busier," she mentions, "and there are more options, which can cut into my business." But overall Victoria doesn't foresee issues with maintaining her livelihood. Video-based education is beginning to make inroads, but an essential ingredient is missing. "I don't think anyone is really going to replace a live teacher. There's a quality there that can't be replaced."

Victoria's advice to those interested in pursuing a career in private instruction is to be courageous. "Give it a try," she says. "Don't be discouraged if it starts small, because most likely it will grow. Care about your students more than you care about the project."

Additional Resources

- *Tutors.com*. Tutor directory and job placement website.
- *North House Folk School*. Traditional craft school in northern Minnesota (https://northhouse.org).
- *Clark*. Tutor management software (https://www.hiclark.com).

13

12. Mason

Bricklayer, Paver, Stonemason

They said to each other, "Let us make bricks and bake them thoroughly." They used brick instead of stone, and tar for mortar.

—Genesis 11:3 NIV (2200 BC)

A gradually-shifting trade, masonry includes stone-cutting, carving, and bricklaying construction activities. In recent decades, concrete has replaced much of the foundation work and wall-building formerly done by stonemasons. Outside of concrete, masonry has followed the residential housing industry into more aesthetic (rather than structural) projects: interior veneers, backyard patios, and outdoor kitchens.

When the thousand-year-old castles were being erected throughout Europe, it is reported that masonry was in such high demand and master stonemasons held in such high regard that they did not need to bow to their monarchs.[1]

Today there are 18,274 masonry businesses generating $24 billion annually in the U.S.[2] While masonry is an essential activity in construction, there are far fewer historically trained masons, particularly in stonework,

1. *Mastercrafts: Stonemasonry.*
2. US Census, "Number of Firms."

than in years past. For every masonry business, there are seven carpentry outfits. So long as demand for stonework continues—which it will—this means increasing incomes for those willing to devote their time and energy to becoming expertly-trained masters.

Despite comparatively smaller numbers relative to construction jobs, masonry jobs are expected to grow much faster than the national average of all professions in the coming years.

Historical Stability: 96 percent

Masons are one of the two highest-scoring trades for historical stability. Over 4,000 years ago, men were building the Tower of Babel with bricks. Masons today are practicing virtually the same trade, with only minor changes to materials and tooling. And these are changes in form, to enhance scale and efficiency, rather than a change in kind. The chisel, the hammer and the trowel are still very much a part of everyday masonry.

Even modern clientele is similar to that in ages past. As with other building trades, every masonry project is unique. Whether laying a brick hearth, paving a walkway, or hewing and setting a stone wall—no two projects are exactly alike.

Resiliency: 67 percent

As a building trade, masonry is vulnerable to recessions and fluctuations in the housing industry. Nevertheless, masons are an integral part of construction and will always be in demand where structures, walls, roads and pathways are needed. The materials used in masonry can be either simple or exotic—from clay brick to polished marble. However, supply chain vulnerabilities increase the rarer the materials become.

Though structural work is becoming less common for masons, decorative work leaves them more vulnerable to recessions and cutbacks in discretionary spending. Specializing in essential, non-discretionary activities, such as foundation repair, can help to protect against market fluctuations.

Though there are brick-laying robots beginning to appear, overall there is low risk of machine automation replacing humans in this industry due to the customized nature and intimate stone working knowledge required to produce finished pieces.

Family-Centeredness: 55 percent

As with other building trades, masonry affords partial opportunities for family work. This is usually limited to men and those ages capable of demanding physical labor. Due to the heavy lifting required, masonry is dominated by men even more so than other building trades.

Masonry businesses can be based from home, but the work will be mostly off-site. Masons leave behind tangible assets mainly in the form of tools, which is likely to be considerable (scaffolding alone comes to mind). Their most valuable asset is skill.

Income: 80 percent

Median incomes for masons were around $22 per hour in 2018, on par with the rest of the construction industry, according to the Bureau of Labor Statistics. However, depending on proximity to metropolitan areas, those rates can go much higher. In San Francisco and Boston, masons earn $70,000 to $80,000 per year.[3] As with other building trades, self-employed masons typically earn double or triple the median hourly wage.

Given the time required to master the craft, a key advantage of masonry work comes in the form of steady, long-term employment as replacements are difficult to find.

Ease of Entry: 72 percent

Masons have mostly low barriers to entry. There is no formal education required, and low startup costs. However those seeking to run their own businesses must undergo an apprenticeship. "Traditionally medieval stonemasons served a seven-year apprenticeship," according to one source. "A similar system still operates today."[4] An apprenticeship today typically lasts three to four years, and combines on-the-job learning and classroom theory.

Competition is moderate among bricklayers and stonemasons, but there is plenty of work to go around for the foreseeable future. After slowing down following the construction rebound in 2012, the Bureau of Labor Statistics predicts a very strong 11 percent rate of growth over the next decade.

---

3. *Career Profiles*, "The Top 10 Most Stable Construction Jobs."
4. *Wikipedia*, "Stonemasonry."

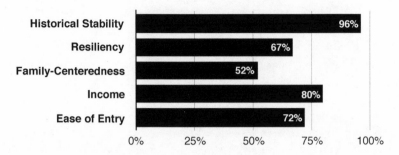

SCORE SUMMARY: MASON

Category	Score
Historical Stability	96%
Resiliency	67%
Family-Centeredness	52%
Income	80%
Ease of Entry	72%

Profile: Top Dawg Masonry

Nick Avila started his career in masonry over 20 years ago. He was working as an assistant manager in Texas for less than $4 per hour when his uncle invited him to join him in Minnesota, shoveling mud for $7 per hour. Nick jumped at the chance to double his pay. Once on the job, he not only shoveled mud but would jump in the line to lay bricks whenever a spare moment presented itself.

"The owner noticed that I wanted to learn," Nick says. "As soon as he gave me the opportunity, I wanted to be the hardest working guy there." Three years later, Nick was the foreman. Nick continued in the trade, learning something new every day. He joined a union and learned the business over time. Seven years ago Nick struck out on his own.

Honesty and quality are what sets Top Dawg Masonry apart from other outfits. Nick says the secret of the trade is not to cut corners. At every step he asks himself: "Would I do this in my own house?" Nick's work speaks for itself: he doesn't do any advertising and doesn't hand out business cards. Every job is from word-of-mouth referrals. As owner, Nick also believes in being the hardest working member of the crew. "You've got to set the example," he says. His employees see it and are inspired to work harder themselves.

A typical day starts with a cup of coffee and planning the day's activities. For an effective crew, Nick needs four bricklayers, two laborers, and an operator who makes sure the bricks and scaffolding are ready. The laborers are babysitters, according to Nick. "They make sure the bricklayers never stop laying brick." After arriving on the job site, Nick will start a wall with the crew then jump out and get another wall started before going back to check on the first wall.

Quality control is Nick's biggest challenge. Masons use a tooling iron to shape and compress mortar between joints, for both aesthetic and water-proofing reasons. One of Nick's responsibilities is to make sure the mortar and joints are struck correctly, otherwise the structural integrity of the wall could be compromised.

Nick's greatest satisfaction is the job itself. "My greatest joy is when I'm laying brick," Nick says. "When it's all said and done you realize, 'Wow! Look what I did with my own hands.'" Over the years, Nick has seen a general decline in work ethic in the industry. Other changes include the many new code requirements such as flashing, mortar fence, and other water-proofing requirements. Looking ahead, Nick mentions brick-laying robots. "But to maintain that robot," he says, "you need three or four guys with it." With automation, there are still many obstacles to overcome.

For those interested in becoming masons, Nick encourages apprentices to learn something new every day and not to let pride get in the way. "There's always going to be someone better than you," he says. "Allow others to give you ideas, and pick up ideas as you learn."

Additional Resources

- *National Concrete Masonry Association (NCMA)*. Education and certification association (https://ncma.org).
- *Mastercrafts: Stonemasonry*. Video documentary (BBC, 2010).

14

13. Silversmith

Goldsmith, Jeweler

As a jeweler engraves signets, so shall you engrave the
two stones with the names of the sons of Israel. You
shall enclose them in settings of gold filigree.

—EXODUS 28:11 (1500 BC)

Students of American history may recall that Paul Revere was a renowned silversmith in Boston prior to the Revolutionary War (and following). Silversmithing, including jewelry-making, was a luxury trade during Colonial times. In a time when most utensils were made of wood or pewter, silver and gold objects were not found in the households of commoners. But most larger cities had at least one silversmith, and the artistic trade goes back much further than Colonial America.

Numerous references can be found throughout the Old Testament to workers and engravers of precious metals. Twenty-five hundred years ago, Uzziel "the goldsmith" worked under the direction of Nehemiah, rebuilding Jerusalem's walls. Thirty-five hundred years ago, after handing down the Ten Commandments, God commanded Moses to create ornate objects from pure gold for use in temple worship. And about four thousand years ago, at a well outside the town of Nahor, Isaac gave his future wife Rebekah golden bracelets. Clearly, precious metals have played a significant role in human history and so have those who shaped them.

Today, jewelers comprise a $7 billion industry in the U.S. with around 2,000 custom jewelry makers in operation.[1]

Historical Stability: 80 percent

Jewelry-making enjoys a generally stable history. This is due in large part to the fact that for many thousands of years jewelry itself was currency. People both adorned themselves while keeping cash close at hand—literally on their hands. The core product, ornamental objects and adornments has not changed in at least 5,000 years. However, industrialization and globalization have had a destabilizing effect on a once-steady source of employment.

Except for large operators who rely primarily on machinery to produce commoditized pieces, the methods of the trade for private operators have largely remained the same. There are new tools, however, with the advent of 3-D printing, which can assist with creating wax models. As in other trades, there are proponents to this new form of automation, who cite improved accuracy and efficiency; there are also opponents, who prioritize uniqueness and traditional craft above modern efficiencies.

The trade has also seen a transformation in clientele: in addition to individuals for whom custom jewelry is made there are now wholesalers and distributors retailing a jeweler's wares in storefronts and shopping malls. Online retailers, such as Etsy, have also emerged providing jewelry-makers direct access to international consumers. However, it can be difficult to compete in an online sphere where makers never see their customers and every product becomes commoditized, both of which push down perceived value.

Resiliency: 58 percent

Jewelry depends on scarce resources: gold and silver. Unless you live on a goldmine, you are not likely to stumble across any of the needed raw materials in your own backyard. Jewelry makers are fully reliant on the international industry for mining precious metals, and its fluctuations in prices. Further, being a luxury item, jewelry is highly vulnerable to recessions. When holding on to cash is a priority, people tend to cut back on luxury purchases.

That having been said, jewelers can do quite well in local markets, as evidenced by the numerous jewelry stores that can be found in every

1. US Census, "Number of Firms."

shopping mall, retail outlet, and increasingly farmer's markets. Jewelry is a popular product with most people, and every wedding, birthday, and anniversary is a baked-in sales opportunity.

Family-Centeredness: 73 percent

Silversmiths, goldsmiths and jewelers can spend most of their time at home, with a proper studio setup. Men and women, children and adults of most ages can be engaged with at least some portion of the assembly, although much training is required to master all elements of the craft.

The trade does produce tangible inheritable assets, not the least of which is the product itself. Also, a reputable brand and trusted name carry a lot of weight in this industry, where uniqueness and quality are prized above utility.

Income: 60 percent

Generating a family-supporting income from jewelry is difficult but not impossible. The industry is full of amateurs and hobbyists who make it difficult for new entrants to stand out. Earning a living from the trade is a long-term proposition. But once a business gets established, the dividends can pay off. The Bureau of Labor statistics puts the median pay for jewelry-makers at $38,000 per year. But stories exist of "momprenuers" who have started home-based jewelry-making businesses that grew into multi-million-dollar enterprises.[2]

Ease of Entry: 84 percent

Aspiring jewelers can get started for very little up-front investment. $500 is enough for basic supplies and low-end jewelry. The price goes up from there with training and materials. There are no formal education requirements, but private instruction and apprenticing will save time and money in the long-run.

There are virtually no government regulations. And while competition is prevalent, uniqueness is the hallmark of the industry. Those with an eye for creativity, whose designs stand out from the crowd, and who can develop loyal relationships with customers and buyers will be able to succeed where others cannot.

2. Ibrahim, "Kendra Scott."

The Bureau of Labor Statistics predicts a decrease in demand for workers in this field, projecting a 7 percent decline through 2028. However, this is due primarily to cheaper, foreign-made goods displacing American-made goods rather than to a reduction in overall demand for jewelry. Custom jewelry-makers with unique, hand-made products will always be able to differentiate themselves in a sea of commoditized products.

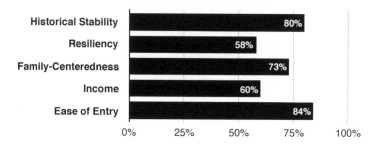

SCORE SUMMARY: SILVERSMITH

Historical Stability	80%
Resiliency	58%
Family-Centeredness	73%
Income	60%
Ease of Entry	84%

Profile: Andrew Beesley Studio & Design

Second-Generation Goldsmith Andrew Beesley

Andrew Beesley grew up around the trades. Born and raised in Provo, Utah, Andrew is a second-generation goldsmith. "My entire life, my father's studio was in our home," he recalls. "It was a big part of our family life because it was so close to home." Andrew remembers from a young age watching his dad. "There was something intriguing about watching him work," he says. Next to his dad was a second workbench where Andrew would learn the tools, getting a feel for running a file. By the time he was a teenager, Andrew was creating finished pieces. After apprenticing with his Dad, Andrew found that it was very natural to transition into working as a jewelry maker as an adult.

After finishing a mission with the LDS Church, Andrew began working with his father full time. Several years later, in 2012, he opened his own studio in downtown Provo. What makes Andrew's practice unique is his adherence to traditional methods and hand-crafting in a time when most practices are embracing new technologies and automating as much as of the work possible. "If jewelry making loses its hand-labor and human touch then it becomes something completely different," he says. "If you turn a product into a commodity, there will come a day when people become completely disenchanted altogether with a fine piece of jewelry. Everything will become disposable."

A typical day for Andrew starts at home. "I'm a husband and a father. Those are my primary jobs," he says. "I happen to be a goldsmith on the side." After dropping the kids off at school, Andrew drives to his office downtown where he can be found ordering supplies, tracking down diamonds, meeting with customers, and pushing paper. As a solo entrepreneur, he may spend only a few hours each day actually making jewelry at his bench.

As a result Andrew is forced to manage his time carefully to stay on task—which can be challenging when working alone with frequent interruptions. On occasion, Andrew returns to his office after supper to work until the early hours of the morning. But he loves working with people and counts that as one of the greatest joys of this trade. "I get to know all of my clients," he says. "When they come in five or ten years later, I still know who they are." Crafting engagement rings and wedding bands, Andrew enjoys being a part of these important events in his clients' lives. "That's an enjoyable interaction between a business owner and a client."

Jewelry is an ever-evolving market, according to Andrew. "Fifty years ago . . . diamonds were diamonds, gold was gold," he says. "Today there's a new synthetic option around every corner." It can be difficult to determine which items offer clients the best combination of quality and value, all while staying competitive. But in a world where everything is becoming increasingly disposable, Andrew has hope for the future. "There's an awakening happening," he says. "People are realizing 'I don't need to live a highly corporate lifestyle. I can live on a farm and be happy.'" Andrew looks forward to a future when there is more appreciation for fine craftsmanship and original artwork.

"You have to work really hard," Andrew says of a career in jewelry. He encourages those considering a career in this trade to find a specific niche in the field that they really love. "Learn it and become an expert in it," he says. "Then stick with it."

Additional Resources

- *GRS Training Center.* Online engraving and setting courses (https://grstc.com).

- *GIA (Gemological Institute of America).* Educational and certification programs (https://gia.edu).

- *Society of North American Goldsmiths.* Association and magazine (https://www.snagmetalsmith.org).

15

14. Interpreter

But Squanto continued with them, and was their
interpreter, and was a special instrument sent of God
for their good beyond their expectation. He directed
them how to set their corn, where to take fish, and to
procure other commodities, and was also their pilot
to bring them to unknown places for their profit,
and never left them till he died.

—WILLIAM BRADFORD (1620)

INTERPRETERS PLAY A CRITICAL role in today's economy. They can be found in hospitals, schools, businesses, courtrooms, and conference centers, connecting groups of people who would otherwise not be able to work together. Nearly every government agency worldwide relies on interpreters to communicate services to their constituents.

Today, due to globalization, demand for interpreters has never been higher. Translation is a $5 billion industry with 2,492 firms operating in the U.S. alone, in addition to an untold number of private contractors.[1] The Bureau of Labor Statistics projects that, with an increasingly diverse population, demand for interpreters will explode in the coming years, increasing 18 percent over the next decade.

1. US Census, "Number of Firms."

Historical Stability: 96 percent

Interpreting is one of the most historically stable professions. The tools, methods, and core product—translating one language into another—have essentially remained unchanged after thousands of years. Interpreters served ancient Egyptian Pharaohs nearly four thousand years ago, just as they serve heads of state today.[2] The only noteworthy changes are very recent advances in computer-aided translation, which is still in its infancy.

The rise of multinational corporations in recent decades has increased commercial demand for interpreters, who are no longer the sole purview of government agencies and diplomatic missions. Starting in the seventeenth century, sign language came into usage as a way to communicate with the deaf and hard-of-hearing. Also worth mentioning are the generations of translators that brought the Bible, originally penned in Hebrew, Aramaic and Greek, to the remotest parts of the world. According to Wycliff Bible Translators, at least some portion of the Bible has been translated into over 3,300 languages.

Resiliency: 66 percent

Language interpreters require a sizable population or proximity to foreign-speaking communities in order to maintain steady work. This may mean they need to travel as a regular part of the job. However, written translation can largely be done at home. With about 1 to 3 percent of the population experiencing hearing loss, deaf and hard of hearing interpreters are needed nearly everywhere, but will find more demand in larger cities.[3]

Insofar as it remains a government-supported activity in schools and local governments, interpreting is less vulnerable to market fluctuations. But, again, this depends to a great extent upon the cultural makeup of each community.

The greatest threat facing traditional interpreters and translators is the emergence of machine automation. After several decades of lackluster results, machines have in recent years improved enough to pose a legitimate threat, specifically to written translation. According to *The Economist*, "Speech recognition has made remarkable advances. Machine translation,

---

2. "They did not realize that Joseph could understand them, since he was using an interpreter." Gen 42:23 (NIV)

3. Mitchell, "How Many Deaf People Are There in the United States?" 112–19.

too, has gone from terrible to usable for getting the gist of a text, and may soon be good enough to require only modest editing by humans."[4]

Family-Centeredness: 50 percent

Interpreting scores lower on family-centeredness, primarily because there are fewer opportunities for children to be involved. The strong verbal skills required to grasp and translate concepts between cultures and languages typically requires many years of education or cultural immersion. Although interpreters can base their business from home, most time is spent working alone, outside the home.

One of interpreting's strengths is the interpersonal trust that develops between the interpreter and his or her clients who cannot speak for themselves. Clients depend on their interpreters and expect to be fairly represented. While this trust leads to long-term, loyal clients, it is not something tangible that can be inherited by future generations.

Income: 80 percent

Being in strong demand, interpreters command a very healthy income, starting around $30 per hour on average. Working through a placement agency means lower per-hour rates but more steady work, whereas freelance interpreters have the opportunity to make much more per hour—double or triple as much as working through an agency—but must find their own clients. Written translation is often priced per project, or even per word.

Interpreting is more regionally affected than other trades, because demographics vary so widely from city to city. The strongest demand for language interpreters is in the south and coastal states, with slightly lower demand in the plains states. Deaf interpreters are needed most everywhere.

Ease of Entry: 78 percent

According to the Bureau of Labor Statistics, employment opportunities for interpreters and translators will increase 19 percent over the next decade— nearly three times faster than the national average for all occupations.

With surging demand, low startup costs, and minimal red tape, interpreting has very low barriers to entry. The chief barrier is education: multilingual fluency cannot be achieved overnight. According to one lifelong

4. Greene, "Language: Finding a voice," para. 4.

interpreter I spoke to, "you can be bilingual but not be able to interpret. It's a different skill and has to be learned."[5]

However, education need not come in the form of advanced degrees. Through mentors, self-education and enough practical experience, anyone can become a skilled interpreter.

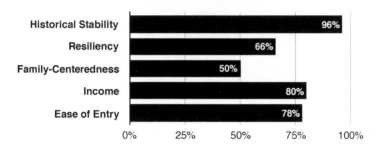

SCORE SUMMARY: INTERPRETER

Historical Stability	96%
Resiliency	66%
Family-Centeredness	50%
Income	80%
Ease of Entry	78%

Profile: Heberto & Ruth Suarez

Heberto began his career in interpreting at the age of 15. His parents were first-generation immigrants, so Heberto took extra classes and summer school to become the family interpreter. As he got older, Heberto was easily able to find work because he was bilingual. Only later did he realize that he was interpreting and translating.

Heberto and his wife Ruth have been self-employed language interpreters now for 30 years. They work mainly in hospitals and clinics. Ruth, a Certified Medical Interpreter, accompanies her clients to eye-doctor or dentist appointments. Sometimes she will spend the entire day with a client who is having surgery.

What sets Heberto and Ruth apart is the relationship they have with their clients. "It's a small community here," says Heberto. "They trust us." Trust is a pivotal issue when it comes to interpreting. Heberto and Ruth are requested locally by both patients and doctors because they have built trust with the community. They have an honest reputation and are known for keeping confidentiality. "We can be advocates for patients," Ruth says. "You're their voice. It's a very rewarding job."

For Ruth, the greatest challenge of this profession is being the bearer of bad news: telling someone that he has cancer or that her baby is disabled or was miscarried. "You have to keep your emotions together," says Ruth. For

5. Herberto Suarez, interview with author, September 18, 2018.

Heberto, the most difficult part is seeing a child suffer and not being able to do anything about it. He will often see a family through the whole medical journey: diagnosis, treatment, and death that leaves behind a wife and children. "Even though it is not physical work, it is mentally challenging," says Heberto. "You can feel drained at the end of the day."

The greatest joys, according to Heberto, are getting to be present for the miracles—a newborn baby—and sharing hopeful news to someone with bad diagnosis that a treatment is working. Ruth finds it rewarding to be paid to help people and to be an advocate in life's most critical moments.

For family members who wish to work together, interpreting can be a home-based business, even if most of the work is off-site. Heberto and Ruth encourage families to train their children in another language. "It's a great idea for children to learn another language," they say, "It can help in other ways."

The biggest threat facing the industry right now is technology. Video interpreting poses a very real challenge, "but the technology is not there yet," says Heberto. And such services can be as expensive or more expensive than a human interpreter. Besides, there are many technical hurdles. "During emergency, what if the computer fails?" asks Heberto. "There are opportunities for technology but still a place for in-person [work]."

Heberto and Ruth's advice to those interested in becoming interpreters is to find a company or mentor who can train you. "You can't become an interpreter overnight," says Heberto. "You have to have certain discipline and attitudes. This is a service. You have to have a heart for people."

Additional Resources

- American Translators Association (ATA). Translation and interpreting association (https://www.atanet.org).
- *Certification Commission for Healthcare Interpreters (CCHI).* Certification and training agency (http://cchicertification.org).
- *National Board of Certification for Medical Interpreters (NBCMI).* Certification agency (https://www.certifiedmedicalinterpreters.org).

16

15. Author

All writing comes by the grace of God, and all doing and having.

—Ralph Waldo Emerson (1844)

Writers have always served a vital function in society, going back to the earliest cuneiform stone tablets of ancient Egypt. Soon after writing was invented, scribes were employed to keep essential government records. The Pentateuch, forming the first five books of the Bible, was recorded roughly 3,500 years ago. Greek and Roman authors produced numerous works in antiquity that remain objects of study today. And through the late middle ages it was again the scribes who translated the Holy Scriptures from Hebrew, Aramaic, and Greek into the common tongue.

An author is anyone who produces original written content for books, journals, and other media. Authored works may take many forms: novels, plays, poetry, and non-fiction works. With over 130 million books in existence, it can be difficult for new authors to break into existing markets.[1] But publishers are always seeking quality work, and opportunities exist for the talented, dedicated, and persistent author. As a renowned author himself, Benjamin Franklin once wrote: "If you would not be forgotten, as soon

---

1. Taycher, "Books of the world."

as you are dead and rotten, either write things worth reading, or do things worth writing."[2]

Today there are approximately 84,000 self-employed authors, who make up part of the $91 billion publishing industry.[3]

Historical Stability: 84 percent

Many languages, many formats, but the act of writing itself hasn't changed since its inception: communicating thoughts and ideas in a format that can be preserved, reproduced, and shared indefinitely.

The tools, however, have changed significantly. With the rise of personal computing in the 1980s, writers switched over to word processors en-masse. Today, through the use of Internet-connected devices, authors can write literally anywhere, sometimes merely dictating while the computer transcribes. None of these advances were available a generation ago.

Audiences have also changed somewhat, with the rise of self-publishing and print-on-demand services. Today many people make a substantial income from self-published books (many more do not) without ever contracting with a traditional publisher.

Resiliency: 67 percent

The nice thing about a finished book is that it doesn't change. A marketable book will continue to sell for many years, if not decades, after its publication. Proven authors with an extensive collection can weather economic cycles and supply chain disruptions just fine.

To earn a living, authors must write on topics, or in genres, with broad appeal and seek publishers that cater to those genres. This usually means at least national rather than local interest and distribution.

Authors are unlikely to be bested by machine automation anytime soon. The fastest supercomputers in the world are currently approaching 1 percent of the human brain's capacity; it will be a long time before they start writing best-selling fiction.[4]

2. Franklin, *Poor Richard's Almanack*.

3. 64 percent of the 131,200 authors in the U.S. are self-employed. BLS, *Occupational Outlook*, "Writers and Authors."; US Census, "Number of Firms."

4. Sakelaris, "New supercomputer mimics human brain."

Family-Centeredness: 70 percent

Certain kinds of writing, such as journalism, may require that work be done in office environments. But the vast majority of authors work from home. This affords flexibility to spend time with family that other trades do not offer. But children have limited options to be involved in the writing process. Certain topics are better suited to women authors than men, and vice versa. Still, the work itself is solitary and difficult to share. However, family members can help with pre-publishing activities such as editing, design, and market research.

While accomplished authors can leave intellectual property to their heirs, which may yield financial benefits for many years, unfortunately, authors do not leave behind anything tangible. Sons and daughters do not inherit their parents' unique writing style and therefore are not automatically granted the same privileges that come from a lifetime of writing. Still, children can learn a marketable skill and sometimes do exceed their parent's achievements.

Income: 60 percent

It is difficult to estimate a published author's income. Authors work out various compensation schemes with their publishers, involving advances and royalties. For example, an author may receive a $2,000 advance and 10 percent royalty on each book sold. But the actual income depends entirely on how well the book sells.

However, there are many writing jobs besides "published author," and the Bureau of Labor Statistics estimates median pay for all writing-related jobs to be close to $30 per hour, or around $60,000 per year.

Ease of Entry: 70 percent

Barriers to becoming a writer are moderately low. Publishers do not require a four-year college degree from prospective authors. But writing is a difficult skill to master. Unless it comes naturally, it will take many years to hone.

Competition is the chief barrier to overcome. Every year there are up to one million books published in the U.S. alone, according to *Forbes* magazine. "On average, they sell less than 250 copies each."[5] This means

5. Morgan "Thinking of Self-Publishing Your Book?" para. 1.

there are more people wanting to earn a living from writing than there are customers willing to buy their books.

There are, however, many jobs for people who *write well.* The Bureau of Labor Statistics lists 131,200 jobs in writing-relating professions, including technical writers, copywriters, and screenwriters.

Besides voluntary education, there are no startup costs, and government regulations won't get in your way. Demand for writers is expected to increase slightly with 3 percent growth over the next decade.[6]

SCORE SUMMARY: AUTHOR

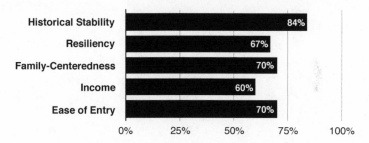

Profile: Lois Walfrid Johnson

Lois knew she wanted to be a writer since she was nine years old. "That's when God called me to be a writer," says Lois, "and I started that evening." Since that time Lois has published over 40 books and hundreds of shorter pieces and magazine articles. She is an internationally acclaimed Christian author with numerous awards including the *C.S. Lewis Medal for Best Series, Award of Merit from Excellence in Media,* and *Dwight L. Moody Award for Excellence in Christian Literature.* Lois has been writing for over 70 years.

"It's fun to see what God can do," says Lois, recounting how her first book *Just a Minute Lord,* a prayer guide for girls, was translated into Japanese. Now Lois' works have been translated into 12 languages. "The Lord blessed my work, enough to keep going," she says.

Lois admits that every writer is different—some work better in the morning, some at night. She always wrote best on a schedule. "To me, I always needed to order my day," she says. In the morning, Lois tackles the "hard creative writing," then spends the rest of the day reworking it. "I want to make sure it is creative, accurate, and godly," she says.

It can be very discouraging to begin writing. Lois' advice is: "Don't give up." There are always going to be rejection slips and people who criticize,

6. BLS, *Occupational Outlook,* "Writers and Authors."

but don't let peoples' opinions stop you. Lois received affirmations through other people. "Someone believing in me kept me going for years."

The greatest joy of writing, according to Lois, is seeing something she has written make an eternal impact. "When I know God has taken my words and brought them alive in the heart and spirit of someone, I am just so grateful," she says.

Lois was raised in a loving family with good parents. On one occasion, she was approached by young parents who had grown up in broken homes. They were seeking parenting advice. Lois knew that fiction would be the perfect vehicle to pass on what she had learned. "It became a goal of mine to tell the very best story possible while showing what it meant to be a family, and a Christian family."

Lois wrote while raising her three children with her husband Roy, but she never allowed her work to take precedence over her family. "I was a mother first and a writer second," she says. Two of Lois' children have gone on to be writers themselves, one of whom is a best-selling author and co-author of over 60 books.

For aspiring authors, Lois shares this advice: "Pray and seek the Lord before you start. It is hard, hard work. Don't put being noticed ahead of everything else. If God wants you to write, you can keep on writing because He will help."

Additional Resources

- *On Writing: A Memoir of the Craft* by Stephen King (Scribner, 2000).
- *Sometimes the Magic Works: Lessons from a Writing Life* by Terry Brooks (Del Rey, 2004).
- *On Writing Well: The Classic Guide to Writing Nonfiction* by William Zinsser (Harper, 1976).

17

16. Butcher

Meat Processor

Bring the fattened calf and kill it, and let us eat and celebrate. For this my son was dead, and is alive again; he was lost, and is found.

—LUKE 15:23–24 (AD 30)

AMERICANS LOVE MEAT. EACH year, they consume more than 58 billion pounds of it. In fact, Americans consume their own body weight in meat annually.[1] That is why meat and poultry represent the largest segment of U.S. agriculture, and the trend isn't slowing down. Around the world, demand for meat is increasing as populations expand and seek out low-carb, high-protein diets.

Custom meat processors play and integral role in connecting suppliers to customers, transforming live animals into packaged meats for sale. Some specialize in certain animals, such as poultry or hogs. Others focus on specialty retail items, such as homemade sausages or home-cured hams. Most processors do a mix of both. Some even bring their services to the farm, driving a truck outfitted for mobile butchering.

1. Per capita consumption of meat and poultry is 179 lbs per year: USDA, "Per Capita Consumption," 28.

Thanks to the local food movement, demand for custom-processed meats is surging. "Buying local has become a huge, huge deal," says Julie Lorentz of the Minnesota Association of Meat Processors.[2] Contrary to occasional media reports, butcher shops are not dying. "In the last ten years we have seen new facilities going up, and new owners taking over existing facilities," Lorentz says.

If you buy local, you are usually buying whole, half, or quartered sections of an animal directly from the farmer who raised it. Farmers rely on custom meat processors to butcher and package their animals for sale. Julie has seen demand for independent butcher shops and custom meat processors increase since the 1980s, but particularly in the last ten to fifteen years. "I don't see this trend going away," she says. "It's really working out well for the consumers and the farmers."

There are currently 2,892 meat processors in the U.S. accounting for $217 billion in revenues annually.[3]

Historical Stability: 84 percent

References to butchers can be found in Ancient Egyptian empires (nineteenth-century BC) and in the writings of Chuang Tzu (fourth-century BC).[4] According to Mosaic law, meat from animal sacrifices went to Levitical priests for food.

At its core, butchering is the same today as it has always been: live animals are slaughtered, skinned, gutted, cut into choice parts, and preserved. The rise of industrialism and refrigeration significantly impacted the scale and methods of traditional butcher shops, but the fact that so many custom processors remain today—and are increasing—is a testament to the endurance of the trade.

The largest change for the typical processor comes by way of tooling. Refrigeration, automatic lifts, and electric bone saws weren't available to butchers a few generations ago. But these are changes in efficiency, primarily. The hand-held knife is never far from the butcher's apron.

2. Lorentz, interview with author. November 13, 2018.

3. US Census, "Number of Firms."

4. Joseph is imprisoned in the guard's house, also translated "butcher" (Genesis 40:3); See *The Dexterous Butcher* by Chuang Tzu.

Author working at a meat processor to learn more about butchering
(Photo: Becca Groves)

Resiliency: 81 percent

As an integral part of the U.S. food supply, butchers generally do well during recessions. However, they are vulnerable to price fluctuations in livestock, itself caused by disruptions to the animal feed supply by weather and drought. The market price of livestock greatly affects meat sales. There is a seasonal dimension as well: poultry, which can be raised in a short amount of time, brings in steady business through the spring and summer months, while larger animals such as hogs, sheep and beef cows bring in business in the fall. And there is always a rush for deer processing during hunting season.

There is roughly one meat processor for every county in the U.S., but many larger cities have dozens of butcher shops. This means butchers do not need to draw from a very large region or population. In fact, for most customers local is better.

While there have been significant strides towards automating aspects of the slaughter business, it is impractical to completely automate. Skinning hides, delicately cutting out organs, and cleaning and inspecting is a human endeavor and will remain so.

Family-Centeredness: 64 percent

Families that operate a butcher shop or meat processor can spend much of their time together. That having been said, it is a time-intensive business, and owners must be prepared to invest far more than the typical 40-hour work week.

There are many roles for various ages and genders, from slaughtering animals to making sausages to working with customers. Young people can help with certain tasks, but there are risks inherent to working with live animals, slaughter tools, and sharp knives.

It would be highly unusual, but not impossible, for butcher shops to be home-based. Depending on state regulations, facilities processing meat must be inspected regularly and must comply with numerous sewage requirements and cleaning codes.

Butchers leave behind many tangible assets. In addition to specialized tools, there are the buildings themselves, which in most cases have undergone extensive makeovers to process animals, including holding pens, lifts and rails, refrigeration rooms, smoke houses, and an array of stainless steel equipment. In addition to this, some butchers may hand down their secret award-winning sausage recipes.

Income: 60 percent

Butchers and meat processors range from very small to industrial-scale. Actual incomes will vary greatly. The Bureau of Labor Statistics cites the median wage for butchers and meat cutters at $31,580 in 2018. However, custom processors who handle many more aspects of the trade, such as slaughter and specialty retail items, can earn far more than grocery-store meat trimmers.

"It can be a very rewarding business," says Lorentz of the Minnesota Association of Meat Processors. "The ones who like it can make a living on it and do really well."

Ease of Entry: 64 percent

Obtaining a suitable building is the primary obstacle. As previously mentioned, meat processors must have a facility that is suitable for handling and storing animals, and that is compliant with food-safety laws. Total investment will be at least a few hundred thousand dollars, whether you are purchasing an existing facility or building from scratch.

Otherwise, barriers to entry for the trade are generally low. No formal education is required—butchers learn on the job from mentors. But the industry is competitive, and butchers must look for ways to stand out from the competition. Lorentz says finding a niche item is one key to success. "If you're the only one in the area who is processing sheep, that is a huge draw." Also, producing sausages or home-cured hams from generational family recipes is a draw that "people will drive for miles to get."

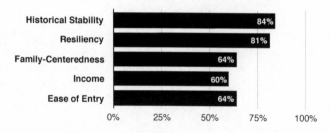

SCORE SUMMARY: BUTCHER

Historical Stability	84%
Resiliency	81%
Family-Centeredness	64%
Income	60%
Ease of Entry	64%

Profile: Dennison Meat Locker

Dori Gregory had no previous experience in the butchering industry when she bought a butcher shop in Dennison, Minnesota. Prior to that she worked as a bookkeeper. Dori and her brother, who worked as a butcher for the previous owner, purchased the company together as partners in 2001. According to Dori, her brother loved the work but didn't want to deal with customers, something with which Dori had plenty of experience. The business did well enough that in 2005, when her brother decided to go another direction, Dori bought him out.

Dennison Meat Locker handles all aspects of butchering, from slaughter to processing. Farmers unload their livestock on one side of the building and several days later pick up packaged cuts of meat on the other side. On any given week, Dennison Meat Locker will process chickens, ducks, turkeys, beef cows, hogs, sheep, goats and deer. This complete, end-to-end service makes Dennison unique at a time when many butcher shops are becoming more selective (i.e., accepting only beef and hogs) or focusing on retail meat sales and forgoing slaughter and processing entirely.

"I think we're more personal and friendly," says Dori, when asked what sets her shop apart from the competition. "We're very careful with how we handle the meat." Emphasis on quality is a crucial factor for both farmers and their customers in a day when people increasingly want to know where their food is coming from.

A typical day for Dori involves processing animals, which means cutting up the animals that have already been slaughtered and refrigerated. Every portion of the animal is cut to customer specifications, from the thickness of steaks to the number of ribs. Other activities include grinding burger and sausages, curing and smoking hams, and making jerky. Slaughter days are once or twice per week, depending on the season. On these days live animals are unloaded into pens by their owners. A crew of about three or four takes care of killing, skinning, and gutting. Then the animals are cleaned, weighed, and refrigerated before processing. And with all of these activities, there is continual "cleaning, cleaning, cleaning," says Dori.

Keeping employees happy and training new employees is a challenge, according to Dori. But overall she is very happy with her job. "I like being here so much," she says, "I can't really consider anything a major challenge." Getting paid for doing something you love is one of Dori's greatest joys. "I've been blessed here," she says.

Dennison Meat Locker is the quintessential family-run business. Dori bought the business with one brother. Her sister, niece and nephew work in the business on a daily basis. Dori's other brother handles payroll.

Since she has been involved, Dori says the industry has changed for the better. There is more emphasis on cleanliness and properly handling meat. "Those are good things," she says. Over the years, Dori has made significant investments in her facility to make it easier to maintain a clean working environment. Going forward, Dori sees increased demand for locally grown food. "Most of my customers want to buy from local farmers," she says, "because then you know what's going into the meat." Dori also started offering healthier alternatives, such as no-nitrate cures for hams. "When we started doing that, it brought in a lot more hogs."

For those interested in butchering, Dori recommends researching the industry before jumping in. "Visit other meat lockers," she says. "See what they do. Make sure it is a profession you would enjoy."

Additional Resources

- *North American Meat Institute.* Association for meat processors (https://www.meatinstitute.org).
- *Farmstead Meatsmith.* Website, podcast, courses and lore about the art of butchering (https://farmsteadmeatsmith.com).

18

17. Apothecary

Pharmacist

*Everyone knows thyme ... Applied with vinegar it
dissolves new swellings and clots of blood, and takes
away thymos and hanging warts.*

—DIOSCORIDES, *DE MATERIA MEDICA* (AD 70)

PHARMACISTS PLAY A UNIQUE but pivotal role in the health and medical
industry, providing generic and prescription-based medicines as well as
counseling to patients in need. Officially, pharmacists as we know them
today came into existence in the seventeenth century when King James I
founded the first pharmacists' guild in England:

> Initially known as "apothecaries," early community pharma-
> cists prepared and dispensed remedies while offering front-line
> medical advice to their customers. Apothecary traditions trav-
> eled to the New World with the English colonists, where they
> flourished for centuries.[1]

But versions of the trade existed well into antiquity. The five-volume
encyclopedia *De Materia Medica* written by Greek physician Dioscorides

1. Zebrowski, "A Brief History of Pharmacy," para. 1.

circa AD 70, became the basis for many medicinal texts in the centuries that followed. The Book of Genesis describes a place called Gilead around 1900 BC, reputed for its balm with healing properties:

> As they sat down to eat their meal, they looked up and saw a caravan of Ishmaelites coming from Gilead. Their camels were loaded with spices, balm and myrrh, and they were on their way to take them down to Egypt.[2]

Also worth mentioning is the practice of alternative medicine and the increasing role it plays in modern health care. Approximately ten million Americans use homeopathy as part of their integrative medical care.[3] Though the two philosophies are diametrically opposed, homeopathy and allopathy have been practiced for centuries and both involve preparing treatments and advising patients on the use of remedies.

There are 19,234 pharmacies in business today accounting for $282 billion annually.[4]

Historical Stability: 68 percent

Apothecaries were around in Colonial America. Often the town doctor served the same role as pharmacist, diagnosing illnesses as well as preparing treatments. It was not uncommon for medicinal herb gardens to be found growing outside of doctors' homes.

Medicine itself has undergone astounding changes over the last century—penicillin was not discovered until 1928. Prior to the medical breakthroughs of the twentieth century, doctors and pharmacists while treating symptoms, relied primarily on the body's ability to heal itself. While this natural approach led to stronger immune systems, it came at a high cost. Infant mortality rates in 17th and 18th centuries were as high as three in ten.[5]

Despite the fact that medicine itself has changed and with it the tooling, the core service provided by pharmacists—preparing treatments and consulting directly with patients—has mostly stayed the same.

---

2. Gen 37:25

3. "Five USA government sponsored health surveys estimated that between 1.7% and 3.1% of the adult population had used homeopathy in the last 12 months." Relton et al., "Prevalence of homeopathy," 69–78.

4. US Census, "Number of Firms."

5. *Plymouth Ancestors*, "Raising Children in the Early 17th Century," 1.

Perhaps even more than the changes in medicine, the paperwork, insurance, and other red tape have shifted the pharmacist's role from previous generations when no third-party payers were involved and government regulation was minimal.

Resiliency: 81 percent

Pharmacy is a highly resilient trade and is not generally correlated to economic cycles. Normally, patients do not discard life-saving therapies to save a buck. In fact, most of the time patients are not paying for their treatments at all, as health insurance "covers" the cost (though pharmacists may beg to differ).

Nearly everyone needs a pharmacist at some point or another. As a result, pharmacists can earn a living serving a local population that does not need to be large. There is some vulnerability in the supply chain, because it is entirely reliant on nationally-sourced, and sometimes internationally-sourced, medicines.

Finally, automation does pose a legitimate threat to the profession, at least on the treatment preparation side. At hospitals, patients are already being prescribed antibiotics fulfilled by vending machines in the waiting room.

Family-Centeredness: 54 percent

Pharmacy receives lower marks for family-centeredness. Formerly, before the twentieth century, apothecaries would have been home-based, but that is unheard of today. That having been said, there are roles for young people, and family members who work in the business will spend much of their time together. The atmosphere is one of service and care, a good environment for mentorship.

As for tangible assets, the apothecary trade does not generate much beyond physical retail locations, if privately owned at all. The primary worth is the business itself and the book value of its customers.

Income: 100 percent

Pharmacy is a fairly high-paying trade. The Bureau of Labor Statistics puts median pay at $126,120 in 2018. On the lower end, staff pharmacists can expect to earn $110,000 per year coming right out of college—but "expect to be worked to the bone," warns one pharmacist I interviewed. For independent owners, the salaries can be much higher, as much as $250,000 to $300,000.

With great rewards come great costs, however, and that is certainly the case with pharmacy. Although it is one of the highest-paying trades, it is also one of the most difficult to enter.

Ease of Entry: 34 percent

The greatest threat to independent pharmacists is the competition from chains and big box stores with embedded pharmacies. CVS and Walgreens currently control at least half of the drugstore business in America, with Walmart, Kroger, and Costco picking up a significant share of the rest.[6] While pharmacy jobs remain, the ability for families to operate independent franchises is rapidly diminishing.

If the competitive landscape weren't discouraging enough, the educational requirements are rigorous. Pharmacists must earn the degree Doctor of Pharmacy. Including undergraduate work, pharmacy degrees require as much as eight years of post-secondary education, in addition to state licensing exams.

Startup-costs of education alone will exceed $100,000. According to the American Journal of Pharmaceutical Education, average indebtedness for pharmacy students exceeds $110,000.[7] Besides education, there are significant expenses in inventory and retail space as well, which put independent pharmacists at a disadvantage.

Job opportunities for pharmacists are expected to remain steady through 2028, according to the Bureau of Labor Statistics.

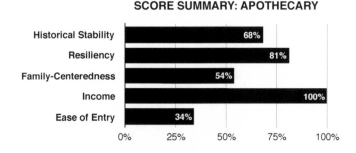

SCORE SUMMARY: APOTHECARY

Historical Stability	68%
Resiliency	81%
Family-Centeredness	54%
Income	100%
Ease of Entry	34%

6. Stern, "CVS and Walgreens."
7. Cain et al., "Pharmacy Student Debt," 5.

Profile: Northfield Pharmacy

Rob Anderson knew he wanted to be a pharmacist since the 5th grade. When a pharmacist from his local community came to his school to give a talk about the profession, it "piqued my interest," says Rob. "I came home and told my parents 'I want to be a pharmacist when I grow up,' and I never changed from that decision." Rob, now practicing for over 40 years, operates an independent community pharmacy with his wife Karen.

For Rob, it's all about the customer experience. "We care more about the person than we do about the money." At Northfield Pharmacy, customers get taken care of individually, like medical patients. "Our customers are our boss," he says. "We have to treat them with that kind of respect. They can hire or fire you."

Northfield Pharmacy has been a family business from the beginning. Rob's wife Karen, a Registered Pharmacy Technician, works alongside Rob. Both of his kids, now grown, worked as clerks in the business. But working in an independently-owned pharmacy rather than in a retail chain is key to making the family dynamic work. "Working together in a community pharmacy that's independent, we get to make the decisions about what we do," says Rob. "You'd never get that in a chain." Both of Rob's kids later told him their experience in the pharmacy taught them how to respect and care for people.

Rob's greatest challenge is dealing with insurance. "I spend 20 percent of my time fighting with insurance companies over drugs they don't want to cover," he says.

Computerization has been the biggest change over Rob's career. It allows him to better track orders, refills, and keep up with patients' needs. The automated phone system will handle up to 170 refill orders in a single day, saving a tremendous amount of time for staff. He has also seen major changes to the role that pharmacists play in a patient's overall care. It's no longer "Count, Lick, Stick, and Pour," as the old saying goes. "More and more duties are being handed to pharmacists," says Rob. "We have become almost a primary care entity."

Rob sees this trend continuing going forward. "There's already starting a process of pharmacists being able to prescribe," he says. "I think more and more responsibility is going to be put on pharmacists." He also sees more consolidation of independent pharmacies into retail chains, a trend not always in patients' best interests. "It's very profit-driven, and it's using as few people as possible to drive that profit higher," Rob says. At his independent pharmacy, Rob overstaffs intentionally. "I would rather make less money and have enough staff so when people come in they feel like they were attended to."

Rob's advice to those interested in a career in pharmacy is "know what you're getting into." Rob advises aspiring pharmacists to work inside different types of pharmacy practices—hospital pharmacies, chain pharmacies, and independent community pharmacies. "I think there's huge market potential for independent pharmacies to be a viable entity well into the future. But it's a lot of work." Pharmacists also need an entrepreneurial spirit, according to Rob. "Money alone won't make you happy," he says. "If you have the ability and desire to care for people to the best of your ability, you will do well."

Additional Resources

- "Life as an Independent Pharmacist." *The Atlantic* (https://www.theatlantic.com/business/archive/2016/05/pharmacist/471195).

- *Pharmacy Times*. Magazine (https://www.pharmacytimes.com).

19

18. Counselor

Consultant, Advisor

In every matter of wisdom and understanding about which the king inquired of them, he found them ten times better than all the magicians and enchanters that were in all his kingdom.

—DANIEL 1:20 (600 BC)

THE COUNSELOR HAS WAXED and waned through history but has generally enjoyed steady employment. As early as societies had leaders, they had advisors to counsel them. Joseph was a counselor to Pharaoh. King David's counselor was Ahithophel (who later betrayed him).[1] Daniel was an advisor to Nebuchadnezzar, Darius and Cyrus. In smaller populations and agrarian societies, counselors were more informal and rare. Miles Standish served as an advisor to William Bradford, governor of the Plymouth Colony soon after the Mayflower passengers disembarked. But advisor was only one of many hats Standish wore as military commander and later treasurer of the Colony. As populations grew in the New World, colonies formed and

---

1. 2 Sam 16

officially-recognized advisors began serving full-time in government as councilors and diplomats.

The advice industry today is broad and varied. It can be summed up as providing strategic counsel to decision-makers. There were no business coaches or certified financial planners in colonial times, but the consulting trade existed nonetheless. The advice-giving industry as we know it today appeared mostly in the latter half of the twentieth century, as small businesses grew into massive corporations, and management theory began to emerge as a way to cope with increasing organizational complexity.

Today, advice is a huge industry, with over 130,000 management consultancies in the U.S., accounting for $218 billion in revenues annually.[2] Consultants can be found in virtually every office building. From management to finance to technology, consultants play a pivotal role in helping leaders at every level navigate the complexities of modern business and government.

Historical Stability: 68 percent

Advisors today provide the same product they always have: advice. But anyone can give advice. What makes professional advisors unique is their proven ability to help leaders reach their goals. As the proverb says, "The way of a fool is right in his own eyes, but a wise man listens to advice."[3]

Modern consulting differs greatly from its ancient counterpart. Today it is common to see young consultants whose advice comes from research and accreditation rather than from life experience. In the case of technology, it is often preferable to work with younger generations who adapt more quickly to the rapidly changing environment—a lingering artifact of the Industrial Revolution where "it is now usual and needful to teach but a single branch" rather than understand complete systems.[4]

Along with the change to methods, tooling has become far more computerized and empirically-based. Consultants are often tasked with researching "best practices" in a given industry because there are so many practices to choose from.

Consultants are hired directly by the people who need them precisely because a custom solution is needed. Although the industry differs from what it was in previous generations, the need for direct contact with clientele has not changed.

2. US Census, "Number of Firms."

3. Prov 12:15

4. Mass. Bureau of Statistics of Labor, *Comparative Wages*, 6.

Resiliency: 68 percent

Advisors score about average on resiliency. In a professional capacity, consultants rather than employees are often the first to go when a business needs to tighten its budgets. But at the same time, consultants are often the first to be hired when companies seek out a new direction. The point is that advisors as a group are generally viewed as discretionary in turbulent times, but individually may be unaffected by economic cycles.

As alluded to earlier, population plays a big role in the advice-giving industry. Consultants will find more opportunities in larger cities. On the other hand, consultants do not need many customers to stay gainfully employed. Often, one customer will suffice.

While there is always a role for the competent individual, consulting has been losing ground to automation for decades and will continue to do so. In technology, this amounts to human automation. Increasingly, businesses are hiring "off-shore" consultants to replace U.S. counterparts at a fraction of the cost. But other advice-giving trades are experiencing a similar phenomenon. Many a legal question that formerly required a lawyer's involvement can be answered through the Internet—whether by searchable online content, or by connecting with offshore advisors conversant in U.S. law.

Most computer scientists will readily agree it's not a matter of *if* machines will be able program themselves someday, but *when*. This means that consulting faces, or will face, a serious threat from automation.

Family-Centeredness: 48 percent

Consulting scores lower on family-centeredness. Although many consultants can and do work from home, the advice-giving work itself rarely invites participation from family members. While supporting roles can include family, the expertise required means vast amounts of research and experience that cannot readily be picked up by family members without equivalent study. There are limited opportunities for children to be involved. However in the many industries, older adults can enjoy a long and steady career—though that too is changing in our rapidly innovating marketplace.

With few exceptions, advice-giving does not generate tangible assets and does not leave any inheritance to future generations, aside from personal earnings.

Income: 100 percent

Consultants typically have a very high earning potential. They are converting years of experience, education and expertise into practical advice for their clients. This is worth a lot of money. The Bureau of Labor Statistics estimates median pay for management consultants at $83,610 in 2018, but there is really no limit for outside consultants. Depending on the industry and individual, rates can be hundreds—or thousands—of dollars per hour.

Ease of Entry: 68 percent

Advisors will typically need at least a college degree, and in many cases post-graduate degrees to find employment in certain industries. Consequently, tuition costs can run into the 5-or 6-digits. But degrees are not always needed. Life experience is still recognized and accepted, though it doesn't come overnight. Prospective consultants must work or study for many years to become established in the trade.

On the upside, there is minimal regulation, and competition is well below average. Reputation is a key differentiator in this trade, which depends more on the person than on a product. Demand for advisors and consultants is projected to surge 14 percent through 2028, much faster than the average increase for other professions.

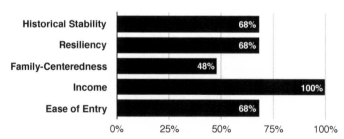

SCORE SUMMARY: COUNSELOR

Historical Stability	68%
Resiliency	68%
Family-Centeredness	48%
Income	100%
Ease of Entry	68%

Profile: Roger Lane Coaching

Roger began his consulting career after working as Vice President of Development for a private university. "I was responsible for raising millions of dollars," he says. During that time he was approached by a camp and conference center and asked to help coach them on a capital campaign. The campaign was a success, and soon "word began to slip out, 'if you need money, give Roger a call.'" After further research and self-study Roger learned the trade of coaching and began his own practice.

What sets Roger apart is his focus on religious entities. "99 percent of my work is with Christian organizations," he says. Earlier in life Roger earned a degree in pastoral studies and has been able to draw from that background in his fundraising work with ministries. "Because of that we're able to fold Christian stewardship and biblical giving into what we do," says Roger, who has been coaching now for 25 years. His clients include churches, universities, camps, schools, and other non-profit ministries such as pregnancy crisis centers. "When somebody needs money, that's when my phone rings."

The work week starts on Sunday night for Roger, when he reviews his appointments. "The week consists of prospecting, coaching, and followup," he says. Coaching entails identifying projects for funding, and defining those projects. "How much money do they need and when do they need it?" There is also ongoing accountability. "You have to make sure clients are making progress," he says.

In the consulting niche of fundraising, a key challenge is building strategies for new organizations with little history or donor base. Often Roger will help these younger ministries that cannot afford regular coaching services. He mentions a proverb: "A generous person will prosper; whoever refreshes others will be refreshed."[5] The greatest joy, according to Roger, is the impact he's had over the course of his fundraising career. "You look back and realize you've raised upwards of $400 million for ministry."

Roger Lane Coaching has been a family business from the beginning. Roger's daughters were involved with back-office activities, and Ann, his wife of 48 years, has been his assistant and indispensable partner. Because of the efficiency of Roger's family-based economy, he has been able to contract twice as many clients as his colleagues. While Roger was meeting new clients, Ann would prepare documents and follow up with existing clients. "She was always ahead of me and knew exactly what I needed."

Roger has seen the industry of consulting change rapidly with technology. Communications are more frequent, and "everything is paperless," he says. "It's highly efficient." At the same time, technology and competition have put downward pressure on consulting fees. Roger is in the process of trying to reduce travel and run campaigns more out of his home. Recently, without ever leaving home, he helped a 5,000-member church in Lusaka, Zambia raise $4.3 million.

5. Prov 11:25 (NIV)

Roger's advice for future advice-givers: identify what you do really well and determine who would be willing to pay for it. "What is it that you bring to the table that I would want, or that somebody would be willing to pay for?" Advisors need to figure out what combination of technology, education, and experience they have that brings the most value to others.

Additional Resources

- *Funded: A Leader's Guide to Raising Money God's Way* by Roger Lane (Bowker, 2019).

- "Interview with a Management Consultant." *JobShadow* (https://jobshadow.com/interview-with-a-management-consultant).

20

19. Sawyer

The Ruwer sends mill-stones swiftly round to grind the corn,
And drives shrill saw-blades through smooth marble blocks,
With never-ceasing din on either bank.[1]

—AUSONIUS (AD 390)

THE SAWYER CONVERTS CUT logs into dimensional lumber, playing a critical role in the construction industry. The earliest sawmill dates to around 250 BC. The Hieropolis Sawmill, located in modern-day Turkey, was the first known machine to harness flowing water to move a sawblade. Before machines assisted, human-powered mills were common, with two people on either end of a saw: the topsawyer positioned above the log and the other in a pit below. Through the ages, sawmills have taken various shapes, sizes, and sources of power. Wind-powered sawmills were built in the Netherlands in the late eighteenth century. The Industrial Revolution spawned numerous advances in the trade, with the advent of steam-powered and then motorized and electric saws.

In an age when industrialization has commoditized just about everything, there remains a role for niche players in the lumber industry. Modern portable machinery has brought a revival to on-site, custom-cut saw-milling. Sawyers can provide milling services to timber owners literally out of the back of a truck and make a good buck at it too. The going rate

1. Ausonius, *Mosella.*

for custom sawyers is as much as $100 per hour or $0.50 per board foot of sawn lumber.[2]

There are 2,824 sawmills in operation today in the U.S., grossing an estimated $32 billion annually.[3]

Historical Stability: 80 percent

Despite breakthroughs in milling that followed the Industrial Revolution, the trade still produces the same product today as it did thousands of years ago. With the breakthroughs came changes to scale and efficiency. Railroads made it possible to transport logs to the sawmill rather than temporarily locating the mill downstream from logger camps.

The tooling has changed along with industrialization, moving from straight, reciprocating saw blades to circular ones. Handling of logs has become more automated as well, with moving log carriages instead of manual lifting and pushing. These changes have contributed to improved quality and more efficient operations but have not displaced the original product and methods altogether. In some parts of the country steam-powered sawmills are still in operation today just as they were a century ago.[4] And in some Amish communities, sawyers run efficient operations entirely on diesel engines.

While the vast majority of milling occurs for wholesale suppliers, which would have also been the case centuries ago, there are still opportunities for direct sales to landowners through the portable sawmilling niche.

Resiliency: 65 percent

Demand for lumber, and therefore sawmilling, follows the construction industry, with some exceptions. Private milling operations with a direct customer base may not be as vulnerable to recession as standard operators who depend on a healthy housing industry.

Geography is important to sawyers. Proximity to forests is a must, but at the same time they must be able to serve a wide enough customer base—at least regional—to support the business. But there are more sawmills in operation than one might think. According to the Minnesota Department

2. Wood-Mizer, "How to Charge for Sawing Services."

3. US Census, "Number of Firms."

4. Phillips Brothers Sawmill and Box Factory in Oak Run, California, family-owned-and-operated since 1897, is the last steam-powered sawmill in the United States. See https://phillipsbrothersmill.com/.

of Natural Resources, there are 326 primary timber producers in Minnesota alone, with 66 using portable sawmills.[5]

The supply chain is short and renewable—trees. And, by necessity, mill operators will be close by. Automation, however, is a threat. As the logging industry and milling industries continue to mechanize, fewer people are required to produce the finished product. This trend will continue to put pressure on the smaller operator who focuses only on primary timber products.

Family-Centeredness: 62 percent

Family-centeredness is higher than average for sawyers for a few reasons. First, families who own and operate a sawmill—the typical arrangement over the centuries—will spend much of their time together. Second, there is an opportunity for the business to be home-based. The Phillips Brothers Sawmill in Oak Run, California, has been family-owned-and-operated since 1897. The family owns both the mill and the timberland from which they harvest trees.

But there are other ways besides on-site sawmilling that families can base the business at home. Portable sawmills allow sawyers to travel to landowners, no matter how far away, to custom-cut lumber to customer specifications. Naturally, this would cut down on the amount of time together as a family, as very young and very old would not be able to participate. But it does present an opportunity for families to produce a viable income through a home-based business.

Although the heavy machinery is dangerous, and caution is warranted, teenagers can be involved as well as older adults. Not all aspects of the trade involve lifting logs and buzzing saws, and it is more predictable than felling trees. The industry is mostly male-dominated, but as with children there are plenty of opportunities for women to be involved operating machinery or managing the business and customer relationships.

Sawmills generate many tangible assets, and if the mill is situated on owned timberland those assets will increase in value with time. The machinery itself, if well-built and well-maintained, can last for generations. The products of manufacture—lumber—can store almost indefinitely in the proper conditions and are a great store of wealth and hedge against inflation. Finally, timberland is valuable in and of itself with a harvestable crop that regrows.

5. Minnesota Department of Natural Resources, "Timber Producers."

Income: 60 percent

It is unusual for sawyers to earn above-average incomes. The Bureau of Labor Statistics does not specify precise incomes for sawyers, but related industries of logging and woodworking range from $31,000 to $38,000 in median salary. Portable sawmill operators charge $65 to $105 per hour, but steady work may be difficult to come by. As with most trades, slow but steady growth fueled by satisfied, repeat customers and word-of-mouth advertising will provide the most reliable employment.

Ease of Entry: 76 percent

Barriers to entry for sawyers are generally low. New portable sawmilling equipment can be had for less than $5,000. However, owning a portable mill doesn't make one a sawyer any more than owning a chainsaw makes one a logger. Understanding how to harvest the most material—and the best material—from a piece of timber is more art than science and can take years to truly master. While there is no formal education requirement, aspiring sawyers would be advised to apprentice under an accomplished sawyer.

Regulations are generally low and vary from state to state. Competition in the trade is about average. However, in this rapidly mechanizing industry the main threat of competition is from larger, higher-capacity mills. It is important to supplement business from a niche, less-commoditized customer base than from dimensional lumber wholesalers. For example, some sawyers will build custom furniture for homeowners using lumber harvested from their own property.

Finally, the trade is projected to stay steady in the near term, declining by 1 percent over the next decade.[6]

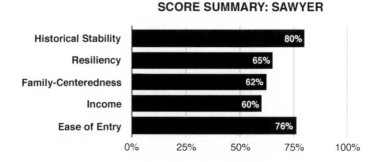

SCORE SUMMARY: SAWYER

Historical Stability — 80%
Resiliency — 65%
Family-Centeredness — 62%
Income — 60%
Ease of Entry — 76%

6. BLS, *Occupational Outlook*, "Woodworkers."

Profile: John Kaliski, Run of the Mill

Sawyer John Kaliski with his portable sawmill

As a successful computer programmer and CTO of a high-tech start-up, John Kaliski was an unlikely candidate to start his own lumber mill. He found inspiration one summer while renovating a one-room schoolhouse in northern Wisconsin. "I was ripping out a wall and got down to the studs and found the worker who built the place had signed his name," he recounts. "The thought that went through my mind was, this guy who probably had a grade-school education, maybe—his work is still standing more than 100 years later. And me, so elegant and full of myself—my line of code is old and gray by the time it hits the hard drive. That was the genesis of all this stuff." John spent the rest of the summer rebuilding the schoolhouse, using a chainsaw jig to mill his own lumber from trees on the property. "It was the best medicine in the world for me," he says. Milling boards was the antithesis of his corporate life with "too many meetings, too many trips, and too much stress."

John's tech company later sold and he started teaching I/T at a state college. But his love of milling and woodworking did not wane. "I hope to retire from teaching someday," he says, "but I will retire from milling when they put me in a box. Preferably one that I made."

The advent of the portable sawmill was a game-changer for John and the small-scale milling industry as a whole. Now there was a man-sized lumber mill that did not require significant up-front investment. John bought his first portable sawmill second-hand on eBay for $11,000. Since the mill is small enough to be towed, milling can be performed at the customer's location without damaging the land.

John's family-owned business, Run of the Mill, is unique in that it offers much more than just sawmilling services. It is a full-service operation providing milling, kiln-drying, woodworking, and finished furniture. John was once hired to remove a walnut tree from a building site, which was then milled and turned into furnishings for a house built on that site. John takes pleasure in the uniqueness and quality of every project. "This isn't IKEA," he tells his customers. "This is something you're going to have the rest of your life. And when you pass, it's going to your kids."

A typical day involves helping customers design what they want to build "from the log up." This may involve routine sawyer activities, such as moving logs with a skid-steer, cutting wood and stacking lumber. Or it may involve more ancillary activities, such as advising customers on how to drop a tree, or estimating how much wood can be harvested from a tree.

John expects demand to continue to increase for small-scale sawmill operators. "There's way more work than I could ever get to," he says. "For a small operation there are always trees coming down naturally." And at $100 per hour, plus trip and equipment charges, the opportunity is a lucrative one.

For John, the greatest challenge is maintaining his equipment. "You very much have to be a jack of all trades," he says. While the equipment is straightforward to operate, it can take a lifetime to master. Different types of trees behave differently when being sawn, and a competent sawyer will need to be able to diagnose problems and come up with creative solutions.

John is up for the challenge. He enjoys working with his hands and building things that will last "a lot longer than I'll be on this earth." He also enjoys making lemonade out of lemons. John can turn negative experiences into positive ones, such as turning a storm-fallen tree into a beautiful dining room table. "It's been a great journey," he says.

Additional Resources

- *Wood-Mizer,* portable sawmills and wood processing equipment manufacturer (https://woodmizer.com).

- *WoodWeb.com,* sawing and drying online forum (http://www.wood-web.com/cgi-bin/forums/sawdry.pl).

- *Phillip Brothers Mill.* Website and documentary about the last family-owned-and-operated steam-powered sawmill in the U.S. (https://phillipsbrothersmill.com).

21

20. Lawyer

It is the trade of lawyers to question everything, yield nothing, and to talk by the hour.

—THOMAS JEFFERSON (1821)

FOR AS LONG AS there have been laws, there have been lawyers—advocates representing aggrieved parties before governing authorities. In the earliest societies, lawyers took the form of family or friends who pleaded the case of a relative before elders at the city gate.[1] Centuries later, orators in ancient Greece and Rome argued cases before governors and judges. The Book of Acts (c. AD 60) records a professional lawyer named Tertullus presenting false charges against Paul in Roman courts.[2]

Many of America's founding fathers were lawyers. "Of the 56 signers of the Declaration of Independence, 25 were lawyers. Of the 55 framers of the Constitution, 32 were lawyers."[3] John Adams, co-author of the Declaration of Independence and second president of the United States, believed so strongly in the right to legal defense in court that he represented the British soldiers accused in the Boston Massacre when no one else would.

1. Job 29:7
2. Acts 24:1
3. State Bar of Michigan, "How Many of the Founding Fathers Were Lawyers?" para. 1.

Today there are 174,340 law firms in America and 1,338,768 lawyers, providing legal counsel in the areas of criminal, family, commercial, estate, and intellectual property law. All combined, the legal defense industry accounts for $298 billion annually.[4]

Historical Stability: 76 percent

The practice of law has certainly changed a great deal, but in essence is very similar to what was practiced generations ago. As populations grew, so did the ranks of lawyers to help make sense of numerous and complex laws. However, animosity existed even in early America where the trade was held in contempt by many.

> The framers of the Fundamental Constitutions of the Carolinas in 1669 declared it a "base and vile thing to plead for money or reward." Connecticut and Virginia during a portion of the seventeenth century prohibited lawyers from practicing.[5]

There were no law schools then, and all lawyers "survived as generalists."[6] Times have certainly changed. There is now one lawyer for every 244 citizens, up from one lawyer for every 755 citizens in 1910—a threefold increase in one hundred years.[7]

With the change in laws came changes to methods and tools used by lawyers to defend their clients and prosecute lawbreakers. Clientele in traditional client-attorney relationships are mostly the same as in previous eras. However class-action lawsuits have opened entirely new approaches, in which it typical for clients never to meet their advocates.

Resiliency: 83 percent

Laws are slow to pass and slower to repeal. They do not disappear during recessions. In fact, they usually grow more complex as governments attempt to intervene in economic matters. Some deference should be given to the type of law practiced. Business law—new company formation, business contracts, and patent applications—will suffer when there is a slowdown in economic activity. But for most, the services of an attorney are more

4. US Census, "Number of Firms."; American Bar Association
5. Hall, *The Magic Mirror,* 21–22.
6. Hall, *The Magic Mirror,* 21–22.
7. US Census 1910, 2017; American Bar Association, "National Lawyer Population Survey."

necessary than discretionary. With one for every 244 citizens, lawyers do not require large populations and need not travel far to sustain themselves.

On the other hand, automation is making inroads into the profession, where online services make it possible to form a new business or obtain contract templates without ever meeting a lawyer in person. As machines continue to improve, lawyers will see increased pressure from automated services as well as from overseas firms that can complete many legal tasks for a fraction of the price of in-house lawyers.

Family-Centeredness: 41 percent

It is possible for lawyers to work from home, but most do not. The nature of the work is better suited to team environments where assistants, para-legals, and other attorneys can collaborate to serve their clients better. Therefore, most of the time working will be apart from family, unless family members are part of the firm.

Both men and women practice law but the enormous investment in education required precludes young children from taking part. Older children may assist in law firm activities and be well ahead of their peers if they choose to practice law. Even so, aspiring lawyers must spend many years studying before taking the bar exam.

Income: 100 percent

Median pay for attorneys was $120,910 in 2018, according to the Bureau of Labor Statistics, placing lawyers alongside physicians and dentists in earning potential. But this includes salaried in-house attorneys who work full-time for large companies.

For independent attorneys the fees can be much higher. It is not uncommon to pay $200 to $400 per hour for expert legal advice from a private business attorney.

Ease of Entry: 44 percent

The barriers to becoming a lawyer are high. A few states do not require law school degrees before taking the bar exam and practicing law; however, they are the minority. The vast majority of lawyers must spend many years earning a law degree before opening their own practices. And because of schooling, startup costs are not trivial. The average attorney begins his or her practice with about $100,000 of debt for law school alone, not including undergraduate debt.[8]

In addition to degrees, lawyers must pass bar exams specific to each state in which they practice law. These exams are expensive and designed to weed out all but the most dedicated students. But despite the fact that competition is fierce, demand for lawyers continues to grow. The Bureau of Labor Statistics projects an increase in the profession of 6 percent through 2028.

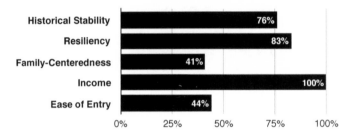

SCORE SUMMARY: LAWYER

Historical Stability	76%
Resiliency	83%
Family-Centeredness	41%
Income	100%
Ease of Entry	44%

Profile: James Y. Prichard, Attorney at Law

Jim Prichard began his law practice 20 years ago after working with a larger firm for several years. Jim's father was a small town attorney, and although he originally planned to go to seminary he decided to obtain his law degree instead. Since that time, he and his wife Tammy have raised seven children.

There are two main types of legal work: transactional practice and litigation. Depending on the kind of work one goes into, the typical day can be very different. Litigation attorneys are always looking towards a court appearance. This includes interacting with people, performing legal research, presenting petitions, conducting depositions, and writing—lots of writing. With litigation "every step has to be performed with the court appearance in mind," says Jim.

Transactional attorneys, on the other hand, primarily work with contracts. This may include real estate, wills, business contracts and tax advice. But anything that starts out as transactional work can also end up in court. "Drafting a will for Dad is transactional," Jim says. But after Dad dies, that will may end up in litigation.

One of the greatest challenges is becoming efficient, according to Jim. Working efficiently is hugely important when practicing law. "A sharp client

---

8. American Bar Association, "Average Amount Borrowed 2001–2012."

will know when they're being over-billed," Jim says. Therefore it is a continual challenge to get quality work done without wasting time. The other challenge is stress. "Everything is either a problem now or could come back to you as a problem later." The greatest joy, according to Jim, is seeing a case settle. Work that you had planned for the next two months is suddenly done, and all the stress is lifted. "Your client is happy and you receive a lot of money all at once."

It is not very common, however, to see family members working together in the trade. Every once in a while you will see a spouse working in the firm, Jim says. If other family members become attorneys it is common to see them work together in the same firm. "That can work out really well," he says. But the high cost of education prevents most from doing so.

Since Jim has been involved in the profession he has noticed a trend towards less congeniality and more toward hostility. The profession is also more stressful than it previously was. Going forward, he expects the legal profession to be squeezed for greater and greater efficiency. "Law 20 to 30 years from now is going to look a whole lot different than it does now," he says.

"The easiest way to practice law is to become an expert and known as a guru in one area," says Jim. That way, you become as efficient as possible, without spreading yourself too thin. Jim advises those interested in becoming lawyers to get an internship before jumping into it. Good grades in law school is also key. "Law is a meritocracy," says Jim. You need to have very good grades to get hired by the big law firms. Honing in on the things that are important for exams will save you from wasting time.

"A law degree is a pretty flexible degree," Jim says. "It can be applied in a lot of ways." There are many well-paying opportunities for those trained to think like a lawyer, even if they are not directly involved in litigation or transactional work. "Just keep your eyes open to the fact that you may not end up where you thought you would."

Additional Resources

- *The University of Chicago Law Review.* Journal, website, and podcast (https://lawreviewblog.uchicago.edu).

- *Revisionist History: The Tortoise and the Hare.* Podcast episode by Malcom Gladwell on entering the legal profession (http://revisionisthistory.com/episodes/32-the-tortoise-and-the-hare).

22

Honorable Mentions

23

21. Baker

'Tis a hard thing, beholding Cyprian loaves, to ride carelessly by, for like a magnet, they do attract the hungry passengers.

—EUBULUS (335 BC)

OF ALL THE FOOD artisans in history, bakers possess a distinctive staying power. They are found in virtually every culture, from ancient Egypt to Colonial America. And bakeries still abound today. Though often reinventing themselves as doughnut or cupcake shops, traditional brick-oven bakeries producing fresh, flour-based breads are also plentiful. While new techniques have been developed, the basic process of mixing flour and yeast, kneading, and baking in an oven has remained the same. Out of this simple framework comes the endless array of baked goods.

Historically, family members have worked together in bakeries, as there are many tasks for young and old alike. However, in our time food regulations prohibit most bakers from working from home, particularly if patrons will be enjoying their pastries on-site.

There are nearly 10,000 retail and commercial bakeries in the U.S. today, generating a combined $54 billion in revenues annually.[1] The Bureau of Labor Statistics estimates that employment for bakers will increase slightly faster than average at 6 percent through 2028.

1. US Census, "Number of Firms."

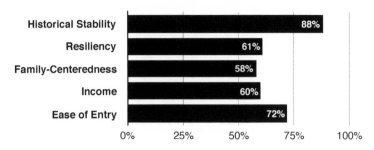

SCORE SUMMARY: BAKER

Historical Stability	88%
Resiliency	61%
Family-Centeredness	58%
Income	60%
Ease of Entry	72%

Additional Resources

- *The Business of Baking.* Online courses and podcast (https://thebizof-baking.com).

- *American Bakers Association.* Wholesale industry association (https://www.americanbakers.org).

24

22. Plasterer

*Suddenly the fingers of a human hand appeared and
wrote on the plaster of the wall, near the lampstand in
the royal palace.*

—Daniel 5:5 NIV (539 BC)

Plasterers provide interior and exterior wall coatings and coverings.
In some cases this is literal plaster, as in lathe-and-plaster. But most commonly this takes the form of drywall, wallpaper and stucco. Plasterers and
painters often work hand-in-hand. In some cases they are the same person.
Plastering is a generally resilient profession with low barriers to entry. And
it has been around for a very long time. According to one historian, "excava-
tions in biblical lands reveal that from very early times, people knew how to
secure lime for plastering walls and for other building purposes." It is also
reported that the temple walls in Jerusalem were plastered white.[1]

Due to declining numbers of professionals in the trade, rates of pay
have been skyrocketing. According to one professional I interviewed, bill
rates for custom plaster work are $150 per hour, primarily because there are
so few tradesmen left.

There are currently 17,780 drywall and wall covering businesses in the
U.S. today with a combined $70 billion in revenues annually.[2] The Bureau

1. Duckat, *Beggar to King*, 175–6.
2. US Census, "Number of Firms."

of Labor Statistics predicts employment in the industry to stay about the same, increasing 2 percent over the next decade.

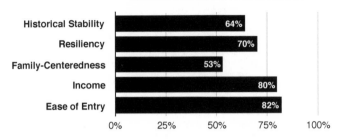

SCORE SUMMARY: PLASTERER

Historical Stability — 64%
Resiliency — 70%
Family-Centeredness — 53%
Income — 80%
Ease of Entry — 82%

0%   25%   50%   75%   100%

Additional Resources

- *Operative Plasterers and Cement Masons (OPCMIA).* Industry association (https://www.opcmia.org).

25

23. Tailor

The glory of God is man, the glory of man is dress.
—Talmud, Derek Erez, Zuta x. (AD 900)

Tailoring involves the assembly of fabrics into finished clothing and accessory end-products such as scarves and hats. Tailoring also includes mending or altering existing attire for better fit and function. As one of the most essential elements to human survival, clothing is almost as ancient as gardening.

Clothing was one of the first home functions to be commoditized by the Industrial Revolution, beginning when Samuel Slater set up his mechanized cotton mill in New England and began producing fabric en masse. Though the industry has since become thoroughly upended, custom tailors and clothiers are still with us today.

There are over 5,678 apparel manufacturing firms in the United States today, grossing $11 billion annually.[1] Although niche opportunities exist, particularly in high-end boutiques, the industry overall continues to contract. The Bureau of Labor Statistics estimates employment will fall by 6 percent through 2028 as overseas competition continues to erode domestic production.

---

1. US Census, "Number of Firms."

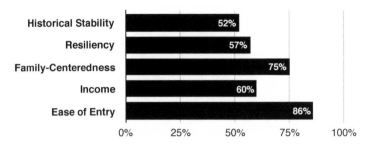

SCORE SUMMARY: TAILOR

Additional Resources

- *How to make a Savile Row Suit.* Video documentary (Museum of Modern Art, 2017).
- *Mastercrafts: Weaving.* Video documentary (BBC, 2010).

26

24. Metalsmith

By hammer and hand all arts do stand.

—THE BLACKSMITH'S GUILD (1325)

BLACKSMITHING, ALSO CALLED METALSMITHING, is one of the earliest known trades, going back at least 5,000 years. Industrialization has all but eradicated the village blacksmith, but metalworking as an industry remains as strong as ever.

Metal fabricators, welders, and other "machine shop" services play a vital role in today's economy. Metalworkers convert raw metals into intermediate parts or finished end-products (e.g., tools). Metalworking may also include forging, but modern industrial forges are beyond the scope of most family-based businesses. While the market for mass-production and standardized parts has largely been captured by overseas manufacturers, there remains strong demand for custom fabricators and machinists who can undertake non-standardized projects and repairs. It can be profitable as well, with bill rates at custom machine shops ranging from $75 to $125 per hour.

There are over 22,000 machine shops in America today grossing $66 billion annually.[1] The Bureau of Labor Statistics estimates the trade will increase gradually by 1 percent through 2028.

1. US Census, "Number of Firms."

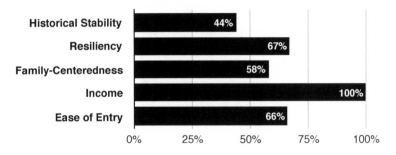

SCORE SUMMARY: METALSMITH

Historical Stability — 44%
Resiliency — 67%
Family-Centeredness — 58%
Income — 100%
Ease of Entry — 66%

Additional Resources

- "What It's Like to Be a Modern Day Blacksmith." *Popular Mechanics* (https://www.popularmechanics.com/adventure/outdoor-gear/a13537816/nicholas-wicks-blacksmith).

- *Modern Machine Shop.* Magazine and website (https://www.mmsonline.com).

- *Mastercrafts: Blacksmithing.* Video documentary (BBC, 2010).

27

25. Barber

The barber, cutting the growth, removing the flourishing roots . . .

—Sᴜᴍᴇʀɪᴀɴ Dɪsᴘᴜᴛᴀᴛɪᴏɴs (2100 BC)

Aꜰᴛᴇʀ ᴅᴇᴄᴀᴅᴇs ᴏꜰ ᴅᴇᴄʟɪɴᴇ, losing business to retail chains, traditional barber shops are making a comeback. Forbes reports that barbering is the fastest-growing profession in the U.S.:

> There was a 23% decrease in barbershops across the country from 1992 to 2012, according to census data. Then there was an uptick in 2013. Now there is a boom.[1]

Professional men's and women's grooming extends back at least 4,000 years. And, fortunately for barbers, you can't get a haircut online. "I think you're going to see a lot more people jumping on this bandwagon," says one researcher for Forbes. "We're going to see a lot of growth in this area."[2]

There are fewer opportunities for family members to work together in this trade, however, as most barber shops are located away from homes in busy shopping malls. But the outlook for barbering is very strong. The Bureau of Labor Statistics projects a 8 percent increase in employment over the next decade.

1. Hagerty, "Barbershops Are Back," para. 3.
2. Hagerty, "Barbershops Are Back," para. 21.

There are over 84,000 barber shops and hair salons in the U.S. today generating a combined $24 billion annually.[3]

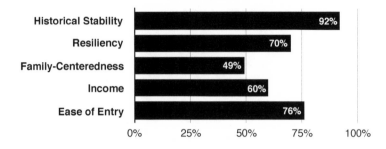

SCORE SUMMARY: BARBER

Historical Stability	92%
Resiliency	70%
Family-Centeredness	49%
Income	60%
Ease of Entry	76%

Additional Resources

- "Barbershops Are Back And Bucking Retail Trends." *Forbes* (https://www.forbes.com/sites/bisnow/2017/07/06/barbershops-are-back-and-bucking-retail-trends).

- "Interview with a Barber." *JobShadow* (https://jobshadow.com/interview-with-a-barber).

---

3. US Census, "Number of Firms."

28

26. Publisher

Oh that my words were written! Oh that they were in-scribed in a book! Oh that with an iron pen and lead they were engraved in the rock forever!

—JOB 19:23–24 (2100 BC)

PUBLISHERS ARE PEOPLE WHO print or publish written material produced by themselves or by other authors. Founding Father Benjamin Franklin was one of the most successful publishers in colonial times. Some of his tomes (for example, *Poor Richard's Almanack*) are still in print today. Most commonly, publishing takes the form of books, newspapers, magazines and journals. In the last 20 years, online publishing has grown from an obscure innovation to a dominating force in the publishing industry. And self-publishing tools, whether online or print, have put publishing within reach of amateur writers. But as the quantity of free, online, and self-published material has increased, the demand for traditionally published material has precipitously declined. As a result, traditional publishing has seen massive contraction over the past two decades. That having been said, publishing has a long track record, and there are many opportunities for family members to work together in a trade, where a profitable niche can be found.

Today, there are 11,793 book, periodical and newspaper publishing firms in the U.S. generating $91 billion annually.[1] The Bureau of Labor

1. US Census, "Number of Firms."

Statistics projects employment in the industry will decline by 16 percent through 2028.

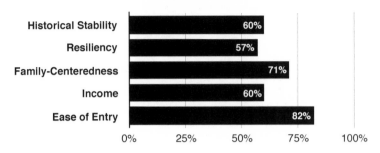

SCORE SUMMARY: PUBLISHER

Additional Resources

- "American Literature Needs Indie Presses." *The Atlantic* (https://www.theatlantic.com/entertainment/archive/2016/07/ why-american-publishing-needs-indie-presses/491618).

- "'They Own the System': Amazon Rewrites Book Industry by Marching Into Publishing." *The Wall Street Journal* (https://www.wsj.com/ articles/they-own-the-system-amazon-rewrites-book-industry-by-turning-into-a-publisher-11547655267).

29

27. Minister

ἐπὶ ταύτῃ τῇ πέτρᾳ οἰκοδομήσω μου τὴν ἐκκλησίαν, καὶ πύλαι
Ἅιδου οὐ κατισχύσουσιν αὐτῆς.

Upon this rock I will build my church; and the gates of
hell shall not prevail against it.

—MATTHEW 16:18 KJV (AD 29)

MINISTRY IS A BROAD profession with many avenues of practice. Some
ministers may be pastors of a local congregation. Others may serve as evan-
gelists, missionaries, worship leaders, youth pastors, or deacons. Generally
speaking, a minister is someone who preaches, oversees religious ceremo-
nies, and shepherds the spiritual growth of a congregation.

Historically, priests served as mediators between man and God.
Melchizedek is the first priest mentioned in the Bible, dating to about 4,000
years ago.[1] Several centuries later, Moses served as mediator when he as-
cended Mount Sinai to receive God's commandments on behalf of the Israelites who "trembled with fear" and dared not approach the mountain.[2] In
the New Testament, Jesus became the final mediator between man and God,

> You have come to God, the Judge of all, to the spirits of the righ-
> teous made perfect, to Jesus the mediator of a new covenant,

1. Gen 14:18
2. Exod 19:16–25

and to the sprinkled blood that speaks a better word than the blood of Abel.[3]

As a profession, ministry affords many opportunities for family members to work together—and it is often expected. However ministry is usually not a high-earning profession, and many pastors are forced to work second jobs to make ends meet. Out of 350,000 religious congregations in the United States, the median church size is only 75.[4] All combined, religious organizations in the U.S. receive $152 billion annually, and the demand for ministers is projected to increase 6 percent over the next decade.[5]

SCORE SUMMARY: MINISTER

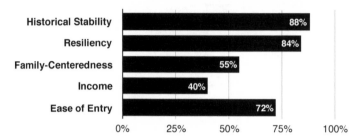

Additional Resources

- *Called to the Ministry* by Edmund P. Clowney (P&R, 1976).

- *IX Marks.* Website and publications for ministers (https://www.9marks.org).

- "A Normal Week in the Life of a Pastor." *The Gospel Coalition* (https://www.thegospelcoalition.org/blogs/jared-c-wilson/normal-week-life-pastor).

---

3. Heb12:23–24 (NIV)
4. Hartford Institute, "Fast Facts about American Religion," para. 1–2.
5. US Census, "Number of Firms."

30

28. Merchant

You, merchant, how small you made the amount of
silver! And how small you made the amount of barley!

—SUMERIAN PROVERB (2100 BC)

LONG BEFORE THERE WERE shopping malls and retail chains, there were traveling merchants who provided wares from distant lands. Retail trade has been in existence for at least 4,000 years. During early American history, merchants played a pivotal role in connecting settlers and pioneers with much needed dry goods and essential equipment in frontiers where there was no industry. Today, it's hard to go any distance without seeing some representation of the retail trade; malls and storefronts dominate most urban and suburban landscapes. And while physical storefronts face challenges from online competitors, the industry as a whole is the largest trade discussed here, accounting for $800 billion annually. According to the National Retail Federation, "retail is the nation's largest private sector employer, supporting one in four U.S. jobs."[1]

Merchants are those who sell goods manufactured by others, traditionally through a physical storefront. There are many such examples of family-owned-and-operated retail establishments. There are over 1 million retail establishments in the U.S., and the Bureau of Labor Statistics expects

---

1. $798.9B net sales, not including food and beverage establishments. National Retail Federation, "The Economic Impact of the U.S. Retail Industry," 2, 12.

employment in this industry to stay steady, declining only 2 percent over the next decade.[2]

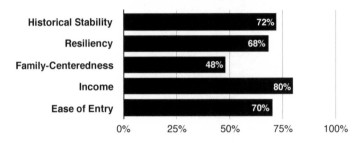

Additional Resources

- *National Retail Federation.* Website, podcast, and research association (https://nrf.com).

---

2. National Retail Federation, "State of Retail."

31

29. Roofer

The people, too, of Mauritania thatch their cot-
tages with rushes; indeed, if we look somewhat closely
into the matter, it will appear that the rush is held in
pretty nearly the same degree of estimation there as
the papyrus is in the inner regions of the world.

—PLINY THE ELDER, *NATURAL HISTORIES* (AD 79)

ROOFING AS A SPECIALIZED building trade is not as common throughout history. The carpenter (or settler) building his house usually put the roof on himself. But there are many examples of the roofing trade existing in other capacities for many centuries. Most notably thatchers in Europe provided coverings for dwellings for thousands of years and are still employed today.

Traditional thatched-roof house (Photo: Peter K Burian/Wikimedia)

In colonial America where timber was abundant, wooden shingles rather than thatch was the obvious choice. Modern roofing materials such as asphalt shingles and steel did not appear until after the early twentieth century. As the materials became more specialized, so did the tradesmen.

Today roofing is a booming component of the construction industry, with over 19,000 roofing businesses earning $41 billion annually.[1] Many roofing companies are family-owned-and-operated, some of them spanning generations. The Bureau of Labor Statistics projects the trade will increase by 12 percent through 2028, much faster than average.

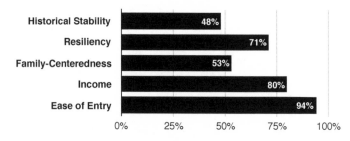

SCORE SUMMARY: ROOFER

Historical Stability	48%
Resiliency	71%
Family-Centeredness	53%
Income	80%
Ease of Entry	94%

1. US Census, "Number of Firms."

Additional Resources

- *Mastercrafts: Thatching.* Video documentary (BBC, 2010).

- *GAF.* Contractor resources and training (https://www.gaf.com/en-us/for-professionals/resources/contractor-resources).

32

30. Embalmer

But this is certain, that before the Persians bury the body in earth they embalm it in wax.

—HERODOTUS, *THE HISTORIES* (440 BC)

MORE COMMONLY KNOWN AS Funeral Directors today, Embalmers, Morticians, and Undertakers are responsible for preparing deceased bodies for ceremonial viewing and burial. Embalming itself was not commonly practiced in America prior to the Civil War, and colonial burials were much less of a production than they are today. But in every culture funeral workers have held long and respected tenures.

Funeral services are also highly resilient. Regardless of innovation, recession, or other societal displacements, there will always be a need for Funeral Directors. Cremation has been the biggest trend to impact funeral services recently, with cremations overtaking burials in the U.S. for the first time in 2015.[1] The industry tends to be male-dominated, and there are fewer opportunities for family members to work together than in other trades, particularly families with young children. On the other hand, the pay is higher on average than other trades surveyed here.

---

1. 48.5 percent of Americans chose cremation in 2015 over 45.4 percent who chose burial. National Funeral Directors Association, "NFDA Cremation and Burial Report."

There are 15,081 funeral homes and cremation services in the U.S. today accounting for $19 billion annually.[2] The Bureau of Labor Statistics
predicts demand for Funeral Directors will increase by 4 percent over the
next decade.

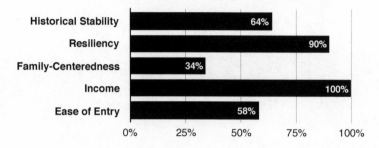

SCORE SUMMARY: EMBALMER

Historical Stability	64%
Resiliency	90%
Family-Centeredness	34%
Income	100%
Ease of Entry	58%

0%   25%   50%   75%   100%

Additional Resources

- *The Undertaking: Life Studies from the Dismal Trade* by Thomas
  Lynch (W. W. Norton, 2009).

- *Frontline: The Undertaking.* Video documentary (PBS, 2007).

2. US Census, "Number of Firms."

33

31. Architect

*In the case of a house the source of motion is the
art and the architect; the final cause is the function;
the matter is earth and stones, and the form is the
definition.*

—ARISTOTLE, *METAPHYSICS* (350 BC)

ARCHITECTURE AS A TRADE goes back many thousands of years to a time
when architects were known simply as "builders." The Tower of Babel described in the Book of Genesis (c. 2200 BC) would have required skilled
architects to conceptualize and attempt the massive structure that "reaches
to the heavens."[1] Regardless the scale, as long as there have been buildings,
there have been architects to design them.

Architecture was refined through the ages, and we see its lasting influence throughout cultures and time: Greek temples, Roman coliseums,
Egyptian pyramids, and Baroque cathedrals. Colonial Americans also
shared a common style with an emphasis on simplicity and utility, befitting
the ethics of their day. Thomas Jefferson is renowned for his architectural
influence on the early American republic, helping to design the U.S. Capitol
and the White House in Washington, D.C.

Though tied to the construction industry, the trade is generally resilient.
Because of its creative requirements, architecture also resists automation.

1. Gen 11:4 (NIV)

But architects must undergo many years of study and earn advanced degrees before opening a practice.

There are 20,894 architecture firms in the U.S. today generating $38 billion annually.[2] The Bureau of Labor Statistics projects that employment in the industry will grow at a strong 8 percent over the next decade.

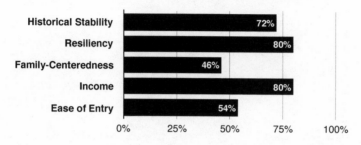

SCORE SUMMARY: ARCHITECT

Historical Stability	72%
Resiliency	80%
Family-Centeredness	46%
Income	80%
Ease of Entry	54%

Additional Resources

- *Life of an Architect.* Blog and podcast (https://lifeofanarchitect.com).
- *American Institute of Architects (AIA).* Licensing and advocacy association (https://aia.org).

2. US Census, "Number of Firms."

34

32. Farrier

The humble petition of our wellbeloved subjects the Brotherhood of Farryers . . . that their art and trade is of great antiquity and of great use and benefitt to our subjects for preserving of horses.

—ROYAL CHARTER OF THE WORSHIPFUL COMPANY OF FARRIERS (1674)

FARRIERS, WHO SPECIALIZE IN trimming and shoeing horses, were closely associated with blacksmiths in colonial America. It was not uncommon for a blacksmith to forge horseshoes or a farrier to repair tools—often they were the same person. But as distinct tradesmen, farriers go back several centuries before the founding of this country. Around 1000 BC Solomon wrote, "The horse is made ready for the day of battle, but the victory belongs to the Lord."[1] Early Roman horseshoes have been found dating to AD 180.[2] However, it was unlikely that horseshoes were in common use until after the ninth century AD, due to the scarcity of iron. By the fourteenth century farrier guilds were forming in Europe, establishing farriers as a distinct trade. Modern farriers spend more time than their predecessors on hoof care and overall equine health. They might be described as a cross between a veterinarians and blacksmiths—at least, they require the skills of both.

1. Prov 21:31
2. BBC, "Early Roman 'horseshoes.'"

With over seven million horses in the U.S., the trade shows no sign of disappearing. Farriers have their own schools, trade associations, and journals. Automation poses almost no risk to this highly unpredictable trade. The pay is good too: full-time farriers reported an average gross income of over $100,000 in 2018.[3] However, most of the work takes place off-site and can be dangerous, limiting opportunities for family involvement. In the U.S. there are 28,000 farriers today, about 80 percent employed full-time, serving an estimated two million horse owners.[4] The Bureau of Labor Statistics projects that jobs in the animal care industry will increase by 16 percent over the next decade.

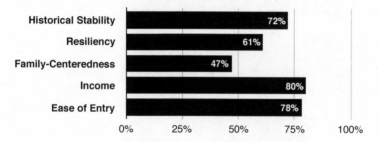

SCORE SUMMARY: FARRIER

Historical Stability — 72%
Resiliency — 61%
Family-Centeredness — 47%
Income — 80%
Ease of Entry — 78%

Additional Resources

- *American Farriers Journal.* Magazine and website (https://www. americanfarriers.com).
- *American Farriers Association.* Education and certification association (https://americanfarriers.org).

3. *American Farriers Journal,* "2019 Farrier Business Practices Report."
4. *American Farriers Journal,* "Employed Farriers: Income Comparison."

35

33. Leatherworker

Make for the tent a covering of ram skins dyed red,
and over that a covering of the other durable leather.

—EXODUS 26:14 NIV (1500 BC)

WHILE TANNING HAS VIRTUALLY disappeared as a distinct trade, there are still several thousand leathercraft businesses in operation today. Leatherworkers are an integral component of the leather goods industry. Leatherworkers turn animal hides into finished consumer goods, including purses, footwear, jackets, and upholstery.

What used to be a sizable industry in the United States has shrunk considerably in recent decades due to intense overseas competition. The U.S. now ranks 8th in the world for leather production, accounting for only 4 percent of the global supply. Other countries such as China, India, Argentina and Brazil now lead the world in leather production and goods.[1]

Niche opportunities still exist, however, for artisanal hand-crafted leather products. And leatherworking businesses can be based from home with family members working in tandem. Today there are 1,139 leather product manufacturers in the U.S. generating $5 billion in annual revenues.[2] Employment in the industry will continue to gradually decline, according

1. United Nations, "World statistical compendium."
2. US Census, "Number of Firms."

the Bureau of Labor Statistics, which projects a 3 percent decrease through 2028.

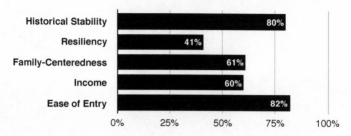

SCORE SUMMARY: LEATHERWORKER

Historical Stability — 80%
Resiliency — 41%
Family-Centeredness — 61%
Income — 60%
Ease of Entry — 82%

Additional Resources

- *Weaver Leathercraft.* Youtube channel.

- *Fine Leatherworking.* Online courses and leatherworking products (https://www.fineleatherworking.com).

- *Leather Crafters & Saddlers Journal.* Magazine (https://leathercraftersjournal.com).

36

34. Sailor

It was manned by one hundred and fifty sailors who were chosen from among the best sailors of Egypt.

—Ancient Egyptian, *Tale of the Shipwrecked Sailor* (2000 BC)

Sailors provide the same service today as they did thousands of years ago. As far back as ancient Egypt, and likely before, captains piloted seafaring vessels in open waters. Sometimes they transported people, other times cargo. Modern innovations such as GPS navigation have revolutionized the transport industry, including sailors' responsibilities. Instead of paper maps, and charting by the sun, moon and stars, GPS uses satellites and computers to chart navigation on digital maps. Still, every ship needs a captain to "take the helm" in unanticipated situations and oversee the vessel's many loading, carrying, and unloading operations.

Because this is one of the slowest forms of transport (it can take three weeks to cross the Atlantic), families involved in the trade are few. Smaller seafaring operations that provide tours or fishing charters near coastal areas and inland lakes do not have this limitation.

Today there are 1,248 water transportation businesses in the U.S. generating $44 billion annually.[1] The Bureau of Labor Statistics estimates a decrease of 2 percent in water transportation workers over the next decade.

1. US Census, "Number of Firms."

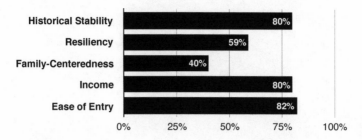

SCORE SUMMARY: SAILOR

Historical Stability	80%
Resiliency	59%
Family-Centeredness	40%
Income	80%
Ease of Entry	82%

0%   25%   50%   75%   100%

Additional Resources

- "How to Become a Sailor." *Maine Maritime Academy* (https://mainemaritime.edu/waterfront/schooner-bowdoin/sail-training/how-to-become-a-sailor).

37

35. Logger

*Now therefore command that cedars of Lebanon be
cut for me. And my servants will join your servants,
and I will pay you for your servants such wages as you
set, for you know that there is no one among us who
knows how to cut timber like the Sidonians.*

—1 KINGS 5:6 (1000 BC)

TREES, WHEN RESPONSIBLY HARVESTED, are the world's greatest sustainable
resource. Early American pioneers were all-in-one lumberjacks, sawyers,
and carpenters, converting stands of trees into human dwellings and commercial outposts. But in most times and places, division of labor has split
loggers into their own trade.

Chainsaws and heavy equipment in modern times have radically altered
the otherwise historically stable trade. Per-capita production has increased
dramatically, but so have the environmental consequences. Deforestation
has led to heavy regulation in the logging industry. Mechanization has also
led to a decline in the number of workers necessary to maintain production,
resulting in rapid loss of jobs in this industry. The Bureau of Labor Statistics
estimates a further 14 percent decline in employment through 2028.

Small, family-run logging and tree-care companies are surprisingly
common in an industry where businesses must be geographically dispersed.
There are plenty of opportunities for family members of proper age to work

together. However, the work is usually offsite, and the demanding physical requirements mean there are fewer opportunities for children and elderly to be involved.

Today there are just under 2,528 forestry and logging businesses in the U.S. generating $13 billion annually.[1]

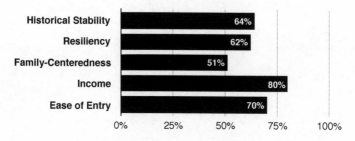

Additional Resources

- "The Life of a Lumberjack." *The Atlantic* (https://www.theatlantic.com/business/archive/2016/11/logger/507848).

- "What it takes to be a logger." Newport News Times (https://newportnewstimes.com/article/what-it-takes-to-be-a-logger).

1. US Census, "Number of Firms."

38

36. Treasurer

So he committed these things to Mithridates, the trea-
surer, to be sent away, with an order to give them to
Sanabassar, that he might keep them till the temple
was built.

Josephus, *Antiquities of the Jews* (AD 93)

Overseeing the financial needs of an organization is a long-running
profession historically awarded to only the most trusted of people. Azma-
veth, one of King David's famed mighty men, was put in charge of the
royal storehouses in Jerusalem (c. 1000 BC). In pre-colonial times, Miles
Standish served as treasurer of Plymouth Colony (1644). Whether looking
after the storehouses of a royal kingdom or fundraising for a present-day
non-profit, treasurers provide an array of financial and auditing services for
their employers. Prior to the corporation there was little need for designated
treasurers outside of government. Families owned and operated their own
businesses using resources that were immediately available to them rather
than relying on external financing. In this respect, the trade has transformed
significantly in the last two centuries. Today, almost every organization regardless of size has a designated treasurer.

Since treasurers are rarely independent from the firm they represent,
independent accounting firms now handle functions traditionally assigned
to treasurers to ensure proper auditing and tax compliance. For these outside

firms there is some degree of flexibility in working from home or involving family members. But most treasury roles are internal to the organization, which reduces opportunities for family involvement. On the other hand, financial managers command a very high income, over $125,000 according to the Bureau of Labor Statistics.

There are over 113,000 accounting firms in the U.S. today comprising a $154 billion industry.[1] The BLS estimates demand for financial managers to be much higher than average in the coming years, with a 16 percent increase in employment through 2028.

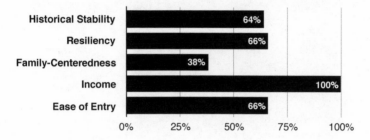

Additional Resources

- *American Institute of CPAs.* Licensing association (https://www.aicpa. org/becomeacpa/gettingstarted.html).

1. US Census, "Number of Firms."

39

37. Physician

According to my greatest ability and judgment . . . I
will do no harm.

—Hippocratic Oath (400 BC)

Diagnosing illnesses and treating the sick is a longstanding profession. In the Old Testament, Job refers to physicians in his defense to his friends.[1] Luke, author of one of the four gospels and the Acts of the Apostles, was himself a physician.[2] Throughout the ages physicians have taken many forms and practices in pursuit of healing their patients. As a result the medical profession has always been in flux, as new technologies, methods, and medicines become available. However, the essence of the trade has not changed for thousands of years.

Barriers to entry are high in this profession. After 11 to 14 years of higher education, the average medical school graduate begins his career $166,750 in debt.[3] But the rewards can also be high. Physicians are the highest-paid professionals of all, with a median salary of $208,000 in 2018, according to the Bureau of Labor Statistics.

Still many professionals are dissatisfied with changes to the medical industry, brought about by insurance requirements and government

1. Job 13:4
2. Col 4:14
3. Kristof, "$1 million mistake."

regulations. Instead of healing the sick, doctors now spend one-quarter of their day filling out paperwork and tending to administrative matters. Further, professional demands prevent family members from working together in the trade. And for the most part work is performed entirely away from home.

There are currently 171,722 primary care doctors in the U.S. working in a $485 billion primary care industry.[4] The need for physicians will continue to increase, with a rise in employment by 7 percent through 2028.

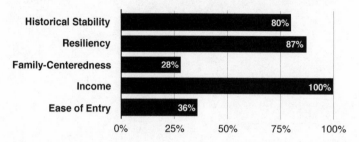

SCORE SUMMARY: PHYSICIAN

Additional Resources

- "The Adventurous Life of a Neurosurgeon." *Penn Medicine* (https://www.pennmedicine.org/updates/blogs/neuroscience-blog/2018/february/life-of-a-neurosurgeon).

- *American Association of Naturopathic Physicians (AANP).* Naturopathy education, accreditation, and advocacy group (https://naturopathic.org).

4. US Census, "Number of Firms."

40

38. Artist

The stone unhewn and cold
Becomes a living mold,
The more the marble wastes,
The more the statue grows.

—MICHELANGELO (1536)

ART IS HIGHLY DISCRETIONARY. But it is also highly valued. Well-crafted pieces from acclaimed artists can hold investment value—and increase in value—over generations. Perhaps that is why art is such an enduring trade. One of the earliest references to professional artists dates back to 1500 BC, when artistic designs were commissioned for the Jewish temple in Jerusalem.[1] But professional artists, including painters, sculptors, and carvers, could be found far earlier in history. In the modern era, auteur filmmakers and animators producing digital art are also considered artists, though of a different class.

While no formal education is required, becoming a self-supporting artist takes extraordinary time and dedication. And art, being an individualized trade, offers limited ways in which family members can work together. Most often one member is the artist and others serve in supporting roles. At the same time, artists often work from home studios and have more flexibility to tend to family concerns.

1. Exod 31:1–5

Today there are an estimated 50,000 craft and fine artists engaged in full-time work in the United States, and the art dealers industry accounts for $9 billion annually.[2] According to the Bureau of Labor Statistics, employment in this trade is expected to increase 6 percent over the next decade.

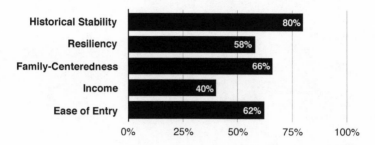

Additional Resources

- *Oil Painters of America.* Education and exhibition association (https://www.oilpaintersofamerica.com).

- "Contemporary Mixed Media Artist." *Job-Shadow* interview (https://jobshadow.com/contemporary-mixed-media-artist-donna-bernstein).

- *MrJakeParker.com.* Professional illustrator's blog and online courses (https://www.mrjakeparker.com).

2. BLS, *Occupational Outlook*, "Craft and Fine Artists."; US Census, "Number of Firms."

41

39. Musician

*His brother's name was Jubal; he was the father of all
who play stringed instruments and pipes.*

—GENESIS 4:21 NIV (3000 BC)

MUSICIANS HAVE A LONG history. Jubal, a descendant of Cain, is highlighted
as the "father of all who play stringed instruments and pipes," which means
that fairly sophisticated musical instruments were in use at least 5,000 years
ago. In ancient Israel, David is found playing the lyre for King Saul,[1] and
later, after becoming king, he appoints professional musicians to accom-
pany the processional of the Ark of the Covenant,

> David told the leaders of the Levites to appoint their fellow Levites
> as musicians to make a joyful sound with musical instruments:
> lyres, harps and cymbals. . . . The musicians Heman, Asaph and
> Ethan were to sound the bronze cymbals; Zechariah, Jaaziel, Sh-
> emiramoth, Jehiel, Unni, Eliab, Maaseiah and Benaiah were to
> play the lyres according to alamoth, and Mattithiah, Eliphelehu,
> Mikneiah, Obed-Edom, Jeiel and Azaziah were to play the
> harps, directing according to sheminith. Kenaniah the head

---

1. "And whenever the harmful spirit from God was upon Saul, David took the
lyre and played it with his hand. So Saul was refreshed and was well, and the harmful
spirit departed from him." 1 Sam 16:23

Levite was in charge of the singing; that was his responsibility because he was skillful at it.[2]

Professionals who provide musical entertainment, sometimes called singers, songwriters, or simply "artists," have seen many changes to their industry since radio made its first musical debut in 1910. Records followed a short time later, making live performances optional for the first time in history. Since the advent of the Internet and digital streaming services in recent years, musicians have endured further upheaval. What used to be a viable, self-supporting career has evaporated for many as widespread use of digital services erodes profit margins of physical merchandise.

Professional musicians have many opportunities to work alongside family. It is not uncommon to see family members comprising several members of a band, for example. Touring musicians may travel with their families. And writing is a process that can be fully home-based. Unfortunately, income is sporadic for most musicians. According to the Bureau of Labor Statistics, "Many musicians and singers find only part-time or intermittent work and may have long periods of unemployment between jobs."[3]

Today there are over 4,849 musical groups and artists the United States generating a combined $6 billion annually.[4] The BLS predicts employment for musicians and singers will remain steady over the next decade.

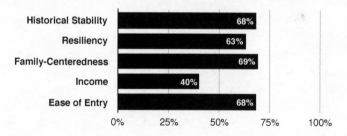

SCORE SUMMARY: MUSICIAN

Category	Score
Historical Stability	68%
Resiliency	63%
Family-Centeredness	69%
Income	40%
Ease of Entry	68%

Additional Resources

- *Chronicles: Volume One* by Bob Dylan (Simon & Schuster, 2005).
- *This Business of Music: Definitive Guide to the Music Industry* by M. William Krasilovsky et al. (Watson-Guptill, 2007).

2. 1 Chr 15:16–22 (NIV)
3. BLS, *Occupational Outlook*, "Musicians and Singers."
4. US Census, "Number of Firms."

42

40. Fisherman

Things may be traded in the city but it is the fisher-man who brings in the food supply.

—SUMERIAN PROVERB (2100 BC)

FISHING, ALONGSIDE HUNTING AND shepherding, is one of the oldest ways people have procured food. The oldest extant records we have from ancient cultures cite fish and fishermen as part of everyday life.

Fishing as an industry has certainly changed much over the last few centuries. Massive rigs now replace the simple row and sail boats used in centuries past. Fish farming, or "aquaculture," has grown from relative obscurity in the 1950s to providing half of all fish consumed globally today.[1] However, at its core, commercial fishing—the wild capture of fish on open waters—still uses tools and techniques that have been in use for millennia.

There are opportunities for families in commercial fishing, but often seasons last for weeks or months, meaning that at least some family members will be separated for long durations. However, many profitable commercial fisheries are family-owned-and-operated.

Commercial fishing comprises 2,528 businesses in the U.S. today and amounts to $3 billion annually.[2] The Bureau of Labor Statistics expects

---

1. FAO, "The State of World Fisheries."
2. US Census, "Number of Firms."

employment to remain mostly steady, decreasing slightly by 2 percent through 2028.

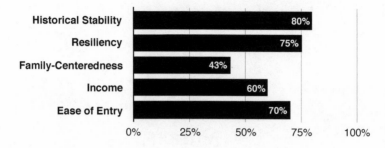

Additional Resources

- "So You Want My Job: Commercial Fisherman." *The Art of Manliness* (https://www.artofmanliness.com/articles/so-you-want-my-job-commercial-fisherman).

- "Beginning Aquaculture." *Texas A&M AgriLife Extension* (https://fisheries.tamu.edu/aquaculture/beginning-aquaculture).

43

41. Miner

*Of occupations attendant on our goods and chattels,
those come first which are natural. Among these
precedence is given to the one which cultivates the
land; those like mining, which extract wealth from it,
take the second place.*

—ARISTOTLE, *ECONOMICS* (350 BC)

MINING IS THE EXTRACTION of resources from the earth's surface, including ore, coal, oil, gold, silver, or other minerals. It is an ancient trade, necessarily existing prior to metalworking. Of all the trades, mining has perhaps undergone the greatest revolution in tooling and methods while still delivering the same core product. That is because the world still relies on materials that lie beneath the earth's surface and will always need miners to extract them. In certain regions of the U.S., mining is a generational trade with family histories going back before the founding of this country.

Mining is a high-risk, high-reward occupation. Capital requirements to open a new coal mine are at least $20 million.[1] Equipment and leases for small-scale gold mines can run into the hundreds of thousands. Though the costs of mining are high, our current living arrangements require coal, oil, and natural gas. And although no modern currency is backed by gold,

---

1. Infomine, "Mining Cost Models."

central banks around the world still hold it, and many nations are aggressively mining it.[2]

Due to the expense, most mining operations today are heavily capitalized corporations with shareholders. They may be family-owned in part, but few if any operations are fully self-funded anymore. There are, however, significant assets associated with mining besides the resources themselves, including land and heavy machinery. Mining can also pay well. According to ABC News, mining is one of the few vocations where workers can earn $70,000 "right out of high school."[3]

Today there are over 19,000 mining operations in the U.S. today generating a massive $403 billion in revenues annually.[4] The Bureau of Labor Statistics estimates employment in this industry will rise by 3 percent through 2028.

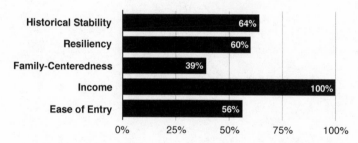

SCORE SUMMARY: MINER

- Historical Stability: 64%
- Resiliency: 60%
- Family-Centeredness: 39%
- Income: 100%
- Ease of Entry: 56%

Additional Resources

- *Mining Journal.* Magazine and website (https://www.mining-journal.com).

- *Mining.com.* Magazine and website (*https://www.mining.com*).

- "What the Backlash Against Coal Feels Like to a West Virginian Miner." *The Atlantic* (https://www.theatlantic.com/business/archive/2016/08/coal-mining/496277).

2. 8,133 tons of gold are currently held in U.S. government reserve. US Dept. of Treasury, "Status Report of U.S. Government Gold Reserve."

3. Dwyer, "Craving Coal Dust," para. 8.

4. US Census, "Number of Firms."

44

42. Banker

Why then did you not put my money in the bank, and
at my coming I might have collected it with interest?

—LUKE 19:23 (AD 30)

BANKS HAVE TAKEN ON many forms over the ages, and bankers many roles. Simply defined, banks are institutions that provide safe-keeping of deposits, interest payments to savers, and capital to borrowers. Bankers, or money-lenders as they were sometimes called, existed long before banks.

> The word "bank" is commonly regarded as derived from the Italian word banco, a bench—the Jews in Lombardy having benches in the market-place for the exchange of money and bills. When a banker failed, his bench was broken by the popu-lace; and from this circumstance we have our word bankrupt.[1]

In the Bible, Jews were forbidden to charge interest on loans made to other Jews, but it was permitted for foreigners.[2] Colonial Americans did not have banks—other than the Bank of England. The first bank in America was not established until 1781.[3] While banking is not as long-lived as

1. Russell, *Banking, Credits and Finance*, 51.

2. "If you lend money to any of my people with you who is poor, you shall not be like a moneylender to him, and you shall not exact interest from him." Exod 22:25

3. The First Bank of North America was the first bank to be established by the new republic. Lewis, *A History of the Bank of North America*, 35.

other trades, it is certainly one of the highest-paying. The median income for loan officers was $63,000 in 2018 and $128,000 for financial managers.[4]

If one has the financial wherewithal to open a bank—requiring up to $30 million in capital and a bank charter—there are opportunities for adult family members to work together.[5] Many banks in this country started as family-owned banks and have continued through multiple generations, although their numbers are declining. Successful bankers generate significant assets for their heirs.

Today there are over 11,000 banks and credit unions in the U.S., comprising a $560 billion industry.[6] The Bureau of Labor Statistics projects a faster-than-average increase of 16 percent in employment in the banking sector through 2028.

SCORE SUMMARY: BANKER

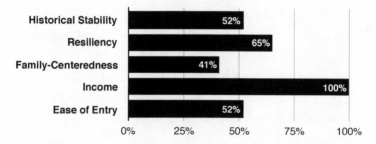

Additional Resources

- "Being an Investment Banker, Far Away From Wall Street." *The Atlantic* (https://www.theatlantic.com/business/archive/2016/11/little-rock-investment-banker/507695).

- *The Warren Buffett Way* by Robert G. Hagstrom (Wiley, 2013).

4. BLS, *Occupational Outlook*, "Loan Officers," and "Financial Managers."
5. Brickley, "How much to start a bank?"
6. US Census, "Number of Firms."

45

43. Courier

It is said that as many days as there are in the whole
journey, so many are the men and horses that stand
along the road . . . and these are stayed neither by
snow nor rain nor heat nor darkness from accomplish-
ing their appointed course with all speed.

—HERODOTUS, *HISTORIES* (440 BC)

COURIERS ENGAGE IN THE delivery of packages and communications between two parties. Historically, this has been by foot, ship, or some form
of ground transportation. Couriers were present at the founding of this
country and before. Prior to the Revolutionary War—and after—Benjamin
Franklin served as Postmaster General to the American colonies.

The basic process of picking up a package, transporting and delivering it has not changed in centuries, but the methods and tools certainly
have. The industry has now become so specialized that end-to-end delivery
is rarely handled by the same person; many hands touch each piece of mail
before it reaches its final destination. But even after the advent of instant and
free delivery through electronic communications for nearly 30 years, letter
carriers continue to be in great demand.

Outside the major players—United States Postal Service, UPS, and
FedEx—there is a myriad of local and regional delivery firms that compete
in this space. The industry has seen tremendous growth in recent years due

to online commerce driving increased demand for shipment. Other innovations include bicycle couriers and grocery store delivery.

Unfortunately, the age restrictions on driving prevent young children from being directly involved. And collection and sorting takes place away from home for larger delivery firms. Despite these challenges, the barriers to entry are low and opportunities exist for enterprising families who want to take part in a rapidly growing industry.

There are over 8,100 courier businesses in the U.S. with $92 billion in revenues annually.[1] The Bureau of Labor Statics projects a sharp decline in U.S. Postal Workers but an increase in couriers and messengers of 3 percent over the next decade.

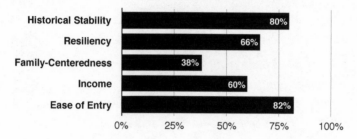

SCORE SUMMARY: COURIER

Historical Stability	80%
Resiliency	66%
Family-Centeredness	38%
Income	60%
Ease of Entry	82%

Additional Resources

- "How To Start A Courier Business." *Profits on Wheels* (https://www.profitsonwheels.com/about).

- "From Clerk to Postmaster at One of the U.S.'s Oldest Post Offices." *The Atlantic* (https://www.theatlantic.com/business/archive/2016/08/postmaster/494498).

1. US Census, "Number of Firms."

46

44. Statesman

The heaviest penalty for declining to rule is to be ruled by someone inferior to yourself.

PLATO, *THE REPUBLIC* (380 BC)

THE STATESMAN—ALSO CALLED POLITICIAN, ruler, or simply, leader—is not typically associated with tradesmen. But the profession is so pervasive throughout history, in all periods and cultures, that it belongs in a discussion of durable trades. Leadership is the most resilient of all trades, found at every level of society and impervious to whims of the marketplace. Even if individual leaders are short-lived, the profession is not. There will always be a need for civil authorities and those with proven leadership ability.

Aside from monarchies, ruling is not a family trade any longer. However, there are opportunities for family members to work together in modern politics, such as during the campaign season. But the day-to-day work of elected officials generally precludes family involvement. Barriers to entry are also sky-high, depending on the level of government. The combined cost of congressional and Presidential races amounted to over $6.5 billion in 2016, not including state and local races.[1] At the gubernatorial level, candidates must raise at least several million dollars—sometimes tens of millions of dollars—to be viable contenders.

1. Center for Responsive Politics, "Cost of Election," Table 1.

Competition is also fierce, with far more politicians than job openings. There are approximately 513,000 federal, state, and local offices in the U.S. Combined expenditures for federal and state races amounted to $10 billion in 2016.[2]

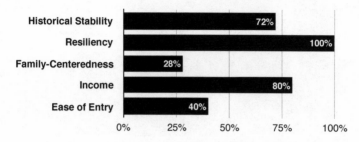

SCORE SUMMARY: STATESMAN

Category	Score
Historical Stability	72%
Resiliency	100%
Family-Centeredness	28%
Income	80%
Ease of Entry	40%

Additional Resources

- *Mitt.* Video documentary (Netflix, 2014).
- *Apostle of Liberty: The World-Changing Leadership of George Washington* by Stephen McDowell (Cumberland, 2007).

2. US Census, "Popularly Elected Officials," 17.

47

45. Professor

*The greatest kindness one can render to any man
consists in leading him from error to truth.*

—THOMAS AQUINAS (1250)

PROFESSORS OF HIGHER LEARNING existed long before elementary schools
could be found in every town in America. The first university, founded in
1088 in Bologna, Italy, is still in operation today. The University of Oxford
was founded a short time later in 1096. Medieval universities grew out of
monasteries and monastic schools, where the emphasis was on studying the
Bible, among other scholastic pursuits. Those pursuing careers in medicine,
law, and particularly theology sought instruction from professors teaching
at these universities.

Today professors remain an integral part of the half-trillion-dollar
industry of higher education in America. The work is solitary and does not
involve family members directly. But the college schedule permits summers
off, and professors usually spend at least some of their time working from
home.

There are over 17,000 colleges, universities and technical schools in
the U.S. employing 1.4 million postsecondary teachers. The higher-educa-
tion industry amounts to $300 billion annually.[1] While acceptance rates at

1. US Census, "Number of Firms."; BLS, *Occupational Outlook*, "Postsecondary
Teachers."

top-rated graduate programs can be low, the Bureau of Labor Statistics projects an overall increase in employment in this field of 11 percent through 2028. However, this number does not account for individual disciplines: Humanities teachers are projected to increase less than half as fast.

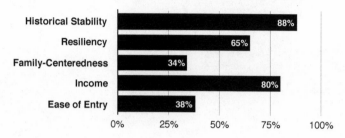

SCORE SUMMARY: PROFESSOR

Category	Score
Historical Stability	88%
Resiliency	65%
Family-Centeredness	34%
Income	80%
Ease of Entry	38%

Additional Resources

- *Getting What You Came For: The Smart Student's Guide to Earning an M.A. or a Ph.D.* by Robert Peters (Farrar, Straus and Giroux, 1997).

- *The Professor Is In: The Essential Guide to Turning your Ph.D. into a Job* by Karen Kelsky, Ph.D (Three Rivers Press, 2015).

48

46. Nanny

And Pharaoh's daughter said to her, "Take this child
away and nurse him for me, and I will give you your
wages." So the woman took the child and nursed him.

—Exodus 2:9 (1600 BC)

Nannies, sometimes referred to as housekeepers or maids, provide in-house keeping and care of children. A less common form is the governess who oversees the in-home education of children. Prior to off-site daycare and public schooling, the presence of nannies was common. Traditionally, nannies served in estates of larger families at the direction of the house-wife. Today families of varying means employ nannies to assist with house chores and childcare, whether or not the mother works outside the home. Placement agencies, which can vet and match candidates with families, are a starting point for both parents and aspiring nannies.

Childcare is a surprisingly stable trade. The basic function of nannies hasn't changed much over the years: playing with or observing play, transporting, preparing meals, and keeping homes tidy. And the clientele is always direct; robots do not make competent substitutes for nannies.

Some opportunities exist for family members to be together in this trade. Nannies who are mothers themselves are sometimes able to bring their own children along. However, the work is by definition away from home, and it is not possible for all family members to engage in the work together. Still, with very low barriers to entry, nannying provides a decent income with very little investment and is a great option for younger women without family obligations of their own.

There are close to 1 million childcare workers in the U.S. today and 77,413 day care services with industry revenues totaling $42 billion.[1] The Bureau of Labor Statistics projects an increase of 2 percent in employment over the next decade.

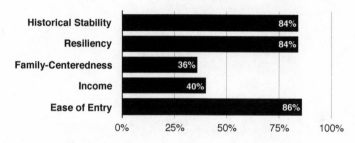

SCORE SUMMARY: NANNY

Historical Stability	84%
Resiliency	84%
Family-Centeredness	36%
Income	40%
Ease of Entry	86%

Additional Resources

- *Care.com*. Caregiver directory and job placement website.
- *International Nanny Association (INA)*. Standards and training association (https://nanny.org).

---

1. US Census, "Number of Firms."

49

47. Judge

Four things belong to a judge: to hear courteously,
to answer wisely, to consider soberly, and to decide
impartially.

—SOCRATES (400 BC)

JUDGES ARE PUBLICLY-APPOINTED OFFICIALS who decide legal cases in a court of law. In the ancient world, the city gate served as a kind of courtroom where victims could plead their cases before appointed elders. In ancient Israel (c. 1500 BC) we find an example of dividing justice into higher courts and lower courts:

> Look for able men from all the people, men who fear God, who are trustworthy and hate a bribe, and place such men over the people as chiefs of thousands, of hundreds, of fifties, and of tens. And let them judge the people at all times. Every great matter they shall bring to you, but any small matter they shall decide themselves.[1]

By the time George Washington was elected in 1789, courts modeled after the English legal system were already well-established throughout the colonies. But judges swore a new oath, "to support the constitution of the United States."

1. Exod 18:21–22

Justice and judges rank high in historical stability and overall resilience. The essential functions of the trade have not changed, and appointed and elected judges are not vulnerable to recessions or supply-chain disruptions. However, judges rank lower on family-centeredness, as the nature of courts and the legal process prevent family involvement in the trade. Barriers to entering the profession are also high, as judges typically begin their careers as lawyers, who require many years of higher education, and they must be appointed or elected.

There are 31,700 state and federal judgeships in the United States with budgets totaling $26 billion.[2] The Bureau of Labor Statistics projects an increase of 3 percent in judgeships through 2028.

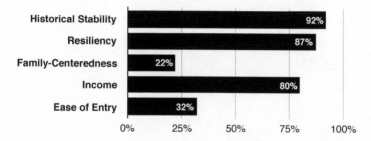

SCORE SUMMARY: JUDGE

Additional Resources

- "A Day in the Life of a Judge." *The Judge's Journal, American Bar Association* (https://www.americanbar.org/groups/judicial/publications/ judges_journal/2017/spring/a_day_in_the_life_of_a_judge)

- *Created Equal: Clarence Thomas in His Own Words.* Video documentary (Manifold Productions, 2020).

2. Univ. Denver, "FAQs: Judges," 3; US Courts, "The Judiciary FY 2021," 3; *Ballotpedia,* "State court budgets," Table 1.

50

48. Scientist

*Finally we shall place the Sun himself at the center of
the Universe.*

—Copernicus (1543)

THE TERM "SCIENTIST" DID not come into use until the nineteenth century,
but forms of this profession can be found throughout history. At the time of
Jesus' birth, Magi from the east traced the movement of heavenly bodies.[1]
Through the middle ages, Copernicus, Galileo, and Newton advanced man's
understanding of the Universe. In Colonial America, the Puritan minister
Cotton Mather was also "a keen scientist who researched in hybrids and
inoculation."[2] At times scientists more resembled magicians than impar-
tial observers of nature. Alchemists of the middle ages sought to transmute
base metals into gold and extend life indefinitely.

Broadly defined, scientists are those primarily involved with conducting empirical research in physical, engineering, or life sciences. Modern
research is extremely specialized as compared to 250 years ago. Anymore it
is rare to find a lone inventor making breakthroughs in his workshop. The
vast majority of research taking place today is funded or utilized by private
companies manufacturing goods to sell. And yet the trade is still concerned

1. Luke 2:1–12
2. Kelly, "John Winthrop—Colonial American Scientist," para. 2.

with the same pursuits—recording observations and understanding natural phenomena.

Because of vast specialization in the trade, there may be many or few opportunities for family members to work together, depending on the specialty. Generally, science is an individual pursuit because it takes so many years to become knowledgeable in one discipline. Children and spouses cannot simply step into the work unprepared. However, modern technologies allow many scientists to work from home as effectively as in a laboratory, permitting some degree of flexibility at least to be near family if not working directly with them.

Today there are 15,323 firms involved in scientific development and research in the U.S. generating $176 billion in annual revenues.[3] This does not include the hundreds of billions of federal dollars spent on research in universities. The Bureau of Labor Statistics projects employment in this field will increase by 7 percent over the next decade.

SCORE SUMMARY: SCIENTIST

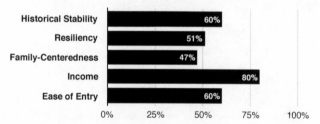

Historical Stability	60%
Resiliency	51%
Family-Centeredness	47%
Income	80%
Ease of Entry	60%

Additional Resources

- "So You Want to Be a Research Scientist." *Medium* (https://medium.com/s/story/so-you-want-to-be-a-research-scientist-363c075d3d4c).

- "The 'Indomitable' MRI: Raymond Damadian's medical imaging machine." *Smithsonian Magazine* (https://www.smithsonianmag.com/science-nature/the-indomitable-mri-29126670).

3. US Census, "Number of Firms."

51

49. Cartographer

As the men started on their way to map out the land,
Joshua instructed them, "Go and make a survey of the
land and write a description of it."

—JOSHUA 18:8 NIV (1400 BC)

CARTOGRAPHY—OR MAPMAKING—IS A RAPIDLY growing trade that has a
long history. George Washington was a surveyor prior to his involvement
in the French and Indian War. Surveying—taking physical measurements
of land—typically went hand-in-hand with mapmaking, but the roles have
become more specialized over time. While the essence of the trade remains,
there is little resemblance to traditional methods and tools used by map-
makers and surveyors of previous generations. Rather than compasses, ink
and parchment, today's Geographic Information Systems (GIS) analysts use
software and imagery from orbiting satellites to draw their maps.

Modern cartography is a highly specialized skill, and entering the
profession will not likely involve family members. But the industry is dominated by small private firms, and starting a home-based consultancy is an
option for some.

There are 8,279 surveying and mapping firms in the U.S. today generating $9 billion annually.[1] The Bureau of Labor Statistics estimates a rapid
15 percent increase in employment in this sector over the next decade.

1. US Census, "Number of Firms."

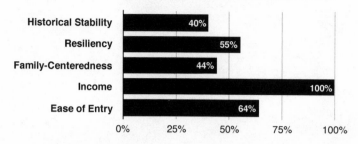

SCORE SUMMARY: CARTOGRAPHER

Additional Resources

- "How a Modern-Day Mapmaker Does His Job." *The Atlantic* (https://www.theatlantic.com/business/archive/2016/03/cartographer/471069).

- *Esri Academy.* GIS products and training website (https://www.esri.com/training).

52

50. Armorer

From the violence of that salt called saltpetre so
horrible a sound is made by the bursting of a thing so
small . . . we find exceeding the roar of strong thunder,
and a flash brighter than the most brilliant lightning.

—ROGER BACON, *OPUS MAJUS* (1267)

VIEWED AS CRITICAL TO a nation's security, armorers repair, modify and manufacture weapons of war. Since the advent of the firearm around AD 1200, gunsmiths have increasingly taken the role of armorers as hand-to-hand combat receded into obscurity. Since the earliest flintlock musket appeared, gunsmiths have played a pivotal role in American history, and they will continue to do so. Colorado School of Trades, one of the top gunsmithing schools in the nation, claims that "with an estimated 357 million firearms in the United States, there will always be a need for a Gunsmith."[1]

Depending on the direction one wishes to go, trained gunsmiths may find individual employment with firearms manufacturers, work in gun stores, or open home-based gunsmithing shops (depending on state and zoning regulations). The latter would permit far more time with family members and in some cases involve them.

---

1. Colorado School of Trades, "About," para. 1.

Today there are 579 firearms manufacturers grossing a combined $13 billion annually.[2] The Bureau of Labor Statistics does not track gunsmiths or armorers specifically but sees a decrease of 8 percent in the general machinist industry over the next decade.

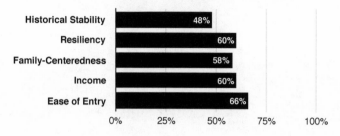

SCORE SUMMARY: ARMORER

- Historical Stability: 48%
- Resiliency: 60%
- Family-Centeredness: 58%
- Income: 60%
- Ease of Entry: 66%

Additional Resources

- "Interview with a Gunsmith." *JobShadow* (https://jobshadow.com/interview-with-a-gunsmith).
- *Colorado School of Trades.* Gunsmithing academy (https://schooloftrades.edu).

2. US Census, "Number of Firms."

53

51. Schoolteacher

In Adam's Fall, we sinned all.

—THE NEW ENGLAND PRIMER (1687)

PUBLIC ELEMENTARY AND HIGH schools as we know them today did not exist prior to 1830 in America. Compulsory education laws had not yet been passed, and primary education was handled locally, by groups of families or in many cases by parents themselves. However, schools were common long before our nation was founded.

Early Sumerian literature (c. 2100 BC) describes the Eduba, a sort of scribal school for children living in ancient Mesopotamia. In colonial New England, Puritan settlers especially prized education and literacy in order to teach their children to read the Bible—an essential rite of their newfound religious freedom. In fact, children and girls in particular in colonial New England had higher literacy rates than children anywhere in the world.[1]

During this time schoolteachers—also called schoolmasters—were in demand, as populations swelled and community school houses began to emerge. In 1647 Massachusetts passed a law that required all towns with at least 50 families to hire a schoolteacher. Towns with 100 or more families were required to establish a grammar, or secondary, school.[2]

---

1. Selcer, *Civil War America*, 301.
2. *Laws and Liberties of Massachusetts*, "Old Deluder Satan Law of 1647."

Today, public education is a massive, $747 billion industry, with just under 100,000 elementary and secondary schools and 4.2 million teachers.[3] Primary education is the second-largest industry surveyed here, bigger even than the military ($738 billion) and commercial banking ($560 billion). Despite its size, the field is highly competitive, and there are generally no opportunities for family members to work together. The Bureau of Labor Statistics estimates a gradual increase for schoolteaching jobs of 3 percent over the next decade.

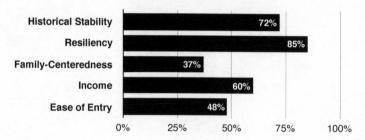

SCORE SUMMARY: SCHOOLTEACHER

Historical Stability — 72%
Resiliency — 85%
Family-Centeredness — 37%
Income — 60%
Ease of Entry — 48%

Additional Resources

- "Interview with a 3rd Grade Teacher." *JobShadow* (https://jobshadow.com/interview-with-a-3rd-grade-teacher).

- *Waiting for Superman.* Documentary film (Paramount, 2010).

---

3. *IBISWorld,* "Public Schools."; BLS, *Occupational Outlook,* "Pre-school Teachers," "Kindergarten and Elementary School Teachers," "Middle School Teachers," "High School Teachers," and "Special Education Teachers."

54

52. Shipwright

The shipbuilder, caulking a boat, heating up fish oil,
with garments not easy to clean.

—SUMERIAN DISPUTATIONS (2100 BC)

SHIPBUILDING IS AN ANCIENT trade. Ancient Sumerian literature references shipbuilders 4,100 years ago. An even earlier reference can be found in Genesis, when God instructs Noah to build an ark roughly 4,600 years ago.[1]

However, Noah was not the first shipwright. Seafaring and shipbuilding was likely around long before this time, and some speculate that Noah may have worked as a shipwright for some period of his life prior to undertaking the largest shipbuilding project in ancient history.

A shipwright is someone who manufactures watercraft for naval, commercial or personal use. He remains an indispensable component of commerce and industry. While the methods used today are vastly different from those in centuries past, shipbuilding can be a high-paying profession. Marine Engineers and Naval Architects earn over $90,000 per year on average.[2] However, there are few opportunities for family members to work together in the modern incarnation of this trade, and startup and equipment costs for private firms are exorbitant.

---

1. Gen 6:14–16
2. BLS, *Occupational Outlook*, "Marine Engineers and Naval Architects."

There are 1,335 ship- and boat-building firms in the U.S. today, accounting for $35 billion in revenues annually.[3] Despite a slowdown in the industry, the Bureau of Labor Statistics projects a 9 percent increase in employment in marine engineering and naval architecture over the next decade.

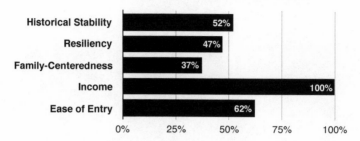

SCORE SUMMARY: SHIPWRIGHT

Additional Resources

- *Tips from a Shipwright.* Youtube channel and website (http://www. tipsfromashipwright.com).

- *American Society of Naval Engineers (ASNE).* Technical society (https://www.navalengineers.org).

3. US Census, "Number of Firms."

55

53. Watchman

Unless the Lord watches over the city, the watchman
stays awake in vain.

—PSALM 127:1 (950 BC)

SECURITY IS A FOREMOST concern in every society. Ancient peoples employed civilian watchmen to stand guard at the entrance to their cities and warn of approaching threats.[1] This practice continued for several thousand years and into early American history, when watchmen and constables provided security to colonial towns and villages. As city populations exploded during the Industrial Revolution, the protection trade transformed to keep apace with surging crime. Policing as we know it today did not exist until well into the nineteenth century. Today there are tens of thousands of protective agencies—from police departments to private security firms—enforcing laws and combating crime.

While it continues to transform in tools, methods, and technologies, policing is a highly resilient trade. Though it can be a competitive field to enter, every community employs security officers, and jobs are generally resistant to economic downturns.

Unfortunately, in its modern incarnation, policing is one of the lowest-scoring trades on family-centeredness, as there is virtually no opportunity for family members to work together. It is rare even for qualified family

---

1. 2 Sam 18:24–25 (NIV)

members to serve in the same department. And there is certainly no opportunity for young children to be involved.

Today there are over 35,000 police departments and private security firms. In total, they add up to a $240 billion industry.[2] The Bureau of Labor Statistics estimates that demand for police and security professionals will increase by 5 percent through 2028.

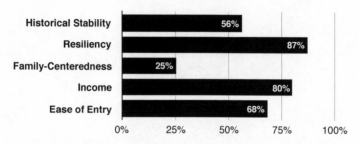

SCORE SUMMARY: WATCHMAN

Historical Stability	56%
Resiliency	87%
Family-Centeredness	25%
Income	80%
Ease of Entry	68%

Additional Resources

- "So You Want My Job: Police Officer." *The Art of Manliness* (https://www.artofmanliness.com/articles/so-you-want-my-job-police-officer).

- *International Association of Chiefs of Police.* Professional association (https://www.theiacp.org).

- *POLICE Magazine.* Magazine and website (https://www.policemag.com).

2. "The U.S. collectively spends $100 billion a year on policing and a further $80 billion on incarceration." McCarthy, "How Much Do U.S. Cities Spend Every Year On Policing?"; 15,388 total law enforcement agencies. US Dept. of Justice, "Local Police Departments."; $62 billion spent on 20,223 private security firms. US Census, "Number of Firms."

56

54. Dentist

When a tooth decays, there is no hurry to extract it,
unless it cannot be helped, but rather to the various
applications described above, we must add more active
compositions for the relief of pain.

—CELSUS, *DE MEDICINA* (AD 100)

DENTISTRY IS A RELATIVELY new trade, historically speaking. The trade did not develop into a distinct profession in America until after the War of Independence. Berkovitz writes,

> Little is known about Baker's early life or training, although he seems to have arrived in America in the early 1760s and was one of the earliest practitioners to call himself a "dental surgeon."[1]

This didn't mean that dental care did not previously exist. General teeth and gum care was provided by doctors and physicians. But the methods were crude: often extraction was the only remedy, and without Novocain. With the dentists appearing in the 18th and 19th centuries, bringing improved practices from Europe, the trade began to flourish as an independent profession.

---

1. Berkovitz, *Nothing but the Tooth,* 209.

Dentists are one of the highest paid professions surveyed here, with median incomes well over $150,000.[2] However, due to the many years of schooling and degrees required to practice dentistry, it is uncommon for family members to work together in the trade, and the barriers to entry are high.

Today there are over 125,000 dentistries in the U.S. generating $126 billion annually.[3] The Bureau of Labor Statistics projects that dentistry will grow faster than average, increasing by 7 percent through 2028.

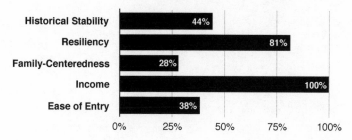

SCORE SUMMARY: DENTIST

- Historical Stability: 44%
- Resiliency: 81%
- Family-Centeredness: 28%
- Income: 100%
- Ease of Entry: 38%

Additional Resources

- "Be a Dentist." *American Dental Association* (https://www.ada.org/en/education-careers/careers-in-dentistry/be-a-dentist).

- *Dentistry Today.* Magazine and website (https://www.dentistrytoday.com).

2. BLS, Occupational Outlook, "Dentists."
3. US Census, "Number of Firms."

57

55. Foundryman

*Every artisan also was to pay tithe, with the exception
of those who were employed in the foundry attached to
the temple.*

—ANCIENT EGYPTIAN, *THE LEGEND OF KHNEMU*
(2000 BC)

FOUNDRIES ARE A CRITICAL link in the steelmaking supply chain, converting mined iron ore into primary materials used by industry. After ore is ex-
tracted, it is smelted and poured into molds to make castings. These castings
are then used by other industries to make finished products. References to
foundries and foundry workers can be found throughout ancient literature
dating back to the 3rd millennium BC. In 1642 the first foundry in America
was established in Saugus, Massachusetts by John Winthrop the Younger.
The Saugus Iron Works smelted, poured, and forged the first iron castings
in America, using water power from the Saugus River. It remains today as a
National Historic Site.

American's first foundry, Saugus Iron Works, was established in 1642. (Photo: Daderot/Wikimedia)

Though essential, foundries and foundrymen have seen dramatic changes and consolidation in their industry over the last 150 years. Less than 700 iron foundries remain in the U.S.—down from 20,000 at the turn of the twentieth century—as fierce competition has driven most of the industry overseas. Further, breakthroughs in machine automation have been eliminating jobs for decades and will continue to put pressure on an industry with highly uniform and repetitive work. That having been said, primary metals manufacturing is an essential underpinning of any society and will never be completely outsourced.

Foundry and forging work is heavy and dangerous, and the industry is dominated by adult men. Because of the massive investment and corporate structure required to operate modern foundries, there are fewer opportunities for family members to work together than in previous generations.

A total of 1,510 ferrous and non-ferrous foundries exist in the U.S. today, generating $30 billion annually.[1] According to the Bureau of Labor Statistics the industry is still contracting, and it predicts an decrease in employment by 11 percent through 2028.

1. US Census, "Number of Firms."

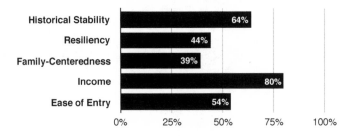

SCORE SUMMARY: FOUNDRYMAN

- Historical Stability — 64%
- Resiliency — 44%
- Family-Centeredness — 39%
- Income — 80%
- Ease of Entry — 54%

Additional Resources

- *Modern Casting.* Magazine (https://www.moderncasting.com).
- *American Foundry Society.* Education and advocacy association (https://www.afsinc.org).
- *Saugus Iron Works.* National Historic Site (https://www.nps.gov/sair).

58

56. Millwright

Around the circumference are fixed paddles, which,
as they are struck by the force of the river, move along
and cause the wheel to turn.

—VITRUVIUS, *ON ARCHITECTURE* (30 BC)

MILLWRIGHTS INSTALL, MOVE, MAINTAIN and repair factory equipment and other industrial machinery. The term originally referred to the master craftsmen who constructed all forms of wind-, water-, and animal-powered mills. In this respect, millwrights have existed for as long as heavy machines have been milling wheat into flour. Today, the profession has expanded into all avenues of industry:

> Today's millwright is concerned with the precision-fitting of machinery to tolerances of a thousandth of an inch. It is the millwright who installs and aligns heavy industrial machinery, including conveyor systems, escalators, electric generators, and cyclotrons, and insures that they operate efficiently. He even puts into effect the vast and complex machines of the nuclear age.[1]

Due to the large-scale and complex nature of the work, millwright-ing is not a family-friendly vocation. Though it is possible for adult family

---

1. *Carpenter*, "North America's Millwrights," 11.

members to work together, professionals can expect to be traveling frequently and spending large spans of time away from their families.

There are currently 21,436 firms providing industrial mechanical services in the United States, generating annual revenues of $70 billion.[2] The trade is expected to grow about as fast as other professions, at 5 percent over the next decade, according to the Bureau of Labor Statistics.

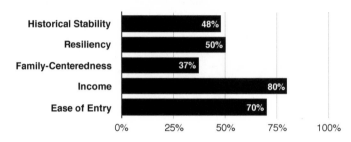

SCORE SUMMARY: MILLWRIGHT

Historical Stability	48%
Resiliency	50%
Family-Centeredness	37%
Income	80%
Ease of Entry	70%

Additional Resources

- *Millwrights and Mechanics Guide* by Thomas Bieber Davis and Carl A. Nelson (Audel, 2010)

- "So You Want My Trade: Elevator Mechanic." *The Art of Manliness* (https://www.artofmanliness.com/articles/so-you-want-my-trade-elevator-mechanic).

2. US Census, "Number of Firms."

59

57. Coachman

After these came Xerxes himself in a chariot drawn by
Nesaean horses; beside him was his charioteer, whose
name was Patiramphes, the son of Otanes, a Persian.

—HERODOTUS, *THE HISTORIES* (440 BC)

THE COACHMAN, CHAUFFEUR, OR simply "driver" as he called today has
served a long tenure in the history of trades. All cultures develop this role
early in their civilizations, and it has adapted to changes in technology well
through the years. From human-powered rickshaws, to horse-driven carriages, to limousines and taxis, to peer-to-peer ridesharing services like
Uber and Lyft, drivers who provide ground-based transportation are found
in every society and always seem to be in demand.

Worth cautioning, however, are the rapid advancements in self-driving
cars and the impact this could have on the transportation industry. Also, it is
not possible for family members to work together in the key function of the
trade: driving. However, most private transport businesses are home-based,
and this permits a greater degree of flexibility than is found in some trades.

Today, there are 1.4 million taxi, limousine and ridesharing services
in the U.S. generating $31 billion annually.[1] Thanks largely to ridesharing,
the Bureau of Labor Statistics predicts that employment in this sector will
explode by 20 percent over the next decade.

1. *IBISWorld,* "Taxi & Limousine."

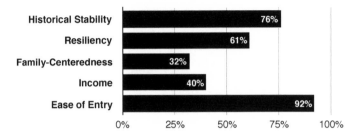

SCORE SUMMARY: COACHMAN

- Historical Stability — 76%
- Resiliency — 61%
- Family-Centeredness — 32%
- Income — 40%
- Ease of Entry — 92%

Additional Resources

- "A day in the life of an Uber, Lyft, and Juno driver." *CNBC* (https://www.cnbc.com/2019/01/30/a-day-in-the-life-of-a-full-time-uber-lyft-and-juno-driver-in-nyc.html).
- *Uber.* Ridesharing service (https://uber.com).
- *Lyft.* Ridesharing service (https://lyft.com).

60

58. Soldier

*Tyranny, like hell, is not easily conquered; yet we have
this consolation with us, that the harder the conflict,
the more glorious the triumph.*

—THOMAS PAINE (1776)

"SOLDIER" IS PERHAPS UNSUITED to a compilation of family-centered trades.
Warfare, if anything, divides rather than unites families. But it cannot be ignored that soldiering is one of the most enduring professions. Defense and
conquest have been part of every human society since time began. Historically, there was a marked difference between officers and the enlisted—or
conscripted—soldiers they raised to fight in war; they were almost entirely
different professions.

The modern American military is a long way from the ragtag conti-
nental army fighting for independence from Great Britain. The tools and
methods of modern warfare have changed in spectacular ways. But the
objectives have not: "to support and defend the Constitution of the United
States against all enemies, foreign and domestic."[1]

Today there are five branches of the U.S. Armed Forces with over 2
million active and reserve soldiers. The defense budget for 2020 is $738 bil-
lion.[2] Near-term growth for this sector is not published by the Bureau of

1. 5 U.S. Code § 3331, "Oath of office."
2. Macias, "Trump signs $738 billion defense bill."

Labor Statistics, but the National Defense Authorization Act of 2019 increases active duty forces by 15,600 service members, a one-year increase of 1.2 percent.[3]

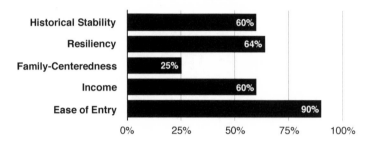

SCORE SUMMARY: SOLDIER

Historical Stability	60%
Resiliency	64%
Family-Centeredness	25%
Income	60%
Ease of Entry	90%

Additional Resources

- *We Were Soldiers Once . . . and Young* by Harold G. Moore and Joseph L. Galloway (Random House, 1992).

- "So You Want My Job: Marine Corps Officer." *The Art of Manliness* (https://www.artofmanliness.com/articles/so-you-want-my-job-marine-corps-officer).

3. Garamone, "President Signs Fiscal 2019 Defense Authorization Act."

61

59. Actor

All the world's a stage . . .

—SHAKESPEARE (1599)

CENTURIES BEFORE CHRIST THEATER was a staple of Mediterranean entertainment. Historian Walter Duckat writes, "as early as the fifth century BC
there were theaters in Greece built on the natural contours of the area."[1]
Theater was viewed then, as it often is now, as a violent and immoral pastime:

> Christianity, too, condemned pagan theater, since Christians as
> well as Jews were slain in the theaters. The church Father Tertul-
> lian declared that the theater was a place of sexual immorality.[2]

Actors today are independent artist who earn a living through live performances, television, or film acting. The methods and technologies have
changed—particularly with the advent of film in the 1920s—but the essence
of acting has not changed since its inception.

Entertainment, being a discretionary expense, is vulnerable to recessions. And, typically, acting is not considered a family-centered trade; actors
are judged on individual talent. However members of the same family are
sometimes naturally gifted and may work well together as troupe actors in
live performances. The pay, unfortunately, is often abysmal. While fortunes

1. Duckat, *Beggar to King*, 1.
2. Duckat, *Beggar to King*, 4.

can be made by a select few, the vast majority of aspiring actors are not employed at all, or must work multiple jobs to make ends meet. According to one Hollywood insider, well over 90 percent of registered members of the Screen Actors Guild do not earn a living by acting.[3]

Today there are currently 64,500 acting jobs in the $84 billion motion picture and performing arts industry.[4] The Bureau of Labor Statistics projects that acting jobs will remain steady, increasing by 1 percent over the next decade.

SCORE SUMMARY: ACTOR

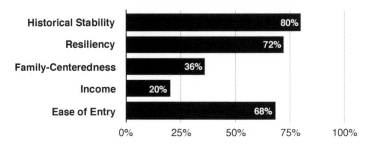

Historical Stability — 80%
Resiliency — 72%
Family-Centeredness — 36%
Income — 20%
Ease of Entry — 68%

0%   25%   50%   75%   100%

Additional Resources

- "So You Want To Be An Actor?" *Forbes* (https://www.forbes.com/sites/alexandratalty/2013/11/21/so-you-want-to-be-an-actor).

- *Backstage*. Magazine and website (https://www.backstage.com).

3. Jeff Lingle, interview with author. December 13, 2018.
4. BLS, *Occupational Outlook*, "Actors."; US Census, "Number of Firms."

62

60. Athlete

If a man is an athlete and makes that his business,
does he pay attention to every man's praise and blame
and opinion or to those of one man only who is a
physician or a trainer?

— SOCRATES, IN PLATO'S *CRITO* (399 BC)

PROFESSIONAL COMPETITION EXISTED FOR many centuries but died out after the Fall of Rome, not to return until after the U.S. Civil War. Professional athletes—those who compete in various sports in front of spectators to win a prize—were not around 250 years ago, but they were around 2,500 years ago:

> In Athens, for example, in the sixth century BC Solon offered 500 drachmas for victors of the Olympic games. . . . On top of that the athletes received free meals for the rest of their lives in the city hall. In many places, for example Egypt, the athletes also obtained exemption from taxes. From the second century AD onwards the once-only awards in money were converted into life-long pensions.[1]

While athletic competition is not a particularly stable trade, it is historical. Sporting events fall under the category of entertainment, and as

1. Remijsen and Clarysse, "Rewards at the home town," para. 2.

such athletes are vulnerable to economic downturns. Salaries range wildly, depending on the sport and individual competency. But as with other entertainers there are many more candidates than there are jobs. The Bureau of Labor Statistics reported median income in 2018 for sports competitors at $50,650 per year.

Generally speaking, athletic competition does not involve family members. However, thanks to the seasonality of professional sports, there is more flexibility, including long breaks for athletes, than can be found in other trades.

At present there are 3,953 spectator sports firms in the U.S. generating $46 billion annually.[2] The Bureau of Labor Statistics projects an increase in athletes of 6 percent over the next decade.

SCORE SUMMARY: ATHLETE

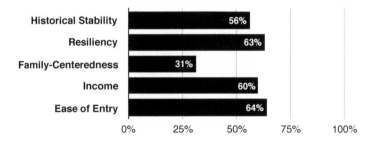

Additional Resources

- "So You Want My Job: NFL Player." *The Art of Manliness* (https://www.artofmanliness.com/articles/so-you-want-my-job-nfl-player).

---

2. US Census, "Number of Firms."

63

61. Tax Collector

As Jesus went on from there, he saw a man named
Matthew sitting at the tax collector's booth. "Follow
me," he told him, and Matthew got up and followed
him.

—MATTHEW 9:9 NIV (AD 28)

TAX COLLECTORS HAVE BEEN around for at least as long as there have been monarchs. In the early 2nd millennium BC, the Egyptian pharaoh imposed a temporary 20 percent tax on the inhabitants of Egypt: "Let Pharaoh proceed to appoint overseers over the land and take one-fifth of the produce of the land of Egypt during the seven plentiful years."[1] One thousand years later, the Old Testament prophet Samuel warns the Israelites what will happen if they appoint a king:

> He will take a tenth of your grain and of your vintage and give
> it to his officials and attendants. . . . He will take a tenth of your
> flocks, and you yourselves will become his slaves.[2]

Far from the temporary 20 percent Egyptian tax, or the intolerable 10 percent Israelite tax, or even the 25 percent tax that defined 'serfdom' in the middle ages, American taxpayers today pay an average 30 percent

1. Gen 41:34
2. 1 Sam 8:11–18 (NIV)

of their income to federal, state, and local taxes, not including property or sales taxes.[3] Those on the upper end of the income scale can pay much more, in excess of 50 percent. This in a country where a threepence tax on tea sparked a revolution?

With so much money claimed by the "king," somebody has to collect it. In fiscal year 2019, federal, state, and local governments collected $5 trillion.[4] While the majority of collection takes place automatically, there are 73,000 IRS agents standing by, ready to assist you in supporting your government. Needless to say, tax collection is a trade that is not going away soon.

But with employee-withholding and electronic-filing, modern tax collectors bear little resemblance to their historical counterparts. As private companies cannot levy taxes, the only employment opportunity for tax collectors is to work for the government. This means limited time with family. However, the pay is good, and with record-breaking revenues almost every year the job security can't be beat.

In total, there are 105,929 federal, state, and local tax collectors operating under a budget of around $17 billion annually.[5] The Bureau of Labor Statistics estimates a slight decline in employment by 2028, decreasing by 2 percent.

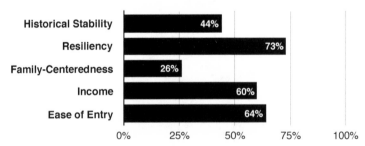

SCORE SUMMARY: TAX COLLECTOR

3. "Serfs in medieval Europe were taxed 20 to 25 percent. I don't think we should be taxed higher than serfs." Elliot, "15 Questions with Grover G. Norquist," para. 10; Frankel, "What's the average American's tax rate?"

4. OMB, "Historical Tables," Table 1.1; US Census, "Quarterly Summary."

5. IRS expenditures were $11.7B in 2018. State and local tax collection expenditures are estimated to be 0.35 percent of revenue (same as IRS), or about $5.2B. IRS, "IRS Budget & Workforce."; BLS, *Occupational Outlook*, "Tax Examiners and Collectors, and Revenue Agents."

Additional Resources

- "Confessions of a former IRS agent." *San Luis Obispo Tribune* (https://www.sanluisobispo.com/opinion/letters-to-the-editor/ article39441198.html).

PART III

Durable Foundations

All that is gold does not glitter,
Not all those who wander are lost;
The old that is strong does not wither,
Deep roots are not reached by the frost.

—J. R. R. TOLKIEN

1

The Vital Lie

A LOCAL CARPENTER ONCE shared a story with me about a conversation between his son and a high school guidance counselor. His son had been evaluating various colleges and their tuition costs when the counselor told him he would be eligible for a lot of scholarships and financial aid because "your parents don't make a lot of money." The counselor had no particular knowledge of the family's financial situation, other than knowing the father was a self-employed carpenter and his mother worked in landscaping.

On another occasion I mentioned to a friend how a college degree didn't seem like a cost-effective solution for everyone when accounting for the high amount of debt so many students incur and the years (or decades) it takes them to pay it back. The friend, whose oldest son had just enrolled in college, took offense at my line of questioning and responded, "I don't want my son to make eight bucks an hour as a plumber."

Now, if anyone knows where I can hire a plumber for $8 per hour, I would be very interested in a referral. But the bigger issue underlying these conversations is the prejudice against trades and the people who work in them. Trades, as the thinking goes, are only for those too poor, ignorant, or lazy to earn a college degree. Only white-collar professionals make real money.

But none of these perceptions has proven true in my experience. I have never worked so hard as when I worked for tradesmen. I am continually amazed at the high rates people will pay for competent carpenters, painters, and, yes, plumbers—rates of pay far exceeding anything I have earned as a software engineer. And if you want to see ignorance, try teaching a computer programmer how to replace the sickle bar on a John Deere 37 mower.

Certainly, poor, ignorant, and lazy people do work in the trades. But they are just as common in the cubicles and corner-offices of corporate America. The issue is not the work itself but perceptions about the people who perform such work. Entering numbers on a spreadsheet does not take much more thought than swinging a hammer—although a lapse in focus in the latter bears more immediate consequences to your digits.

If the perceptions are false, why do they persist? This phenomenon can be best explained by what Norwegian playwright Henrik Ibsen referred to as "the vital lie." In society there are certain truths that are too painful to accept. It is more comfortable in these situations to embrace a lie rather than confront the truth. To the professional guidance counselor earning $50,000 per year, or the recent college graduate $100,000 in debt, it can be difficult to accept the idea of an unschooled, blue-collar laborer earning double, or triple, his white-collar salary.

The Millionaire Next Door

The carpenter's son, in fact, did not qualify for any financial aid; his parents make too much money. Between the construction and landscaping businesses, his mom and dad gross approximately $500,000 annually. By age forty, his parents paid off their mortgage and now live debt-free with net assets of just under $1 million.

Plasterers in our county charge $150 per hour to perform work that no one else knows how to do. And plumbers, electricians, and machinists are not far behind. The painter I interviewed for this book left his corporate job to start a painting business because he found the cubicle life unfulfilling. He earns more now as a painter than he did as a corporate executive. His schedule is more flexible too, allowing him to spend more time with his wife and daughters, who are also getting involved in the business.

The Costumes We Wear

Occasionally, after working a day in construction, I will run errands on my way home. I can't help but notice the stares I get when I arrive at the library, the post office, or the bank dressed in Carhartt overalls with sawdust in my hair. It's a markedly different reaction from the one I get when I show up in slacks and sweater with a laptop bag on my shoulder.

The same goes for the greasy mechanic or the mortar-stained mason: why do we presume to know another's intelligence—or financial situation— by the costume he wears? The farmer who lives down the road from us has been farming his whole life and has raised children who have been farming their whole lives. He's the one I call when my tractor breaks down with half a field left to bale. Unassuming as he looks, in a t-shirt and usually sunburned, the man possesses more knowledge of agriculture and machinery than I'll ever have.

The fact is, our perceptions about trades and the people who work in them are mostly false. Uncomfortable as it may be, there is more money, intelligence, creativity and flexibility involved in trades than in most white-collar jobs. Many trades are more conducive to family life than demanding, high-powered corporate jobs. Most tradesmen do not need to travel far to find work; there is plenty of demand locally. And trades—at least the ones discussed here—are not as likely to become displaced by the next autonomous robot or software upgrade. They have stood the test of time and, in all likelihood, will continue to do so.

2

The Dignity of Work

WHEN WE FIRST STARTED raising broiler chickens, we had no idea how to turn the grown birds into oven-ready chickens. We found a great butcher shop nearby that would process our chickens and have them ready for pick-up the following day, bagged and frozen, for a mere $2 per bird. Considering what was entailed in butchering a chicken—killing, de-feathering, cutting into pieces—two dollars was much too good a deal to pass up.

When we started raising sheep and goats a few years later, the same butcher would turn our grass-eaters and brush-clearers into gourmet cuts of meat. We would choose the assortment of steaks, chops, and ground burger, and everything was conveniently packaged and frozen when we stopped by to pick it up the following week. All we had to do was deliver the animal and write a check.

Getting pigs to the butcher was more of a task. It turns out you can't move a pig into a trailer if he doesn't want to go. But with a little perseverance (and a lot of chocolate brownies), we found it a huge relief to simply write a check and pick up hundreds of pounds of hams, bacons, and sausages a few days later.

It was on one of these glorious pickup days that I casually mentioned to the owner my interest in learning how to butcher our own animals. At some point between the chickens and sheep and hogs it started to dawn on me that I really have no idea how to turn our animals into food. It was a total "black box" to me: we drop off clucking chickens or baaing sheep, then pick up oven-ready dinners a few days later.

So on a whim I asked the very friendly owner if she ever needed part-time help. If I really wanted to learn how to butcher and not quickly forget,

I felt that I needed to work in the trade for a little while. The owner asked me, "Are you good with a knife?" I replied, "No. I'm a computer programmer!" But she told me I could be taught, and we left the matter alone as I awkwardly made my exit. My surprise came about three weeks later when I got a call from the owner: "Do you still want to work here?" I thought to myself, "I'm not sure I was really serious about that."

A Different Perspective

The biblical perspective on work is unique. In his book on ancient trades, Walter Duckat explains how the Israelites' view of work departed radically from other ancient peoples:

> Contempt for labor prevailed in ancient Greece where even a citizen who was a laborer was held in contempt. While the gods of all nations of antiquity, such as the Olympians, are described as spending their lives in either debauchery or pleasures, or, like the Hindu gods, passively in everlasting repose, God of the Bible is the Master Worker who is Maker and Sovereign of the world.[1]

According to Duckat, "The Hebrews were virtually the only ancient people who preponderantly viewed work as dignifying rather than demeaning." God created man in his own image and placed him in the garden "to tend and keep it."

"Unlike other peoples of antiquity who despised both slaves and workers, humble workers attained exalted positions in Israel," Duckat explains. Abraham, Isaac, and Jacob were shepherds. Saul was a farmer before being anointed the first King of Israel. David, his successor, was a shepherd. Elisha, the farmer, was ploughing with a yoke of the oxen when Elijah, the prophet, found him. Amos both tended sheep and tended sycamore trees. Moses, who was raised in Pharaoh's palace, was not ordained until after tending flocks for 40 years. Before leading Israel's armies, Gideon could be found threshing wheat. And Jesus, a carpenter, found his first disciples fishing in the Sea of Galilee.

Not only does the Bible dignify humble occupations, it also condemns idleness. "Greater is the merit of industry than idle piety," comments Jewish rabbi Ben Sameos on Psalm 128: "Blessed is everyone who fears the Lord, who walks in his ways! You shall eat the fruit of the labor of your hands." In

---

1. Duckat, *Beggar to King*, xx.

Proverbs we are given the example of the ant who diligently stores up food for the winter.

In the New Testament, Paul exhorts us to "make it your ambition to lead a quiet life: You should mind your own business and work with your hands, just as we told you, so that your daily life may win the respect of outsiders and so that you will not be dependent on anybody."[2]

Therefore we need not be ashamed of labor, no matter how humble. God, the Master Worker, gives purpose and meaning to every occupation.

Back to Work

My first day at Dennison Meat Locker was grueling. I was thrown into the fray from the beginning. There was no employee orientation, safety video, or even a guided tour. Instead I was shown once how to clean a hanging side of beef, then handed a knife as my teacher walked away to skin another cow.

On a typical day we slaughtered six beef cattle, four to six hogs, and several sheep or goats. On poultry days we processed up to 1,200 chickens. Once we finished slaughtering, cleaning, weighing, and refrigerating, we still had two hours of cleanup. And let me tell you, you haven't cleaned anything until you've cleaned a "kill room."

It is a surreal experience to learn ancient trades like butchering. The work certainly is not glamorous—it is often smelly, gross, and repetitive. As a software engineer, I am used to writing code from a comfy chair in an air-conditioned office. But there's a satisfaction in learning something new, in re-learning forgotten skills of previous generations. The "black box" of butchering is no longer a mystery to me. And I'm a lot better with a knife than I used to be.

2. 1 Thes 4:11–12

3

The Discipleship of Work

WHEN WE MOVED TO our farm several years ago with a toddler and new-born in tow, we mainly had it in mind to experience a bit of the country life: to plant a large garden and perhaps raise a few chickens. We didn't expect much else to change. But the land has had its own effect on us.

The chickens and gardens are here, to be sure. But so are sheep, goats, pigs and honeybees. We also find ourselves baling hay, pitching manure, splitting wood, and repairing fences. Always repairing fences. At some point our hobby farm became a working farm, and nearly every aspect of our lives now revolves around this labor we undertake together, as a family.

The work is real. It's dirty, smelly, sweaty, and tremendously physical. Cutting, splitting, stacking firewood. Weeding, mulching, harvesting from the garden. Hauling water and cleaning stalls. There are easier ways to ac-quire food. Cleaner ways. Cheaper ways. But that's not why we do it.

A friend once quipped that growing tomatoes is "the best way to de-vote three months of your life to saving $2.17." In a way, he's right: food has never been cheaper or more abundant than it is today. According to the Bureau of Labor Statistics, U.S. expenditures on food have dropped from 44 percent of the annual household budget in 1901 to a mere 13 percent in 2017. Over the last century, the industrial agricultural system with its fac-tory farms has brought us a previously unimaginable abundance of cheap food. But it has come at a very steep price.

Around the turn of the twentieth century, industrialists and bureau-crats alike were patting themselves on the back for the unprecedented economic growth of the previous century. Nearly every aspect of the Amer-ican economy had been upended by the Industrial Revolution. Official government documents hailed the arrival of "the factory system." Statisticians wrote with uncharacteristic praise for this newfound way of work (and unmerited derision of the former):

> [Prior to the Industrial Revolution] the factory system had not yet displaced the domestic or individual system of labor. Nothing was known of the development of special skill by the subdivision of labor and the confinement of each workman to one particular step in a series of progressive operations, an expedient by which the productive capacity of the modern operative has been brought to the maximum and the time required to complete the product reduced to the minimum.[1]

The expedients gained came at the price of relationships lost: factory production meant the end of the apprenticeship model, the method by which generational skill had been passed on for thousands of years. Families that divided into factories no longer educated, mentored, and discipled their children at home. Dependency on the family and community was replaced with dependency on the employer. Work became an end unto itself rather than an opportunity for mentorship.

But it is at work that true discipleship takes place, more so than at church or in the classroom. Work is where the real person resides. The true nature of a man is revealed when he is swinging a hammer, felling a tree, or negotiating a contract. For good or ill, we speak loudest to those around us when we are at work. Integrity, perseverance, and faith in divine providence cannot be transmitted in a lecture hall. They must be modeled.

Jesus taught in the synagogues. But he discipled his followers along the way—in boats, along seashores, in towns and villages, while *at work*. The apostle Paul mentored Aquila and Priscilla while working: "because he was a tentmaker as they were, he stayed and worked with them."[2] He also admonished the Thessalonian church to "acknowledge those who work hard among you . . . and hold them in the highest regard in love because of their work."[3]

Scripture makes it clear that work is not solely about making stuff. God intended something else to occur in the process. We may be growing tomatoes or crafting fine furniture. But we are also shaping souls.

That is why we don't mind the sweat and dirt or the inefficient methods of production we employ here on our farm. For us it's not about doing it faster or cheaper. Relationships are what matter. I want to be there beside

---

1. Mass. Bureau of Statistics of Labor, *Comparative Wages*, 10.

2. Acts 18:3

3. 1 Thes 5:12–13

my son as he struggles to lift bales into the barn, or kneel beside my toddlers as they pick blueberries and manage to save a few for the bucket. In the garden I can tell my children about spiritual truths and our responsibility to care for God's creation. They get to see how their dad reacts to uncooperative weather, broken-down tractors, and raccoons in the henhouse. In these trying moments, will I give in to anger and despair, or will I demonstrate my faith by trusting in God's provision?

It is at work where our faith is most on display. It is here that disciples are made.

4

A Resilient Future

*Unless the LORD builds the house, the builders labor
in vain.*

—Psalm 127:1 (NIV)

When we first began to consider a move to the country, we wondered what it might be like to live off the land as our great-grandparents did. We looked forward to the day when we could grow enough food to last the winter. That day hasn't come yet. But over the last several years we've made gradual progress—we have animals, gardens, tractors and a barn. However, I can assuredly say that at present we would not survive the winter without grocery stores.

What we have learned is that building a new family economy takes time. Lots of time. But the journey of a thousand miles begins with a single step. While I can't tell you how to arrive at a durable future, I can tell you where to begin.

A Firm Foundation

The first step is faith. Without faith, there is no hope for a resilient future. Jesus said, "Everyone then who hears these words of mine and does them will be like a wise man who built his house on the rock. And the rain fell, and the floods came, and the winds blew and beat on that house, but it did not fall, because it had been founded on the rock."[1]

Faith is not wishful thinking lacking in any real substance. Faith *is* real substance. Attempting anything of true significance begins in faith. Faith is the inward belief that manifests the outward reality: "By faith we understand that the universe was created by the word of God, so that what is seen was not made out of things that are visible."[2]

A story was once shared with me about shipwrecked survivors during World War II. When rescue vessels finally found the lifeboats in the icy North Atlantic sea, sailors came upon a baffling, yet tragic sight. Despite their superior physique, all of the younger soldiers had died. But the older soldiers were still alive. It turned out that the older surviving soldiers had fought in World War I; they had faced death before and survived. They had faith they could endure this trial too. But the younger soldiers, having never experienced war or the limits of their endurance, lost all hope before their rescuers arrived.

The Psalmist tells us that "the righteous shall be in everlasting remembrance. He shall not be afraid of evil tidings: his heart is fixed, trusting in the Lord."[3] If we align our purposes with God's, we need not worry about the future. "Are not two sparrows sold for a penny? Yet not one of them will fall to the ground outside your Father's care. . . . So don't be afraid; you are worth more than many sparrows."[4] We begin, therefore, by acknowledging God as the source of our provision and trusting in his providence—not in riches, politicians, hard work, retirement nest-eggs, or even historically-stable trades.

Farming Knowledge

My son was not yet two years old when we moved to our farm. His sister was nine days old. At the time we knew next to nothing about farming, shepherding, or repairing machinery. My first-ever building project was a cabin I built in our woods that was to become my home office.

The cracking of our first eggs and harvesting our first honey were huge milestones for us. We planted a garden and some apple trees. A barn was built, and we added a few dairy goats and sheep to graze the orchard. Now we are cutting and baling our own hay and storing food for the winter.

1. Matt 7:24–27
2. Heb 11:3
3. Ps 112:6–7 (KJV)
4. Matt 10:29–31 (NIV)

Every step along the way has been a learning experience. Neither my wife nor I comes from farming backgrounds. Through trial-and-error, helpful neighbors, and a lot of stubborn persistence we have pieced together the beginnings of a family farm.

In our journey toward a new family economy, my chief observation is that it takes much longer than I ever imagined it would. There is no rushing this process. The accumulated skill of previous generations literally takes a generation to pass on. Those not raised in a family of farmers, shepherds, woodworkers, or other master craftsmen will have a difficult time learning the trade from scratch. But those who persevere and dedicate themselves to building something that will last will pass on a rich inheritance to their own children in the process.

My son is now nine years old. He can plant a garden, split firewood, drive a tractor, handle livestock, and tend an orchard. I was 35 before I built my first structure; he is already using power tools. His sister is seven, and three more siblings have arrived in the meantime. All of them are learning right alongside my wife and me. They are inheriting our hard-fought lessons. If the journey of a thousand miles begins with a single step, the journey toward a lasting family economy begins with a single generation.

Durable Families

Durable trades are not an individual pursuit. For too long, work has driven a wedge into families, dividing husband from wife, father from son, mother from daughter, and family from home. Building something that will last requires a radically different perspective of family from what is common or encouraged today. It requires total devotion to each other and the well-being of the family. It means individual sacrifice for the betterment of the whole.

For thousands of years it was the family economy that provided the context in which family members spent time together, achieved goals together, cared and provided for one another's needs, gave and received mentorship, and transmitted faith, culture, and values to the next generation.

In his book *Family Life*, Kevin Swanson likens the family economy to an ax and handle. "An ax head by itself is of little use to take down trees," he writes. "Place an ax head on an ax handle, and the capability for useful work has increased a hundred fold. This demonstrates the basic elements of the family economy as designed by God."[5]

---

5. Swanson, *Family Life*, 113.

The family economy encompasses more than business and entrepreneurship, though that is an essential part of it. It also integrates education, discipleship, worship, and recreation. It is the melding of individual aspirations into a common purpose. More importantly, it has been the context by which parents pass their faith, culture and values on to their children for most of human history.

If there is anything that can withstand the nihilistic effects of modernity and the uncertain outcomes of our high towers, it will be families that are reclaiming critical functions at home—education, apprenticeship, discipleship—and working together towards a common vision to which they have been called.

Appendix
Additional Resources

TRADE-SPECIFIC RESOURCES ARE LISTED at the end of each chapter. The following are additional resources that the reader may find helpful:

Family Economy

- *The Natural Family Where it Belongs: New Agrarian Essays* by Allan C. Carlson (Routledge, 2014).
- *One with Everything* by Mike Cheney (Generations/AME, 2017).
- *Family Life: A Simple Guide to the Biblical Family* by Kevin Swanson (Generations, 2016).
- *The Household and the War for the Cosmos* by C.R. Wiley (Canon, 2019).
- Genesis 2
- Deuteronomy 6
- Psalm 127
- Proverbs 31

Culture, Faith, Agrarianism

- *The Collapse of Complex Societies* by Joseph Tainter (Cambridge University Press, 1988).
- *The World-Ending Fire: The Essential Wendell Berry* compiled by Paul Kingsnorth (Counterpoint, 2019).

- *The Benedict Option: A Strategy for Christians in a Post-Christian Nation* by Rod Dreher (Sentinel, 2018).

- *Amusing Ourselves to Death: Public Discourse in the Age of Show Business* by Neil Postman (Penguin, 1986).

- *Local Culture: A Journal of the Front Porch Republic* (https://frontporchrepublic.com).

- *The Natural Family: An International Journal of Research and Policy* edited by Allan C. Carlson (http://familyinamerica.org).

Farming, Homesteading, Self-Sufficiency

- *The Self-Sufficient Life and How to Live It* by John Seymour (DK, 2009).

- *The Backyard Homestead* by Carleen Madigan (Storey, 2009).

- *Frontier House.* Video documentary series (PBS, 2002).

- *The Grovestead.* Our family's quarterly homesteading newsletter (https://thegrovestead.com/newsletter).

Historical Trades & Traditional Skills

- *Shop Class as Soulcraft: An Inquiry into the Value of Work* by Matthew B. Crawford (Penguin, 2010).

- *Mastercrafts* with Monty Don. Video documentary (BBC, 2010).

- *Townsends: 18th-century cooking.* Youtube channel.

- *American Experience: The Amish.* Video documentary (PBS, 2012).

- *Homestead Heritage: An Exodus.* Video documentary (https://homesteadheritage.com/videos/an-exodus).

Tours & Attractions

- *Colonial Williamsburg.* Historic re-enactment community in Williamsburg, Virginia (https://colonialwilliamsburg.com).

- *North House Folk School.* Traditional craft school in Grand Marais, Minnesota (https://northhouse.org).

- *The Ploughshare.* Traditional skills school near Waco, Texas (https://sustainlife.org).

- *Saugus Iron Works.* Historic foundry in Saugus, Massachusetts (https://www.nps.gov/sair).

- *Phillip Brothers Mill.* Steam-powered sawmill in Oak Run, California (https://phillipsbrothersmill.com).

- *Farm America.* Nineteenth- and twentieth-century farms in Waseca, Minnesota (https://www.farmamerica.org).

Continue the Conversation . . .

Are you pursuing a more durable future with your family? I invite you to share your story with us at: TheGrovestead.com.

Table: Durable Trades

#	Trade	Historical Stability	Resiliency	Family-Centeredness	Income	Ease of Entry	Total Score
1	Shepherd	88%	93%	100%	80%	74%	90.0%
2	Farmer	68%	80%	100%	80%	68%	83.4%
3	Midwife	84%	91%	67%	100%	56%	79.5%
4	Gardener	84%	85%	76%	60%	90%	77.2%
5	Woodworker	68%	55%	91%	60%	82%	73.9%
6	Carpenter	76%	78%	62%	80%	92%	73.8%
7	Painter	88%	71%	56%	80%	94%	73.3%
8	Cook	84%	75%	61%	80%	72%	72.6%
9	Brewer	72%	77%	69%	80%	64%	72.5%
10	Innkeeper	84%	63%	67%	80%	64%	72.1%
11	Tutor	88%	75%	55%	80%	76%	71.7%
12	Mason	96%	67%	52%	80%	72%	70.7%
13	Silversmith	80%	58%	73%	60%	84%	70.7%
14	Interpreter	96%	66%	50%	80%	78%	70.4%
15	Author	84%	67%	70%	60%	70%	70.35%
16	Butcher	84%	81%	64%	60%	64%	69.8%

#	Trade	Historical Stability	Resiliency	Family-Centeredness	Income	Ease of Entry	Total Score
17	Apothecary	68%	81%	54%	100%	34%	68.1%
18	Counselor	68%	68%	48%	100%	68%	67.4%
19	Sawyer	80%	65%	62%	60%	76%	67.1%
20	Lawyer	76%	83%	41%	100%	44%	66.4%
21	Baker	88%	61%	58%	60%	72%	66.3%
22	Plasterer	64%	70%	53%	80%	82%	66.1%
23	Tailor	52%	57%	75%	60%	86%	65.8%
24	Metalsmith	44%	67%	58%	100%	66%	65.75%
25	Barber	92%	70%	49%	60%	76%	65.7%
26	Publisher	60%	57%	71%	60%	82%	65.6%
27	Minister	88%	84%	55%	40%	72%	64.7%
28	Merchant	72%	68%	48%	80%	70%	64.4%
29	Roofer	48%	71%	53%	80%	94%	64.2%
30	Embalmer	64%	90%	34%	100%	58%	64.0%
31	Architect	72%	80%	46%	80%	54%	63.9%
32	Farrier	72%	61%	47%	80%	78%	63.8%
33	Leatherworker	80%	41%	61%	60%	82%	63.7%
34	Sailor	80%	59%	40%	80%	82%	63.1%

#	Trade	Historical Stability	Resiliency	Family-Centeredness	Income	Ease of Entry	Total Score
35	Logger	64%	62%	51%	80%	70%	63.0%
36	Treasurer	64%	66%	38%	100%	66%	62.6%
37	Physician	80%	87%	28%	100%	36%	62.5%
38	Artist	80%	58%	66%	40%	62%	62.0%
39	Musician	68%	63%	69%	40%	68%	62.0%
40	Fisherman	80%	75%	43%	60%	70%	61.3%
41	Miner	64%	60%	39%	100%	56%	61.1%
42	Banker	52%	65%	41%	100%	52%	59.7%
43	Courier	80%	66%	38%	60%	82%	59.4%
44	Statesman	72%	100%	28%	80%	40%	59.2%
45	Professor	88%	65%	34%	80%	38%	59.1%
46	Nanny	84%	84%	36%	40%	86%	58.6%
47	Judge	92%	87%	22%	80%	32%	58.4%
48	Scientist	60%	51%	47%	80%	60%	58.1%
49	Cartographer	40%	55%	44%	100%	64%	58.05%
50	Armorer	48%	60%	58%	60%	66%	57.5%
51	Schoolteacher	72%	85%	37%	60%	48%	56.9%
52	Shipwright	52%	47%	37%	100%	62%	56.6%

#	Trade	Historical Stability	Resiliency	Family-Centeredness	Income	Ease of Entry	Total Score
53	Watchman	56%	87%	25%	80%	68%	55.8%
54	Dentist	44%	81%	28%	100%	38%	54.6%
55	Foundryman	64%	44%	39%	80%	54%	54.5%
56	Millwright	48%	50%	37%	80%	70%	53.1%
57	Coachman	76%	61%	32%	40%	92%	52.8%
58	Soldier	60%	64%	25%	60%	90%	51.4%
59	Actor	80%	72%	36%	20%	68%	50.2%
60	Athlete	56%	63%	31%	60%	64%	49.9%
61	Tax Collector	44%	73%	26%	60%	64%	47.3%

Methodology

Each trade was scored on a sliding scale across 20 criteria. These scores were weighted and summarized according to the five main categories used in the book. In the case of a tie, Historical Stability was prioritized. A detailed breakdown of categories and weights is as follows:

Historical Stability (20 percent of total):

- Change to Core Product/Service (40 percent of category)
- Change to Method (20 percent)
- Change to Tools (20 percent)
- Change to Clientele (20 percent)

Resiliency (15 percent of total):

- Minimum Population Requirement (20 percent of category)
- Supply-Chain Vulnerability (25 percent)
- Economic Cycle Vulnerability (20 percent)
- Market Diffusion (local or foreign) (20 percent)
- Automation Risk (15 percent)

Family-Centeredness (35 percent of total):

- Time Together, while working (30 percent of category)
- Age Variability (20 percent)
- Gender Compliment (5 percent)
- Home-Based (30 percent)
- Inheritable Tangible Assets (15 percent)

Income (20 percent of total):

- Based on Federal Poverty Guidelines, BLS median wage data, and other primary research

Ease of Entry (10 percent of total):

- Startup Costs (30 percent of category)
- Competition (20 percent)
- Education Requirements (30 percent)
- Government Regulation (10 percent)
- Growth Projections (10 percent)

Bibliography

Ali, Muneeb. "Toasters are breaking the Internet." *Medium* (October 22, 2016). https://medium.com/@muneeb/toasters-are-breaking-the-internet-c1d153c33f78.

Allen, Frederick. *The Shoe Industry*. New York: Henry Holt and Company, 1922.

American Bar Association. "Average Amount Borrowed 2001–2012." (2012). https://www.americanbar.org/content/dam/aba/administrative/legal_education_and_admissions_to_the_bar/statistics/avg_amnt_brwd.authcheckdam.pdf.

———. "National Lawyer Population Survey." (2018). https://www.americanbar.org/content/dam/aba/administrative/market_research/Total_National_Lawyer_Population_1878–2018.authcheckdam.pdf

American Farriers Journal. "2019 Farrier Business Practices Report." Lessiter Media (2019).

———. "Employed Farriers: Income Comparison." Lessiter Media (June 16, 2017). https://www.americanfarriers.com/articles/9213-employed-farriers-income-comparison.

American Hotel and Lodging Association."Frequently Asked Questions." (2020). https://www.ahla.com/faq.

Aron, Paul. "Paint the Town." *Trend & Tradition* (Summer 2016). https://web.archive.org/web/20190804100530/https://www.history.org/Foundation/magazine/Summer16/paint.cfm.

Ausonius. *Mosella*. Translated by David Parsons (2003). http://www.parsonsd.co.uk/moselle.php

Automation and the Future of Jobs. Directed by Magnus Sjöström. Indigenius, 2016.

Ballotpedia. "State court budgets and judicial salaries." (September 2017). https://ballotpedia.org/State_court_budgets_and_judicial_salaries.

Barna. "Six Reasons Young Christians Leave Church." (September 27, 2011). https://www.barna.com/research/six-reasons-young-christians-leave-church/.

Batchelder, Samuel. *Introduction and Early Progress of Cotton Manufacture in the United States*. Cambridge: Little, Brown, and Company, 1863.

BBC. "Early Roman 'horseshoes' dug up from Vindolanda fort ditch." (August 4, 2018). https://www.bbc.com/news/uk-england-tyne-45034623.

Berkovitz, Barry. *Nothing but the Tooth: A Dental Odyssey*. London: Elsevier, 2012.

Berry, Wendell. *The Art of the Commonplace: The Agrarian Essays of Wendell Berry*. Edited by Norman Wizba. Berkley: Counterpoint, 2002.

Boquet, Shenan. "1.72 billion abortions worldwide in the last 40 years." *LifeSite News* (April 1, 2013). https://www.lifesitenews.com/opinion/1.72-billion-abortions-worldwide-in-the-last-40-years.

Bosker, Bianca. "The Binge Breaker." *The Atlantic* (November 2016). https://www.theatlantic.com/magazine/archive/2016/11/the-binge-breaker/501122/.

Bowles, Nellie. "Early Facebook and Google Employees Form Coalition to Fight What They Built." *The New York Times* (February 4, 2018). https://www.nytimes.com/2018/02/04/technology/early-facebook-google-employees-fight-tech.html.

Brickley, Peg. "How much to start a bank?," *Philadelphia Business Journal* (November 30, 1998). https://www.bizjournals.com/philadelphia/stories/1998/11/30/story5.html.

Brody, Hugh. "Nomads and Settlers." In *Town and Country*, edited by Anthony Barnett and Roger Scruton. London: Johnathan Cape, 1998.

Bureau of the Census. *Historical Statistics of the United States Colonial Times to 1970, Part 1*. U.S. Department of Commerce (September 1975). https://www.census.gov/library/publications/1975/compendia/hist_stats_colonial-1970.html.

Bureau of Labor Statistics. "American Time Use Survey Summary." (June 6, 2018). https://www.bls.gov/news.release/atus.t09.htm.

———. "Consumer Expenditures—2017." (September 11, 2018). https://www.bls.gov/news.release/cesan.nro.htm.

———. *History of Wages in the United States From Colonial Times to 1928*. (October 1929). https://fraser.stlouisfed.org/title/4126.

———. *National Longitudinal Surveys: Frequently Asked Questions*. "Number of Jobs Held in a Lifetime." (2015). https://www.bls.gov/nls/nlsfaqs.htm#anch41. "People born in the years 1957 to 1964 . . . held an average of 11.7 jobs from ages 18 to 48."

———. *Occupational Outlook Handbook*. (2019). https://www.bls.gov/ooh/.

———. "Series Report: Butter, salted, grade AA, stick, per lb. (453.6 gm) in U.S. city average, average price, not seasonally adjusted." Online database (1980–2010). https://data.bls.gov/cgi-bin/srgate.

Cain, Jeff, et al. "Pharmacy Student Debt and Return on Investment of a Pharmacy Education." *American Journal of Pharmaceutical Education* 78 no. 1 (2014).

Campaign for a Commercial-Free Childhood. "Open letter to Mark Zuckerberg." (January 30, 2018). https://assets.documentcloud.org/documents/4361648/Child-experts-letter-to-Facebook.pdf.

Carlson, Allan. "The Family-Centered Economy." *Front Porch Republic* (August 1, 2011). http://www.frontporchrepublic.com/2011/08/the-family-centered-economy/.

———. *Family Cycles: Strength, Decline, and Renewal in American Domestic Life*. New York: Routledge, 2017.

———. *The New Agrarian Mind: The Movement Toward Decentralist Thought in 20th Century America*. New York: Routledge, 2017.

———. "Sweden and the Failure of European Family Policy." *The Natural Family* 31 no. 2 (2018).

Career Profiles. "The Top 10 Most Stable Construction Jobs." (2018). http://www.careerprofiles.info/most-stable-construction-jobs.html.

Carpenter. "North America's Millwrights Have Prospered with Industrial Change." United Brotherhood of Carpenters and Joiners of America (October 1979). https://archive.org/details/carpenter99unit/page/n347.

CDC. "Births: Final Data for 2016." *National Vital Statistics Reports* 67 no. 1 (2018). https://www.cdc.gov/nchs/data/nvsr/nvsr67/nvsr67_01.pdf.

———. "Excessive Drinking is Draining the U.S. Economy." (July 13, 2018). https://www.cdc.gov/features/costsofdrinking/index.html.

———. "Number and Percent of Births to Unmarried Women, by Race and Hispanic Origin: United States, 1940–99." https://www.cdc.gov/nchs/data/statab/t991x17.pdf.

———. "STDs at record high, indicating urgent need for prevention." (September 26, 2017). https://www.cdc.gov/media/releases/2017/p0926-std-prevention.html.

The Center for Responsive Politics. "Cost of Election: 2016 Cycle." *OpenSecrets.org* (2018).

Cellan-Jones, Rory. "Stephen Hawking warns artificial intelligence could end mankind." *BBC* (December 2, 2014). http://www.bbc.com/news/technology-30290540.

Cherlin, Andrew, et al. "Changing Fertility Regimes and the Transition to Adulthood: Evidence from a Recent Cohort." John Hopkins University (2012). http://krieger.jhu.edu/sociology/wp-content/uploads/sites/28/2012/02/Read-Online.pdf.

Cleary, Vern. "Effects of the Industrial Revolution." *Modern World History: Interactive Textbook,* Bellarmine College Prepartory (2014). https://webs.bcp.org/sites/vcleary/modernworldhistorytextbook/industrialrevolution/IREffects.html#Urbanization.

Colonial Williamsburg. "Cabinetmaker." (2019). https://web.archive.org/web/20160727121357/http://www.history.org/Almanack/life/trades/tradecab.cfm.

Colorado School of Trades. "About." https://schooloftrades.edu/about/.

Crews, Ed. "Plain and Neat." *CW Journal* (Summer 2003). https://web.archive.org/web/20191005031942/http://www.history.org/foundation/journal/summer03/cabinet.cfm.

The Daily Record. "Historical Prices: 1913: Morristown, New Jersey, November 21–25." (1913). https://mclib.info/reference/local-history-genealogy/historic-prices/1913-2.

Declercq E. "Midwife-attended births in the United States, 1990–2012." *Journal of Midwifery & Women's Health* 60 no. 1 (2015).

Delainey, Erin, and Matt Haines. "Industry on Tap: Breweries." BLS, *Spotlight on Statistics* (December 2017). https://www.bls.gov/spotlight/2017/industry-on-tap-breweries/pdf/industry-on-tap-breweries.pdf.

Desanctis, Alexandra. "Iceland Eliminates People with Down Syndrome." *National Review* (August 16, 2017). https://www.nationalreview.com/2017/08/down-syndrome-iceland-cbs-news-disturbing-report/.

Desjardins, Jeff. "How Currency Debasement Contributed to the Fall of Rome." *Business Insider* (February 21, 2016). http://www.businessinsider.com/how-currency-debasement-contributed-to-fall-of-rome-2016-2.

Dmitri, Carolyn, et al. "The 20th Century Transformation of U.S. Agriculture and Farm Policy." USDA, Economic Research Service (June 2005). https://www.ers.usda.gov/publications/pub-details/?pubid=44198.

Dreher, Rod. *The Benedict Option: A Strategy for Christians in a Post-Christian Nation.* New York: Sentinel, 2017.

Duckat, Walter. *Beggar to King: All the Occupations of Biblical Times.* New York: Doubleday, 1962.

Durden, Tyler. "Venezuela Slashes 5 Zeros From Currency In 'One Of Greatest Devaluations Ever.'" *ZeroHedge* (August 8, 2018). https://www.zerohedge.com/news/2018–08–20/venezuela-slashes-5-zeros-currency-one-greatest-devaluations-ever.

Dwyer, Devin. "Craving Coal Dust 'Like Nicotine': Why Miners Love the Work." *ABC News* (April 7, 2010). https://abcnews.go.com/US/Mine/west-virginia-coal-miners-allure-dangerous-profession/story?id=10305839.

Elliott, Rebecca. "15 Questions with Grover G. Norquist." *The Harvard Crimson* (November 18, 2010). https://www.thecrimson.com/article/2010/11/18/nbsp-government-percent-fm/.

Facebook. "Hard Questions: Is Spending Time on Social Media Bad for Us?" (December 15, 2017). https://newsroom.fb.com/news/2017/12/hard-questions-is-spending-time-on-social-media-bad-for-us/.

Fearnow, Benjamin. "Number of Witches Rises Dramatically Across U.S. as Millennials Reject Christianity." *Newsweek* (November 18, 2018). https://www.newsweek.com/witchcraft-wiccans-mysticism-astrology-witches-millennials-pagans-religion-1221019.

Federal Reserve Bank of New York. "Household Debt Tops $14 Trillion." (February 11, 2020). https://www.newyorkfed.org/newsevents/news/research/2020/20200211.

Feingold, Spencer. "Field of machines: Researchers grow crop using only automation." *CNN* (October 7, 2017). http://www.cnn.com/2017/10/07/world/automated-farm-harvest-england/index.html.

Financial Times. "KFC runs out of chicken in logistics fiasco." (February 19, 2018). https://www.ft.com/content/223d4df0–1595-11e8–9376-4a6390addb44.

Flemming, John. "Gallup Analysis: Millennials, Marriage and Family." Gallup (May 19, 2014). https://news.gallup.com/poll/191462/gallup-analysis-millennials-marriage-family.aspx.

FranchiseHelp. "Courtyard by Marriott Franchise Cost and Opportunities." (2020). https://www.franchisehelp.com/franchises/courtyard-by-marriott/.

Frankel, Matthew. "What's the average American's tax rate?" *USA Today* (March 10, 2017). https://www.usatoday.com/story/money/personalfinance/2017/03/10/whats-the-average-americans-tax-rate/98734396/.

Franklin, Benjamin. *Poor Richard's Almanack.* 1738 ed.

Frey, Carl, and Michael Osborne. "The Future of Employment: How susceptible are jobs to computerisation?" University of Oxford (2013). https://www.oxfordmartin.ox.ac.uk/downloads/academic/future-of-employment.pdf.

Future of Life Institute. "Autonomous Weapons: An Open Letter From AI & Robotics Researchers." (July 28, 2015). https://futureoflife.org/open-letter-autonomous-weapons/.

Gallo, Amy. "The Value of Keeping the Right Customers." *Harvard Business Review* (October 29, 2014). https://hbr.org/2014/10/the-value-of-keeping-the-right-customers.

Garamone, Jim. "President Signs Fiscal 2019 Defense Authorization Act at Fort Drum Ceremony." U.S. Department of Defense (August 13, 2018). https://dod.defense.gov/News/Article/Article/1601016/president-signs-fiscal-2019-defense-authorization-act-at-fort-drum-ceremony/.

Gates, Bill. "Ask Me Anything: Bill Gates." *Reddit* (January 28, 2015). https://www.reddit.com/r/IAmA/comments/2tzjp7/hi_reddit_im_bill_gates_and_im_back_for_my_third/.

Gatto, John Taylor. *The Underground History of American Education: A School Teacher's Intimate Investigation Into the Problem of Modern Schooling.* Oxford Village Press, 2001.

Geisendorfer-Lindgren, Peter. "Stadiums, cathedrals: Marks of their eras." *Star Tribune* (September 2, 2016). http://www.startribune.com/stadiums-cathedrals-marks-of-their-eras/392207411/.

Gibbs, Samuel. "Apple's Tim Cook: 'I don't want my nephew on a social network.'" *The Guardian* (January 19, 2018). https://www.theguardian.com/technology/2018/jan/19/tim-cook-i-dont-want-my-nephew-on-a-social-network.

Gitlen, Jeff. "How Much Does It Cost to Start a Brewery?" *LendEDU.com* (October 3, 2018). https://lendedu.com/blog/how-to-start-a-brewery/.

Godard, Thierry. "The Economics of Craft Beer." *SmartAsset* (May 18, 2018). https://smartasset.com/credit-cards/the-economics-of-craft-beer.

Greene, Catherine. "Growth Patterns in the U.S. Organic Industry." USDA, Economic Research Service (October 24, 2013). https://www.ers.usda.gov/amber-waves/2013/october/growth-patterns-in-the-us-organic-industry/.

Greene, Lane. "Language: Finding a voice." The Economist, *Technology Quarterly* (May 1, 2017). https://www.economist.com/technology-quarterly/2017–05-01/language.

Hagerty, Kyle. "Barbershops Are Back And Bucking Retail Trends." *Forbes* (July 6, 2017). https://www.forbes.com/sites/bisnow/2017/07/06/barbershops-are-back-and-bucking-retail-trends.

Hall, Kermit. *The Magic Mirror: Law in American History.* New York: Oxford University Press, 1989.

Hamilton, Brady, et al. "Births: Provisional Data for 2017." *Vital Statistics Rapid Release,* CDC (May 2018). https://www.cdc.gov/nchs/data/vsrr/report004.pdf.

Harl, Kenneth. "The Later Roman Empire." *Tulane University,* Course Handout (2001). https://web.archive.org/web/20160609161744/http://www.tulane.edu/~august/handouts/601cprin.htm.

Harris, Tristan. "The Eyeball Economy: How Advertising Co-Opts Independent Thought." *Big Think* (April 10, 2017). http://bigthink.com/videos/tristan-harris-the-attention-economy-a-race-to-the-bottom-of-the-brain-stem.

Hartford Institute. "Fast Facts about American Religion." (2006). http://hirr.hartsem.edu/research/fastfacts/fast_facts.html.

Hartmann, Thom. "Good German Schools Come to America." *The Hartmann Report* (November 1, 2007). https://www.thomhartmann.com/articles/2007/11/good-german-schools-come-america

Hinckley, David. "Average American watches 5 hours of TV per day, report shows." *New York Daily News* (March 5, 2014). https://www.nydailynews.com/life-style/average-american-watches-5-hours-tv-day-article-1.1711954.

Hoffman, Christopher. "Time is on your side." *Woodshop News* (October 20, 2013). https://www.woodshopnews.com/features/time-is-on-your-side.

Howard, Jacqueline. "Americans devote more than 10 hours a day to screen time, and growing." *CNN* (June 29, 2016). https://www.cnn.com/2016/06/30/health/americans-screen-time-nielsen/index.html.

IBISWorld Industry Reports. "Public Schools in the US." (January 2020). https://www.ibisworld.com/united-states/market-research-reports/public-schools-industry/.

―――. "Sports Medicine Practitioners in the US." (December 2018). https://www.ibisworld.com/united-states/market-research-reports/sports-medicine-practitioners-industry/.

―――. "Taxi & Limousine Services in the US." (December 2019). https://www.ibisworld.com/united-states/market-research-reports/taxi-limousine-services-industry/.

Ibrahim, Jeanine. "Kendra Scott: How a small business owner turned $500 into millions." *CNBC* (May 12, 2013). https://www.cnbc.com/id/100724099.

Iceland Monitor. "Iceland's first pagan temple in 1000 years ready in late 2018." (December 2, 2017). https://icelandmonitor.mbl.is/news/culture_and_living/2017/12/02/iceland_s_first_pagan_temple_in_1000_years_ready_in/.

Ikerd, John. "Is Sustainable Capitalism Possible?" Lecture at The Life Economy Session of The World Life-Culture Forum—2006, Gyengong'gi Province, Republic of Korea (June 20, 2006). http://web.missouri.edu/ikerdj/papers/KoreaSustainableCapitalism.pdf.

Infomine. "Mining Cost Models: 5,000 ton per day open pit." (2018). http://costs.infomine.com/costdatacenter/miningcostmodel.aspx.

IRS, "IRS Budget & Workforce." (2020). https://www.irs.gov/statistics/irs-budget-and-workforce.

Irwin, Neil. "If we go off the fiscal cliff, the Fed can't save us." *The Washington Post* (December 5, 2012). https://www.washingtonpost.com/news/wonk/wp/2012/12/05/if-we-go-off-the-fiscal-cliff-the-fed-cant-save-us.

Jarmoc, Jeff. Twitter post (October 21, 2016, 8:21 PM). https://twitter.com/jjarmoc/status/789637654711267328.

Jefferson, Thomas. Letter to Edward Carrington on May 27, 1788, https://founders.archives.gov/documents/Jefferson/01-13-02-0120.

―――. Letter to John Jay on August 23, 1785, http://tjrs.monticello.org/letter/69.

―――. Letter to John Taylor on May 28, 1816, https://founders.archives.gov/documents/Jefferson/03-10-02-0053.

―――. *Notes on the State of Virginia,* Query XIX. (1782). https://en.wikisource.org/wiki/Notes_on_the_State_of_Virginia_(1853)/Query_19.

Jones, Jeffrey. "U.S. Church Membership Down Sharply in Past Two Decades." Gallup (April 18, 2018). https://news.gallup.com/poll/248837/church-membership-down-sharply-past-two-decades.aspx.

Kadlec, Dan. "Organic Food Sales Remain Strong" *Time* (July 22, 2009). http://content.time.com/time/specials/packages/article/0,28804,1911974_1911972_1911956,00.html.

Kelly, Martin. "John Winthrop—Colonial American Scientist." *ThoughtCo* (December 8, 2017). https://www.thoughtco.com/john-winthrop-colonial-american-scientist-4079663.

Khimm, Suzy. "A gallon of milk could cost $8 in 2013. Here's why." *The Washington Post* (December 26, 2012). https://www.washingtonpost.com/news/wonk/wp/2012/12/26/a-gallon-of-milk-could-cost-8-in-2013-heres-why/.

Kimball, Josh. "Wicca Experts Encourage Christians to Engage America's 'Fastest-Growing' Religion." *Christian Post* (September 21, 2008). https://www.

christianpost.com/news/wicca-experts-encourage-christians-to-engage-america-s-fastest-growing-religion-34408/.

Kipling, Rudyard. "The Gods of the Copybook Headings." The Kipling Society. http://www.kiplingsociety.co.uk/poems_copybook.htm.

Koerth-Baker, Maggie. "32 Innovations That Will Change Your Tomorrow." The New York Times Magazine (June 1, 2012). http://www.nytimes.com/interactive/2012/06/03/magazine/innovations-issue.html.

Koppel, Ted. Lights Out: A Cyberattack, A Nation Unprepared, Surviving the Aftermath. New York: Broadway, 2016.

Kotlikoff, Laurence. "America's Hidden Credit Card Bill." The New York Times, (August 1, 2014). https://www.nytimes.com/2014/08/01/opinion/laurence-kotlikoff-on-fiscal-gap-accounting.html.

Kristof, Kathy. "$1 million mistake: Becoming a doctor." CBS News (September 10, 2013). https://www.cbsnews.com/news/1-million-mistake-becoming-a-doctor/.

Kumco, Aylin, and Abigail Okrent. "Methodology for the Quarterly Food-Away-from-Home Prices Data." USDA, Economic Research Service (May 2014). https://ageconsearch.umn.edu/bitstream/184292/2/tb-1938.pdf.

Lawless, Jill, and Aritz Parra. "World cyberattack cripples UK hospitals, demands ransoms." AP News (May 12, 2017). https://www.apnews.com/076a9045d94645a2c052ba0456c666.

The Laws and Liberties of Massachusetts, 1648 ed. Cambridge: Harvard University Press, 1929. https://www.mass.gov/files/documents/2016/08/ob/deludersatan.pdf.

Lewis, Lawrence. A History of the Bank of North America, the First Bank Chartered in the United States. Philadelphia: J. B. Lippincott & Co, 1882.

Library of Congress. "The Industrial Revolution in the United States." Teaching With Primary Sources. http://www.loc.gov/teachers/classroommaterials/primarysourcesets/industrial-revolution/pdf/teacher_guide.pdf.

Lifeway Research. "Church Dropouts: How Many Leave Church between ages 18–22 and Why?" (Spring 2007). http://lifewayresearch.com/wp-content/uploads/2014/01/Church-Dropouts_How-Many-Leave-Church-and-Why-8.07.2007.pdf

Sen. Lodge, Henry Cabot. Letter to Sen. Weeks on December 17, 1913. In Hearings Before the Committee on Rules, House of Representatives, 72nd Congress, First Session on H. Res. 68 and H. Res. 249 (1932) 12.

Logsdon, Gene. Letter to a Young Farmer: How to Live Richly Without Wealth on the New Garden Farm. Vermont: Chelsea Green, 2017.

Lowenthal, Bennett. "The Jumpers of '29." The Washington Post (October 25, 1987). https://www.washingtonpost.com/archive/opinions/1987/10/25/the-jumpers-of-29/17defff9-f725-43b7-831b-7924ac0a1363.

Macias, Amanda. "Trump signs $738 billion defense bill." CNBC (December 20, 2019). https://www.cnbc.com/2019/12/21/trump-signs-738-billion-defense-bill.html.

MacDorman, Marian F., et al. "Trends in Out-of-Hospital Births in the United States, 1990–2012." CDC, NCHS Data Brief 144 (March 2014). https://www.cdc.gov/nchs/data/databriefs/db144.pdf.

Maddison, Angus. "Statistics on World Population, GDP and Per Capita GDP, 1–2008 AD." University of Groningen (2010). http://www.ggdc.net/MADDISON/oriindex.htm.

MANA. "Legal Status of U.S. Midwives." (2019). https://mana.org/about-midwives/legal-status-of-us-midwives.

————. "Midwives & the Law." (2019). https://mana.org/about-midwives/midwives-and-the-law.

Manyika, James, et al. "Jobs Lost, Jobs Gained: Workforce Transitions in a Time of Automation." McKinsey Global Institute (December 2017). https://www.mckinsey.com/featured-insights/future-of-work/jobs-lost-jobs-gained-what-the-future-of-work-will-mean-for-jobs-skills-and-wages.

Massachusetts Bureau of Statistics of Labor. *Comparative Wages, Prices and Cost of Living*. Boston: Wright & Potter printing co, 1889. https://lccn.loc.gov/07028681.

Mastercrafts: Stonemasonry. Directed by James Dawson, presented by Monty Don. BBC, 2010.

McCarthy, Niall. "How Much Do U.S. Cities Spend Every Year On Policing?" *Forbes* (August 7, 2017). https://www.forbes.com/sites/niallmccarthy/2017/08/07/how-much-do-u-s-cities-spend-every-year-on-policing-infographic/.

McCloskey, Deirdre. Review of *The Cambridge Economic History of Modern Britain*, edited by Roderick Floud and Paul Johnson. *Times Higher Education Supplement* (January 15, 2004). http://deirdremccloskey.org/articles/floud.php.

Minnesota Department of Natural Resources, "Timber Producers." (2020). https://webapps15.dnr.state.mn.us/timber_producers/companies.

Mitchell, Ross. "How Many Deaf People Are There in the United States?" *Journal of Deaf Studies and Deaf Education* 11 no. 1 (2006). https://doi.org/10.1093/deafed/enj004.

Morgan, Nick. "Thinking of Self-Publishing Your Book?" *Forbes* (January 8, 2013). https://www.forbes.com/sites/nickmorgan/2013/01/08/thinking-of-self-publishing-your-book-in-2013-heres-what-you-need-to-know/.

Musk, Elon. "Centennial Symposium: One-on-one with Elon Musk." *Massachusetts Institute of Technology* video blog post (October 31, 2014). https://www.youtube.com/watch?v=PULkWGHeIQQ.

National Funeral Directors Association, "NFDA Cremation and Burial Report Shows Rate of Cremation at All-time High." (July 18, 2017). https://web.archive.org/web/20191117093617/http://www.nfda.org/news/media-center/nfda-news-releases/id/2511/nfda-cremation-and-burial-report-shows-rate-of-cremation-at-all-time-high.

National Retail Federation. "The Economic Impact of the U.S. Retail Industry." (September 2014). https://nrf.com/retails-impact.

————. "State of Retail." (2020). https://nrf.com/insights/economy/state-retail.

Olsen, Olivia. "A Norse temple for the 21st century." *Aljazeera America* (January 24, 2016). http://america.aljazeera.com/opinions/2016/1/a-norse-temple-for-the-21st-century.html.

OMB. "Historical Tables." The White House (2020). https://www.whitehouse.gov/omb/historical-tables/.

Ong, Thuy. "Sean Parker on Facebook." *The Verge* (November 9, 2017). https://www.theverge.com/2017/11/9/16627724/sean-parker-facebook-childrens-brains-feedback-loop.

PAII, "About The Industry." https://paii.wildapricot.org/About-the-Industry.

Paul, Rand. *Proceedings and Debates of the 11th Congress, Second Session: Vol 164 No. 25*. Congressional Record (February 8, 2018). https://www.congress.gov/crec/2018/02/08/CREC-2018–02-08.pdf.

Payscale, "Salary for Certification: ISA Certified Arborist." (May 2020). https://www.payscale.com/research/US/Certification=ISA_Certified_Arborist/Salary.

Peden, Joseph. "Inflation and the Fall of the Roman Empire." Lecture at the Seminar on Money and Government in Houston, Texas (October 27, 1984). https://mises.org/library/inflation-and-fall-roman-empire.

Pew Research Center. "America's Changing Religious Landscape." (May 12, 2015). http://www.pewforum.org/2015/05/12/americas-changing-religious-landscape/.

Plymouth Ancestors. "Raising Children in the Early 17th Century: Demographics." New England Historic Genealogical Society. https://www.plimoth.org/sites/default/files/media/pdf/edmaterials_demographics.pdf.

Potter, Gary. "History of Policing in the United States." Eastern Kentucky University. http://plsonline.eku.edu/insidelook/history-policing-united-states-part-1

Rabouin, Dian. "Total global debt tops 325 pct of GDP as government debt jumps: IIF." *Reuters* (January 4, 2017). https://www.reuters.com/article/us-global-debt-iif/total-global-debt-tops-325-pct-of-gdp-as-government-debt-jumps-iif-idUSKBN1401PQ.

Rayome, Alison. "Report: Ransomware attacks grew 600% in 2016, costing businesses $1B." *TechRepublic* (March 15, 2017). https://www.techrepublic.com/article/report-ransomware-attacks-grew-600-in-2016-costing-businesses-1b.

Relton, C., et al. "Prevalence of homeopathy use by the general population worldwide: a systematic review." *Homeopathy* 106 no. 2 (2017).

Remijsen, Sofie, and Willy Clarysse. "Rewards at the home town." *Ancient Olympics* (2012). http://ancientolympics.arts.kuleuven.be/eng/TD008EN.html.

Robinson, Harriet. *Loom and Spindle.* New York: Thomas Y. Cromwell & Company, 1898.

Rosenberg, Matt. "The 5 Sectors of the Economy." *ThoughtCo* (June 25, 2018). https://www.thoughtco.com/sectors-of-the-economy-1435795.

Russell, Thomas. *Banking, Credits and Finance.* Chicago: Whitman, 2016.

Sakelaris, Nicholas. "New supercomputer mimics human brain, researchers say." *UPI* (November 6, 2018). https://www.upi.com/New-supercomputer-mimics-human-brain-researchers-say/1361541441333/.

Selcer, Richard. *Civil War America, 1850 To 1875.* New York: Infobase, 2006.

Sirrine, Rob, et al. "Estimated Costs of Producing Hops in Michigan." Michigan State University Extension (2014). https://www.canr.msu.edu/uploads/resources/pdfs/estimated_costs_of_producing_hops_in_michigan_(e3236).pdf.

Somerville, Scott. "The Politics of Survival: Home Schoolers and the Law." Home School Legal Defense Association (April 2001). https://files.eric.ed.gov/fulltext/ED461177.pdf.

State Bar of Michigan. "How Many of the Founding Fathers Were Lawyers?" *SMBBlog* (July 4, 2011). https://sbmblog.typepad.com/sbm-blog/2011/07/how-many-of-the-founding-fathers-were-lawyers.html.

Stern, Corey. "CVS and Walgreens are completely dominating the US drugstore industry." *Business Insider* (July 29, 2015). https://www.businessinsider.com/cvs-and-walgreens-us-drugstore-market-share-2015-7.

Stewart, Andrew. *One Hundred Greek Sculptors, Their Careers and Extant Works.* Yale University Press, 1990.

Sutcliffe, Rick. *The Fourth Civilization.* Arjay, 2002. http://www.arjay.ca/EthTech/Text/Ch1/Ch1.2.html.

Swanson, Kevin. *Family Life: A Simple Guide to the Biblical Family.* Generations, 2016.

Tainter, Joseph. *The Collapse of Complex Societies.* Cambridge: Cambridge University Press, 1988.

———. "Will Our Society Survive Complexity?" *McAlvany Weekly Commentary* audio podcast (October 1, 2014). https://mcalvanyweeklycommentary.com/complexsocieties/.

Taycher, Leonid. "Books of the world, stand up and be counted! All 129,864,880 of you." *Google Book Search* (August 5, 2010). http://booksearch.blogspot.com/2010/08/books-of-world-stand-up-and-be-counted.html.

Toronto Sun. "Adult diapers expected to outsell baby diapers soon." (March 3, 2016). https://torontosun.com/2016/03/03/adult-diapers-expected-to-outsell-baby-diapers-soon/wcm/0eacd840-bf42-4d04-bada-2e9317e6c2af.

Tung, Liam. "iPhone throttling: Class actions pile up as Apple hit with 32nd lawsuit." *ZDNet* (January 11, 2018). http://www.zdnet.com/article/iphone-throttling-class-actions-pile-up-as-apple-hit-with-32nd-lawsuit/.

Turtel, Joel. *Public Schools, Public Menace.* New York: Liberty, 2005.

Tuttle, Brad. "Is Organic Milk Worth the Extra Money?" *Money* (May 4, 2017). https://money.com/organic-milk-costs-new-report/.

United Nations. "The State of World Fisheries and Aquaculture 2016." FAO (2016). http://www.fao.org/3/a-i5555e.pdf

———. "World Population Prospects: The 2017 Revision." Department of Economic and Social Affairs (June 21, 2017). https://www.un.org/development/desa/publications/world-population-prospects-the-2017-revision.html.

———. "World statistical compendium for raw hides and skins, leather and leather footwear 1999–2015." FAO (2015). http://www.fao.org/3/a-i5599e.pdf.

US Census Bureau. "New Census Data Show Differences Between Urban and Rural Populations." (December 8, 2016). https://www.census.gov/newsroom/press-releases/2016/cb16-210.html.

———. "Number of Firms, Number of Establishments, Employment, Annual Payroll, and Preliminary Estimated Receipts by Enterprise Employment Size for the United States, All Industries." *2017 Economic Census* (March 2020). https://www.census.gov/data/tables/2017/econ/susb/2017-susb-annual.html.

———. "Popularly Elected Officials." (1992). https://www.census.gov/prod/2/gov/gc/gc92_1_2.pdf.

———. "Quarterly Summary of State and Local Government Tax Revenue." First–Fourth Quarters 2019 (2019–2020). https://www.census.gov/programs-surveys/qtax.html.

———. "Real Median Household Income in the United States." (2018). https://fred.stlouisfed.org/series/MEHOINUSA672N.

US Courts. "The Judiciary FY 2021 Congressional Budget Summary." (February 2020). https://www.uscourts.gov/sites/default/files/fy_2021_congressional_budget_summary_0.pdf.

USDA. "2012 Census of Agriculture." National Agriculture Statistics Center (2012). https://www.nass.usda.gov/Publications/AgCensus/2012/Full_Report/Volume_1,_Chapter_1_US/.

———. "Farm to School Census." (2014). https://farmtoschoolcensus.fns.usda.gov/farm-school-works-stimulate-local-economies.

———. "Food and alcoholic beverages: Total expenditures." Economic Research Service. (2015). https://web.archive.org/web/20160514203431/http://www.ers.usda.gov/datafiles/Food_Expenditures/Food_Expenditures/table1.xls

———. "Nominal food and alcohol expenditures, with taxes and tips, for all purchasers." Economic Research Service (2018). https://www.ers.usda.gov/data-products/food-expenditure-series/.

———. "Per Capita Consumption of Red Meat, Poultry, Boneless Equivalent, 1970–2017." *Meat & Poultry Facts* (2017).

US Department of Justice. "Local Police Departments, 2013: Personnel, Policies, and Practices." *Bureau of Justice Statistics* (May 2015). https://www.bjs.gov/content/pub/pdf/lpd13ppp.pdf.

US Department of Treasury. "Alcohol Beverage Authorities in United States, Canada, and Puerto Rico." Tax and Trade Bureau (September 25, 2018). https://www.ttb.gov/wine/state-ABC.shtml.

———. "Status Report of U.S. Government Gold Reserve." (2019). https://www.fiscal.treasury.gov/reports-statements/gold-report/current.html.

University of Denver. "FAQ: Judges in the United States." (2014). https://iaals.du.edu/sites/default/files/documents/publications/judge_faq.pdf;

Vincent, James. "Former Facebook exec says social media is ripping apart society." *The Verge* (December 11, 2017). https://www.theverge.com/2017/12/11/16761016/former-facebook-exec-ripping-apart-society.

Walker, Jon. "Family Life Council says it's time to bring family back to life." Southern Baptist Convention (June 12, 2002). http://www.sbcannualmeeting.net/sbc02/newsroom/newspage.asp?ID=261.

Watson, Thomas. *The Beatitudes: An exposition of Matthew 5:1–12*. 1660.

Weeks, Jos. D. *Report on the Statistics of Wages in Manufacturing Industries*. United States Census Office, Washington: GPO, 1886.

Wilson, Woodrow. "The Meaning of a Liberal Education." Address to the New York City High School Teachers Association on January 9, 1909 in *The Papers of Woodrow Wilson 1908–1909*. Princeton: Princeton University Press, 1974.

Wines & Vines. "North America Winery Count Is Now 9,872." (January 24, 2017). https://winesvinesanalytics.com/news/article/179538/North-America-Winery-Count-Is-Now-9872.

———. "Number of Wineries Grows to 8,391 in North America." (January 27, 2014). https://winesvinesanalytics.com/news/article/127266/Number-of-Wineries-Grows-to-8391-in-North-America.

Winthrop, John. "A Model of Christian Charity." Sermon delivered onboard the Arbella, 1630.

Wood-Mizer. "How to Charge for Sawing Services." https://woodmizer.com/.

The World Bank. "Fertility rate, total (births per woman)—United States (1960–2017)." (2019). https://data.worldbank.org/indicator/SP.DYN.TFRT.IN?locations=US.

Zahn, Max. "'The true religion of America': Why one TV mogul is going all in on sports." *Yahoo Finance* (November 2, 2019). https://finance.yahoo.com/news/byron-allen-on-sports-121350249.html.

Zebrowski, Robert. "A Brief History of Pharmacy." St. Louis College of Pharmacy. https://www.stlcop.edu/practice/about.html.

Zillow. "United States Home Prices & Values." (February 29, 2020). https://www.zillow.com/home-values.

Made in the USA
Columbia, SC
11 July 2022

63305251R00190